Water in the West

Recent Titles in the
CONTEMPORARY WORLD ISSUES
Series

Religious Belief and Science
Glenn H. Utter

Foster Care in America
Christina G. Villegas

Women in Media
Amy M. Damico

Income Inequality in America
Stacey M. Jones and Robert S. Rycroft

Rape and Sexual Assault
Alison E. Hatch

Campus Free Speech
Lori Cox Han and Jerry Price

Global Terrorism
Steven J. Childs

Food Insecurity
William D. Schanbacher and Whitney Fung Uy

Conspiracy Theories
Jeffrey B. Webb

Advertising in America
Danielle Sarver Coombs

Cyber Warfare
Paul J. Springer

Extremism in the Police
Carla Lewandowski and Jeff Bumgarner

The U.S. Criminal Justice System
Sarah Koon-Magnin and Ryan J. Williams

Women and Girls in STEM Fields
Heather Burns Page

Remote Learning and Distance Education
William H. Pruden III

Water in the West

A Reference Handbook

Jacqueline Vaughn

BLOOMSBURY ACADEMIC
NEW YORK • LONDON • OXFORD • NEW DELHI • SYDNEY

BLOOMSBURY ACADEMIC
Bloomsbury Publishing Inc
1385 Broadway, New York, NY 10018, USA
50 Bedford Square, London, WC1B 3DP, UK
29 Earlsfort Terrace, Dublin 2, Ireland

BLOOMSBURY, BLOOMSBURY ACADEMIC and the Diana logo are trademarks of Bloomsbury Publishing Plc

First published in the United States of America 2025

Cover image: Glen Canyon dam aerial view. shuvro ghose/Adobe Stock

A catalog record for this book is available from the Library of Congress.

ISBN: HB: 979-8-2161-8262-7
ePDF: 979-8-2161-8263-4
eBook: 979-8-2161-8264-1

Series: Contemporary World Issues

Typeset by Integra Software Services Pvt. Ltd.
Printed and bound in the United States of America

Contents

Preface

In the early 2020s it sometimes seemed like all the headlines in the West were about water. Water that was scarce or totally non-existent. Water that drenched the California coast, causing billions of dollars in damage. Water in the form of snow that delighted Utah skiers but turned to floods when the sun came out. Water that helped to refill reservoirs in Arizona after decades of drought. Water that gave hope to millions of people who thought the drought might be over. Water that made states unable to reach agreement on what to do. In 2024, the European Union's Copernicus Climate Change Service announced that 2023 had officially become Earth's hottest year on record, with July 2023 Earth's hottest month on record. In the West, Phoenix experienced thirty-one consecutive days of temperatures of 110 degrees or hotter, and the 128-degree reading in Death Valley, California was a near world record.

During that same time, the language that was being used to describe what was happening became increasingly dire, with phrases like "looming catastrophe" and "an uncertain future" employed with greater frequency. Calls were made for "urgent action" to deal with "one of the most profound issues facing the U.S. today." Solutions were plentiful but often vague. Water users were told to use the resource "responsibly" because "no one will come out of this unscathed." One state official suggested eliminating lawns; an environmental group called for draining Lake Powell. By 2024, the language was slightly less apocalyptic but, in some ways, still intense. One climate scientist said that the West was still "on the edge." Predictions and comparisons were all over the place.

This book puts those events in perspective and context.

This book focuses on the western region of the United States, which faces different water issues and challenges than the Great Plains and states east of the Mississippi, due to variations in precipitation, geography, and land-use history. In the East, where water is generally abundant due to more than adequate snowfall and rainfall, along with a complex of myriad streams and rivers, the nation's early history of industrialization led policymakers to focus on *water quality*. Pollution, which became a major concern after the turn of the twentieth century due to rapidly growing urbanization, drew the attention of the federal government, and congressional legislation such as the Clean Water Act. The environmental movement that began to coalesce in 1970 with the observance of the first Earth Day, seized on events such as the time Ohio's Cuyahoga River burst into flames, and then transitioned into issues such as civic environmentalism, environmental justice, and the globalization of environmental problems.

In the West, where cities developed more slowly and where the climate and geography is demonstrably different, water concerns focus on supply and control, only some of which is controlled by humankind. Here, it is *water quantity* that lies at the forefront of how we live, with surface water and groundwater management more critical. States, rather than the federal government, have become the platforms from which the legal and regulatory systems controlling water have emerged, and along with them, a complicated, circuitous maze of disputes and court cases that underscore how important water is to our life.

For the purposes of this book, the West refers to the following eleven states: Arizona, California, Colorado, Idaho, Montana, Nevada, New Mexico, Oregon, Utah, Washington, and Wyoming. However, each of these states faces challenges all their own in supporting communities and policies that use their water resources wisely and sustainably.

In order to understand why water is so important in the West, it is first important to delineate the history and basics of western water principles and laws and how they came to be developed, the focus of Chapter 1. Those legal concepts parallel the history of the West itself, from the region's origins in Spanish and Mexican land ownership, to the transition from territories to states, and the decisions made about how to control what limited water existed in the region. Western efforts to control surface waters through reservoirs, dams, and canals has been almost entirely negotiated by a series of specialized state-level administrative bodies, and regional or interstate agreements. Chapter 2 discusses the challenges related to the Colorado River, and key issues and solutions faced by each state.

In Chapter 3, the book looks at the West and its water from the perspective of four stakeholders who have different vantage points on water scarcity and management. Those perspectives are expanded in Chapter 4 with profiles of historical figures and contemporary activists deeply embedded in the history of water policy in the West.

Chapter 5 provides a suite of primary documents that illuminate broad trends and shifts in public and political attitudes about water in the American West over time, including landmark legal opinions, historic laws, and statements from such figures as President Theodore Roosevelt, explorer John Wesley Powell, and Clinton-era Secretary of the Interior Bruce Babbitt. Chapter 6 consists of an annotated bibliography of books, magazine and journal articles, government publications, and electronic media. Chapter 7 is an annotated chronology of some of the key events in the development of water resources and policies. The final section is a Glossary of key terms used throughout the book in the realms of hydrology, legislation, and the law.

Water in the West

1

Western Water Conflicts: Background and History

Introduction

There is a critical difference in how water issues are perceived between the eastern and western states. In the East, where water is generally abundant due to more than adequate precipitation, along with a complex system of rivers and streams, the nation's early industrialization led to a focus on water *quality*. Pollution, which became a major concern after the turn of the twentieth century due to rapidly growing urbanization and industrialization, drew the attention and concern of the federal government and the American public. Agencies like the Environmental Protection Agency were created in response to this concern, and the enactment of environmental laws such as the Clean Water Act gave these agencies considerable legal authority. As the population grew, so, too, did the demand for clean water.

In the West, where cities developed more slowly and where the climate and geography are demonstrably different, water policy has focused on supply and control. States, rather than the federal government, have become the platforms from which the legal and regulatory policies managing water supplies have emerged, along with some of the most innovative ideas on how to increase our supply of water—ideas borne out of necessity in an arid land.

Chapter 1 begins by illustrating the historical challenges that have faced the West when it comes to managing water by examining what happened in Los Angeles in the early twentieth century. The megalopolis has often been the

---

The Glen Canyon Dam, near Page, Arizona, was built between 1956 and 1966 as a water storage facility for the Lower Colorado River Basin. Perhaps the most contested dam in America, environmental groups continue to rally for its removal. (U.S. Bureau of Reclamation.)

personification of both what *to* do and what *not* to do, with much of the rest of the country following the city's lead.

The chapter then moves on to an explanation of the types of water and what each type is utilized for, and a discussion of how water rights evolved differently in the early western frontier, including water rights belonging to Native Americans. It also covers interstate water agreements and international water treaties involving Mexico and Canada, along with a summary of the role of three major federal agencies that broaden our understanding of water management. Included in that discussion are non-state actors like non-governmental and non-profit organizations, whose influence has increased substantially since the 1970s with the growth of the environmental movement. The chapter concludes with an analysis of the nature and severity of the West's water scarcity problems in an age of intensifying climate change.

Bringing Water to Los Angeles

In 1781, the Pueblo de Nuestra Señora Reina de los Angeles was founded by forty-four settlers and four soldiers who had come to the region from New Spain (what is now Mexico). By 1811, the area's population was more than 500, and by 1841, that number had more than tripled to 1,680. Early on, with the help of the native Indian people, the new residents built a series of ditches, called *zanjas*, to irrigate their fields and water their livestock.

With the Treaty of Guadalupe Hidalgo, which ended the Mexican–American War in 1848, the United States took over parts of the territory. At the time, the 3,000 or so Pueblo inhabitants received their water from the Rio Porciuncula (Los Angeles River), whose source was an aquifer under the San Fernando Valley, as well as some mountain rainfall. When Los Angeles was incorporated as a US city in 1850, the city was beginning to show signs of growth, with the census estimating the population at 1,610.

Upon incorporation, the community members quickly built the Zanja Madre (Mother Ditch), an open earthen aqueduct, to store the water from the river in a small reservoir, and from there, the water traveled through a series of smaller zanjas. In 1867, the city council authorized a French wine grower who owned property near the central city area to begin the transition from a system of earthen ditches to iron pipe. Jean Louis Sansevain was not very successful in his efforts, and in 1868, the city offered a thirty-year lease to the Los Angeles Water

Company (LAWC). When the lease expired in 1898, the city's mayor began negotiating the purchase of the company, and at a cost of $2 million, Los Angeles now owned its own water company.

This was just the beginning of a lengthy, tortuous, embittered effort to bring water to a city that was built in an arid desert that many considered worthless and uninhabitable. When the city took over the task of bringing water to its citizens, the region was in the tenth year of drought. Livestock were dying, lakes had dried up, and the city was told that it was time for Los Angeles to supplement the river from another source. That source, the Owens Valley, was home to the Indigenous Paiute and Shoshone people, who called the area Land of the Flowing Water for 15,000 years. When settlers arrived in the 1850s, they murdered the natives and took over the land.

What happened next is synonymous with the name William Mulholland (profiled in Chapter 4). Along with the former mayor of the city of Los Angeles, Fred Eaton, Mulholland embarked on an ambitious plan around 1904, stealthily buying up land and water rights to build a 250-mile-long aqueduct from the Owens Valley using canals that would bring snowmelt from the Sierra Nevada to LA. At the same time, the National Reclamation Service was in the process of considering making the Owens Valley the center of a large-scale irrigation project that would benefit local farmers and ranchers. Realizing the importance of moving quickly to out-compete the federal project, Mulholland and Eaton convinced city leaders to back what was expected to be a $23 million aqueduct that could supply water for 2 million Los Angeles residents.

The farmers and ranchers of the Owens Valley were irate when they found out about the plan by the city, and people in Los Angeles were equally infuriated by the cost of the project. Critics questioned whether land speculators were driving the project more than they needed for the city to bring water to Los Angeles. Despite these qualms, however, the voters passed a bond issue in September 1905 by a margin of fourteen to one. Less than a year later, a second bond issue for even more money was passed by a ten to one vote.

Mulholland's project began in 1906 with surveys of the area, followed by a massive effort to build roads to the remote location. A Southern Pacific Railroad line had to be built to ferry in the equipment that was needed, as well as the 4,000 workers, 1,300 mules, and support for 57 work camps along the aqueduct's route. As was typical of projects like this one, saloons accompanied the building of the 233-mile-long aqueduct. Despite political intrigue and accusations of boondoggles and corruption, the Los Angeles Aqueduct project was completed with a celebratory observance on November 5, 1913, six years after it had begun.

Unfortunately for Mulholland, his predictions about how much water Los Angeles would need quickly proved to be woefully low, given the population explosion that ensued. Census figures for the city showed 4,385 in 1860, but that number grew to 50,395 by 1890, and in 1910, the same year the Los Angeles Aqueduct was completed, the population had grown to 319,198.

Those figures were for the city of Los Angeles alone, and did not include any of the other cities that had grown up outside the main perimeter of what had started out as a Pueblo plaza.

Other problems began to arise besides the population explosion, only it was a real explosion in 1924. A blast from an estimated 500 pounds of dynamite destroyed a portion of the aqueduct near the town of Lone Pine, an act of sabotage that was not totally unexpected given the animosity and distrust that had been simmering in the Owens Valley for two decades. There had been threats against the aqueduct employees, and in November, vigilantes from the area took over one of the aqueduct's gatehouses and opened up the floodgates, releasing the water down a spillway. The protesters sought $12 million in compensation for the damage done to the area's businesses and its agriculture. After four days of occupation, with a promise of mediation, the group dispersed. In 1925, the California state legislature enacted a bill that would subsequently make cities responsible for damages to businesses or property values caused by water diversions such as the aqueduct. Perhaps sensing a lesson from the Owens Valley incidents, Mulholland decided to build reservoirs and a dam in other parts of the region to insulate Los Angeles from further disruptions.

But what came to be known as the California Water War did not end. In May 1927, another huge explosion rocked the aqueduct and the canyons in a remote part of the Mojave Desert. The next day, and then a week later, more bombs destroyed the pipeline, with more bombings following in June. Sometimes the "war" involved explosives; other battles were limited to a war of words in the newspapers. Federal agents, saboteurs, detectives, and the curious brought visibility to the conflict, but the outcome was not what some would have expected. In November 1927, brothers who previously had led some of the Owens Valley protests were convicted of something totally different. Mark and Wilfred Watterson, local Owens Valley bankers, were convicted on thirty-six counts of embezzlement and fraud, and the doors of the banks they owned closed. Although seven people had been arrested in connection with the bombing, and one had confessed to sabotage, all seven were released by a local justice of the peace. No one else was ever arrested.

One more incident from the 1920s characterized the challenges Los Angeles was facing. Mulholland, having decided to build reservoirs closer to the city, had chosen a site in San Francisquito Canyon, about 50 miles northwest of Los Angeles, for a 600-acre reservoir created by the new St. Francis Dam. Construction of the 208-foot-tall concrete dam began in August 1924 and the project was completed in May 1926. The city began filling the dam with water from San Francisquito Creek, and eight months later, two large cracks appeared on the downside face of the dam. Mulholland dismissed the cracks as perfectly normal. Mulholland also was unconcerned two months later, on March 12, 1928 when the head dam-keeper notified him of leaks on the sides of the dam, which Mulholland also considered normal. He did, however, order the level of the reservoir's water to be lowered.

Just after midnight, 12.5 billion gallons worth of turbulent water, along with debris including trees, mud, and pieces of roofs, began hurtling down the narrow walls of the canyon. Two hours later, the 75-foot wall of floodwater toppled the orchards and reached the agriculture workers in the Santa Clara Valley and the community of Santa Paula. Over five hours after the initial rumbling of the dam's destruction, the flood reached the ocean near Ventura. When the dam broke, it created a 65-mile-long path of destruction, left more than 400 people dead, and caused untold millions of dollars in damage. Hoping to avoid even more unwanted publicity about the scale of the disaster, the Los Angeles City Council agreed to provide $1 million in flood relief funds.

Unpredictably, despite an influx of attorneys eager to represent the families of the human victims of the flood, only a few dozen lawsuits were filed against the city, and all but one was settled out of court. There were also charity events held to benefit the flood victims, and multiple investigations launched to determine what had caused the dam to collapse. The Los Angeles County coroner held a lengthy inquest and in April 1928, the jury returned a complicated verdict, blaming Mulholland for choosing a location for the dam that had a poor underlying rock structure, the lack of adequate safety features, and criticizing the Department of Water and Power for relying on a single man's judgment. A few months later, Mulholland resigned as Chief Engineer of the Department. No charges of criminal negligence were ever filed.

Surface Water Sources and Challenges

As the name implies, surface water consists of bodies of water like lakes, rivers, reservoirs, creeks, wetlands, and swamps that are permanent or perennial in nature. There is also a classification called ephemeral surface water that is less permanent or seasonal, including streams, lagoons, and water holes. Surface water comes from rain and snowfall that replenishes the body of water, but other processes, including evaporation, seepage into the ground, or use (whether by humans, animals, or plants), are also responsible for water loss.

Surface water is used primarily for drinking water, everyday use by people, irrigation, and by certain types of industries such as hydropower. Although most of our drinking water begins as surface water, that varies from one state to another, in large part depending on how much surface water is available. Surface water and groundwater are also sometimes blended, depending on the use. For example, people in seven western states get most of their water from the Colorado River, whereas those in the Seattle area get their water from the Cedar and Tolt rivers.

The United States Geological Survey has an interesting way of showing how much surface water is found in each state as part of its "How Wet Is Your State?" statistics. Although Alaska wins the overall prize for the country, the figures for the states in the West may be a surprise. The figures below represent the perennial water area percentage, using data derived from the US Census.

Arizona	0.3
California	4.8
Colorado	0.4
Idaho	1.1
Montana	1.0
Nevada	0.7
New Mexico	0.2
Oregon	2.4
Utah	3.2
Washington	6.8
Wyoming	0.7

Source: usgs.gov/special-topics/water-science-school/science/how-wet-your-state-water-area-each-state.

Groundwater Sources and Challenges

All groundwater starts out as surface water, which then percolates into basins naturally, or water can be artificially injected into wells for storage and future use. The basins are not empty like underground tanks used by gasoline service stations, but rather consist of water found in unconsolidated material like sand or gravel called aquifers. The groundwater fills the porous spaces around the sediment, and then it can be extracted. In certain types of soil, the aquifer can be artificially refilled after it has been pumped out, referred to as groundwater recharge. In other instances, such as clay, there is no way to resaturate the soil and the result is often the collapse of the ground, called subsidence. During wet winters, natural processes like rain and snow do the recharging.

Historically, groundwater has been pumped out and used primarily for agricultural use, but in more recent years, it has become a source for urban areas as well. The increase in global temperatures due to climate change has shrunk surface water and snowpack in some areas, requiring users to pump groundwater instead. One of the impacts of excessive groundwater pumping in the West is the development of giant cracks or fissures where the ground literally splits open. As water is pumped out of aquifers, the level lowers and the ground begins to sag. These are not naturally occurring cracks, and if rainwater is insufficient to replenish the aquifer, the features may never recover. Arizona has been monitoring the fissures since at least 2002, and the Arizona Geological Survey has already charted 169 miles of the cracks within the state.

In 2023, *The New York Times* published the results of a months-long analysis of groundwater depletion throughout the country. The analysis showed that there is virtually no federal regulation of groundwater, leaving states to enact, or not enact, their own rules. Colorado, for instance, allows groundwater to be pumped from some regions until it is gone. Arizona has little regulation of the groundwater in its Ice Age aquifers, and attempts to enact a statewide groundwater law have been unsuccessful. Arizona has little information on how much groundwater, or storage, it has, making a statewide policy difficult, along with fierce resistance from lawmakers. Known as a business-friendly state, Arizona has not enacted groundwater legislation since 1980. In California, the *Times* study showed that in 2022, the aquifers in at least seventy-six basins were being pumped out faster than they could be replenished by precipitation, called overdrafting. Many observers believe that the current levels of overdrafting and use of groundwater will be the most critical issues in the West's water scarcity debate for decades to come without significant change, and soon.

The Evolution of Western Water Rights and Law

Western water law represents an amalgamation of customs, often localized decision-making, negotiations, and trade-offs made in an atmosphere that ranges from how early miners approached disputes during California's Gold Rush to contemporary legislation and rulemaking at the state and local levels. Still there are remnants of English common law, a bit of Eastern practicality, and the debate over rights that are the underpinnings of how this scarce resource is allocated and managed. Along with the legal evolution of water law are numerous policies, court cases, and regulatory procedures that make any discussion difficult to follow. Add in the political forces that ebb and flow and shape water laws and the complexity of technical and science-based information, and then climate change and the unpredictability of natural resources in the West, and the evolutionary process can seem haphazard. Many of these changes will be explored in Chapter 2, but the section that follows explores the primary stakeholders and history that shaped the background of water law in the West.

Two words best describe how water rights developed in the West: prior appropriation. Also known as "first in time, first in right," the term began to be used during the period of western expansion as miners, settlers, and speculators began to lay claim to lands that had previously been the home of Native Americans, such as the Paiute who lived in the Owens Valley. Basically, it meant that once a person claimed water as their own, they could use as much of it as they wanted. Picture, for instance, a man who chose to build a homestead for his family along the banks of a river in Montana. He used that source for drinking water, irrigating his crops, and feeding his livestock. The state recognized his claim, issued him a permit to use that water, but not to own it. The settler who came after him might also claim a right to that water, but his rights were considered secondary, or junior, to the earlier settler, who was the senior rights holder. Prior appropriation water rights are not subject to any time limit—they are issued in perpetuity—and in times when there are shortages, such as a drought, the senior rights holder's claim must be satisfied before any other rights holder.

The term "prior perfected rights" is used to describe the situation in California's Imperial Valley, where a series of court cases, good timing, intermarriage, and political maneuvering have legally allowed the water district, which holds the water in trust, and twenty families to use one-seventh of all of the water in the Colorado River—about 1,186,200 acre-feet—as their own. The 1862 Homestead Act limited farmers to 160 acres of free land, but officials ignored the limitation as speculators, developers, and their extended families bought up vast swaths of the region in one of the poorest counties in California. In 1980, legislation designed to reform the Bureau of Reclamation also exempted Imperial County farmers from the Homestead Act-era limit. These twenty families now use more of the Colorado River water than all of Wyoming, New Mexico, or Nevada, according to a study by the group ProPublica.

Native American Water Rights

Among the most vexing water problems in the West are those involving the water rights of Native American tribes. The issues relate not just to securing rights to water, but also to bigger issues of tribal sovereignty and governance. As explained earlier, water rights in the West have historically been governed by the doctrine or principle of prior appropriation, or more simply "first in time, first in right," which means that entities with the oldest rights to water are the last ones to have their allocations cut in times of shortages. Before Indian water rights were established through the courts, the West's water was used by the indigenous, or ancestral peoples who lived there, believed to be as early as 800 CE. The US Supreme Court has ruled that a tribe's water rights date to the year in which its reservation was established by Congress under the Indian Appropriations Act in 1851, a date which often is long before the creation of many communities and cities. The term reservation refers to an area of land "reserved" for the tribe through an agreement, such as a treaty or an executive order, with the federal government serving as trustee. According to the US Department of the Interior's Bureau of Indian Affairs (BIA), there are now about 56.2 million acres comprising 326 land areas held in trust by the federal government for Native American tribes. The reservations may also be called *rancherias* or Pueblos. The Navajo Nation is the largest reservation at about 17.5 million acres across the Four Corners region of Arizona, New Mexico, and Utah.

The smallest reservation is just 1.32 acres in California—the Pit River Tribe's cemetery—but most are less than 1,000 acres.

Montana was one of the territories that chose to apply the concept of prior appropriation in determining who had rights to water. That principle was at the heart of one of the early landmark court cases involving Native American tribes. The dispute began in 1898 when the superintendent of the Fort Belknap Reservation complained to the Bureau of Indian Affairs that the reservation's 1,300 Indians, primarily members of the Gros Ventre and Assiniboine tribes, had not received water from the Milk River to irrigate their crops. He predicted that the Indians would face a winter of starvation unless something was done. The problem arose because the Indians had made an agreement in 1888 ceding their lands to the federal government except for a small tract of dry land that would be set aside as a reservation, and that they would receive sufficient water for irrigation. A decade later, the federal government had built houses and other buildings, diverting water from the river for the fort's use. The Indians began diverting water from the Milk River in 1898, primarily to irrigate about 30,000 acres of grain, grass, and vegetables.

The land that the tribes had ceded to the federal government became part of the public domain, and were then opened for settlement to anyone. The Matheson Ditch Company, Cook's Irrigation Company, and the Empire Cattle Company (owned by Henry Winters, the defendants in the case, *Winters v. United States*) homesteaded the land and began constructing dams, ditches, and reservoirs to provide Milk River water for the settlers for whom they had built churches, schools, roads, and other amenities, along with water for their families' crops. They argued that this was the only supply of water that was available to them, and unless they were allowed to use the river's waters, their lands could not be cultivated and the homes could not be lived in by the settlers. The federal government brought suit on behalf of the tribes, and the lower court ruled in favor of the tribe. Winters then appealed the case to the US Supreme Court.

In their 1908 decision, the majority upheld the Indians' right to the Milk River's waters. The opinion noted that when the reservation was created, the designation carried with it the setting aside of water as well as land, basically creating an implied water right. Along with that right, the justices ruled that Native tribes had the earliest possible priority date for their claim to the river's waters, as their use of the water began at time immemorial; in essence, the beginning of time. This meant that tribes were granted prior appropriation status because they were on the land and used its water before any non-native settlers. The court did not address several of the other issues raised in the case, and implementation of what came to be called the Winters Doctrine was not specified. There was no discussion in the opinion of how much water the tribes should receive, or how that water should be delivered—issues that would continue to be debated in the decades that followed.

In 1963, the US Supreme Court sought to clarify the *Winters* decision in *Arizona v. California*. In this case, the federal government supported the claims of five reservations in three states—Arizona, California, and Nevada—to their legal right to Colorado River water that was needed to irrigate their lands. The state of Arizona disagreed, in part because the water used by the tribes meant less water was available for Arizona to use. The justices affirmed the Winters Doctrine, noting that the federal government would not have created the reservations and the arid lands where the tribes were sent without also assuming the land would be irrigated to support the people's needs. As was the case in *Winters*, the Court believed the federal government intended to deal fairly with the tribes, and the rights to water on their lands, or else those lands would be useless.

Some of the federally recognized tribes in the West have managed to resolve their water rights claims through negotiations, and others have claims for "unresolved rights" to water they believe are theirs. Tribes may have to wait years for resolution—some have been in negotiations for decades. The *Aamodt* case is one of the longest of those negotiations, starting with plans drawn up in the 1960s as part of the San Juan-Chama Diversion Project. This was a Bureau of Reclamation interbasin water transfer project in New Mexico and Colorado. The water was to be taken from the San Juan River Basin as a supplement to the water in the Rio Grande watershed, bringing water to cities along the river, including Santa Fe and Albuquerque. "Modest" amounts of water were to be allocated from the Rio Grande to several watersheds, including the Rio Pojoaque Basin, considered a tributary irrigation unit. The plans also called for the building of the Nambe Falls Dam and an adjacent reservoir to provide water for the Pojoaque Valley Irrigation District and the Pueblos of San Ildefonso, Nambe, Tesuque, and Pojoaque.

The case is somewhat unique because unlike disputes arising from an Indian reservation, where the government had set aside land for a tribe's use, the court took a different view of the water rights of Pueblos. The court ruled that the Pueblos had water rights under the 1848 Treaty of Guadalupe Hidalgo, which preserved the property rights of owners of land grants. In that sense, the court noted that the Pueblo lands, and the water they used, had been owned prior to European colonization, a concept known as "aboriginal priority" or "immemorial priority." However, this left open the question of how much water was included in the Pueblos' land grant rights. The court held that lands that had been irrigated for cultivation between 1848 and 1924, when the Pueblo Lands Act was enacted, would be considered "historically irrigated acreage," or HIA.

The years of negotiations and litigation that followed were part of the state adjudication process under the McCarran Act of 1952. In 2006, the parties completed the Aamodt Litigation Settlement and sent it on to Congress for approval and funding. It took four more years for Congress to approve the settlement in the 2010 Claims Resolution Act. It was not until 2013 that the parties reconciled the settlement with the Claims Resolution Act and it was officially signed. It took until 2017 for the parties to the adjudication to sign off on a Final Decree. Complicating this lengthy process was the sheer number of parties involved: the state of New Mexico, about 5,600 non-Indian claimants, the Pueblos, governmental entities such as Santa Fe County, the acequias, the irrigation district, and numerous federal and state agencies.

Negotiations are particularly contentious in Arizona, where there are twenty-two federally recognized tribes living on lands that are mostly arid. Although US Supreme Court decisions appear to have made clear that tribes have an implied right to water on their lands, getting that water from the source to the tribe's members has been another matter. For one thing, the *Winters* case did not settle the issue of how much water the tribes were entitled to, and how they were to get the water to their reservation from a source such as the Colorado River.

Between 1978 and October 2023, the federal government reached thirty-nine Indian water rights settlement agreements which were approved by Congress, with another four agreements reached through administrative actions. The majority were reached during the 1990s and 2000s, and they continue to be amended and litigated. By 2023, an investigation by *High Country News/ ProPublica* found that ten of the twenty-two tribes in Arizona have unsettled claims to water. The investigation noted that Arizona has created "additional hurdles" that tribes must overcome in pursuing water claims, and the state has attempted to impose conditions that the tribes find completely unacceptable. In 2020, for instance, state legislators attempted to block tribal gaming licenses if the tribe had outstanding water rights litigation with the state of Arizona. Tribes in Arizona that have tried to reach a water rights claim settlement that is still not resolved have waited an average of thirty-four years, with an average of eighteen years for even a partial settlement, according to the investigation. Part of the reason for the lengthy process is because Arizona requires hydrological studies conducted by the state's Department of Water Resources—studies that take years to complete. In other cases, water that runs from one state to another means that tribes must deal with both states' requirements to file a claim.

Another ruling in a 2023 US Supreme Court case was considered especially significant because of its implications for other tribes. In 2003, the Navajo Nation sued the state of Arizona and the federal government, arguing that the government had failed to protect the tribe's water rights.

The parties negotiated for ten years before a federal judge dismissed the Navajos' case in 2013. On appeal to the Ninth Circuit Court of Appeals, the tribe won a partial victory, and in 2022, the US Supreme Court agreed to hear the case. In *Arizona v. Navajo Nation*, excerpted in Chapter 5, the tribe contended that the 1868 Treaty of Bosque Redondo gave the federal government an affirmative duty as trustee to make sure that the tribe would have full access to water it needed to be sustainable. The treaty established the Navajos' lands as the tribe's permanent home, which the Navajo interpreted as meaning it also guaranteed them a sufficient supply of water. In their arguments, the tribe sought to compel the federal government to take affirmative steps to secure the water supply, but also to assess the tribe's water needs. The tribe also sought to make the government develop a strategic plan to get the water needed to the reservation, which potentially could mean building pipelines, pumps, and other elements of water infrastructure. Whereas New Mexico and Utah have settled agreements with the Navajo on their shared border with the Colorado River, Arizona did not, becoming the other party to this case.

The justices, in their five-to-four opinion, said that their interpretation of the 1868 treaty did not require the government to take those types of affirmative steps. Although those writing the 1868 treaty could not have anticipated the consequences of over 150 years of history and how the tribe's need for water may have been affected, "Under the Constitution's separation of powers, Congress and the President may update the law to meet modern policy priorities and needs." The minority included not only the court's three most liberal justices but also Justice Neil Gorsuch, who dissented. He pointed out that the Navajo Nation was not asking the government to take the affirmative steps outlined in the majority opinion, but merely to have the government identify which water rights belonged to the tribe in its role as trustee. Had the Navajo Nation won, their needs for additional water would have been subtracted from other states' portions and the reduced flow of the Colorado River due to evaporation and climate change. It might also have been interpreted as making the federal government foot the bill for untold dollars for water infrastructure, a precedent the court was not willing to set.

Federalism and Interstate Water Agreements

One of the primary tenets of the US Constitution is the concept of federalism, broadly defined as the way in which power is divided and shared by various levels or layers of government.

Usually, that means that the national government is limited in what it can and cannot do with clearly defined powers, and the states are given the authority to govern somewhat autonomously. The term dual federalism is often used to describe this vision of shared powers. Federalism is expressed in numerous sections of the Constitution and in interpretation and decisions by the courts. Somewhat ironically, the Supremacy Clause, found in Article VI, holds federal law to be superior to state law, but the Tenth Amendment of the Constitution holds that "the powers not delegated to the United States by the Constitution, nor prohibited by it to the States, are reserved to the States respectively, or to the people."

Those ideas might have found their way into a national water policy at some point over the last 250 years or so, but this is a complex and evolving area of the law. On the one hand is the Constitution's emphasis on national supremacy, whereas on the other is a desire for local autonomy and decision-making. Those competing views of federalism have been tested frequently as state capacity has increased in some regions, and as interest groups began to play a larger role in the development of environmental policy.

During the nation's early history, the balance of intergovernmental power, which was decidedly state-centered, played out in the eastern half of the country over a broad range of issues, based on customs, norms, and laws brought over from Europe. That model fit well until the end of the Civil War and a rebalancing that focused on nation-centered "cooperative federalism" between the states and the federal government. However, in the West, where a frontier mentality emerged from the open (often uncontrolled and unmanaged) spaces, officials sometimes relied on their distance from the nation's capital and eastern ways to allocate and manage water. Local ways of doing things, influenced by Spanish tradition and the desire to develop the land and its resources, led to permit systems and the doctrine of prior appropriation, leaving little room for any type of federal regulation and enforcement. Then, as is often the case now, Native American tribes who had been on the land and used its resources first were seldom a part of the conversation over water rights.

Because the federal government owns much more of the land in the West than it does in the East, there are bound to be conflicts over which level of government is in charge, leading to fragmentation and, more recently, partnerships. Through the twentieth and twenty-first centuries, the federal government has also used its sizable treasury to guide western water policy by funding dams, reservoirs, and other water infrastructure projects that states would not have been able to pay for on their own. It could be argued, however, that as groundwater resources have become increasingly critical to meeting the demand for water in the West, the federalism pendulum has shifted once more back to the states and, in some cases, to local governments.

State-required groundwater management plans in places like California have developed from legislative and administrative mandates, whereas local governments have experimented with restrictions on the planting of decorative turf and even building moratoriums. The result is a hybrid model of water policymaking, which in some ways is dependent on where you live.

To complicate matters even more, water is not a resource that recognizes state boundaries. Most of the nation's major river systems flow through numerous states; the Columbia, Missouri, Colorado, and Rio Grande, for example, cross state political boundaries and ignore them, making interstate cooperation essential. "Megaregions," as they are sometimes called, that share resources like water do not always value or share those resources in the same way. Add in the boundaries shared with Mexico and Canada, and there is the need for there to be national-level policies for shared waterways. As issues like climate change and patterns of extreme weather have made their way to the policy agenda, the federal government has assumed a key role in determining how water is managed. But as short-term water crises have arisen and innovative ideas have begun to develop, it is at the local level of government where decisions are increasingly being made.

Historically, disputes between states on all sorts of land and resource issues have been common. Sometimes those disputes reach a point where efforts at negotiation, wheeling (and dealing), mediation, and discussion are just not effective. The two sides fail to reach a compromise, or may decide not to continue any further attempts to sit down together. There are a variety of legal instruments that allow states to work out their differences among themselves—an interstate agreement—and other platforms that allow parties to a dispute within a state to create an intrastate agreement. Interstate agreements, which involve two or more states, stem from Article I, Section 10, Clause 3 of the US Constitution, also known as the Compact Clause. This section of the Constitution requires the states to get congressional approval to form such an agreement, a way in which the balance of power between the states and the federal government is maintained.

Historically, many of the disputes between the states involved arguments over boundaries, but in more recent times, compacts have been used as an administrative tool. The compact may divide up the authority of government, may serve as a communications tool so that the parties can conduct business, or memorialize decisions that have been made by those involved. The agreements may create a commission, identify shared resources, or provide management through agencies or bureaus.

Many disputes between states over water resources concern allocations from rivers that pass through two or more states. A compact, agreed to by the states involved and then ratified by both Congress and the legislature of each state involved, is how disagreements over the allocation of the resource are resolved. There are currently twenty-two Interstate Water Allocation Compacts in place, 16 of which involve rivers flowing through twelve western states (see Figure 5.3). The oldest of these compacts were formed in 1922; the most recent dates to 1978.

However, even where there is an agreement in place, the states may still disagree over how the agreement is being administered or complied with, and they may seek legal remedy. In that situation, because it is a dispute between states, the case is heard by the US Supreme Court, bypassing action at a lower court level, called original jurisdiction. Water resource cases are some of the most common ones that go directly to the US Supreme Court. University of Maryland professor Robert Percival notes that the justices are not eager to hear cases of original jurisdiction like those involving interstate water issues because they involve highly technical problems. It thus becomes difficult for the court to intervene in cases involving one state's position over another's.

An example of how such a dispute gets adjudicated involves the 1938 Rio Grande Compact, an agreement that divided up the Rio Grande's waters that flow nearly 2,000 miles from Colorado to Texas. According to the stipulations of the agreement, Colorado (the upriver state) cannot keep all of the river for itself, but must instead deliver a proportion of its flow to downstream New Mexico. A system of stream gauges determines whether Colorado is abiding by the compact.

Then, New Mexico must deliver a portion of its allotment to downstream Texas. The states, however, have argued for decades about the implementation of the compact, and the arguments became more acute during the drought that struck the region in the early 2000s. The court cases have been complicated by the fact that the Bureau of Reclamation is involved because it constructed the Rio Grande Project, a series of dams, reservoirs, and canals that deliver the river's waters to irrigation districts and to Mexico. Two of the irrigation districts filed suit against the Bureau in 2008, and the parties settled by creating a document that dealt with water allocations during times of drought. The parties were back in court in 2011 when New Mexico sued the US government and one of the irrigation districts, and then Texas filed a complaint in the US Supreme Court in 2013, arguing that New Mexico was not fulfilling its obligation to give the state its fair share of the Rio Grande.

The US Supreme Court chose to appoint a federal judge to oversee the procedures and facts of the case as Special Master in 2014. New Mexico filed counterclaims against Texas and the Bureau in 2018, and various parties gave testimony. Despite attempts to reach agreement on who owed what to whom over the next few years, Texas and New Mexico were not able to settle their case, although they announced they had agreed on a proposal in late 2022. Although they were not parties to the lawsuit itself, other groups' attorneys were involved in the settlement discussion, including the city of Las Cruces, New Mexico State University, the Public Service Company of New Mexico, the Southern Rio Grande Diversified Crop Farmers Association, and the New Mexico Pecan Growers. The federal government, representing the Bureau, said that the proposal violated the Rio Grande Compact, and the two irrigation districts also opposed the settlement. In late January 2024, in one tersely worded sentence, the US Supreme Court announced that it would hear arguments in Case Original No. 141 Texas v. New Mexico and Colorado, "in due course," without any date being set.

Managing Water across International Borders: Mexico and Canada

In addition to the agreements that the states have reached to manage the waters that cross their boundaries, there are additional treaties and agreements that have been established between the United States, Mexico, and Canada for the management, protection, and use of water resources that the nations share. Those with Mexico date back to the end of the 1846–1848 Mexican–American War and the Treaty of Guadalupe Hidalgo. Some have involved land acquisitions, such as the 1853 Gadsden Purchase, the last major territorial acquisition between the two countries. Others concern steps to resolve boundary disputes, such as the Banco Convention of 1905 and the 1994 North American Trade Agreement.

When it comes to the issue of water, most of the attention has focused on the Colorado River and the Rio Grande, which constitute two-thirds of the 1,900-mile-long border between the two countries. One key agreement, the 1906 Convention between the United States and Mexico for the Equitable Distribution of the Waters of the Rio Grande, dealt primarily with the northwestern El Paso/Juarez Rio Grande Basin. Although Mexico signed the agreement, the leaders were not satisfied with its terms and plans to build a dam at Elephant Butte, New Mexico that was not finished until 1916. Mexico was not allowed to participate in the subsequent negotiations for the Colorado River Compact, and although the United States and Mexico agreed to resume talks in 1928, the discussions went nowhere.

The Water Treaty of 1944 and the IBWC

The broader Treaty on Utilization of Waters of the Colorado and Tijuana Rivers and of the Rio Grande, better known as the 1944 Water Treaty, covered the southwestern Lower Rio Grande Basin and its tributaries. Unlike interstate compacts where a river's flow is shared between the upper and lower water rights holder, this bilateral agreement splits water between two nations, and as a result, the United States gives Mexico some of its water share, and Mexico gives some of its water to the United States. It may be thought of as a type of multilateral agreement that involves not only the two national governments but also eight US states and seven Mexican states that comprise the Colorado and Rio Grande basins.

Under this agreement, the United States granted a minimum of 1.5 million acre-feet of Colorado River water to Mexico, or about 10 percent of the Colorado's annual flow. However, when the treaty was made, the annual flow was estimated at 16.8 million acre-feet per year; it is currently estimated to be closer to 13–14 million acre-feet, depending on the season and year. It is as if there was an assumption that the river's flow would never change, nor would the allotments from each state ever change into perpetuity.

The Morelos Dam, about a mile downstream from the boundary between the United States and Mexico, is administered by both countries, serving as the gateway for the water that flows to irrigate the agricultural land in the Mexicali Valley, as well as providing water to Tijuana and Tecate. Other stipulations dealt with the Rio Grande and the Rio Conchos, its primary tributary. Under the treaty's provisions, Mexico retains the water rights to two-thirds of the water from the six Rio Grande tributaries on its side; whereas the United States gets all water from those tributaries that are on its side, plus one-third of the six on the Mexican side. The United States is required to deliver 60,000 acre-feet from the northwestern portion of the Rio Grande to the Mexican state of Chihuahua. On the other hand, Mexico must give the United States an average of 350,000 acre-feet of water (measured in five-year cycles) from the tributaries of the Rio Grande.

Key to the implementation of the 1944 agreement is the International Boundary and Water Commission (IBWC, or CILA—Comisión Internacional de Limites y Aguas—in Mexico). Although the IBWC dates back to 1889, the organization was disbanded in 1941 with its diplomatic functions transferred to the International Boundary Commission (IBC). The 1944 treaty expanded the power and duties of the commission by making it the primary arbiter over water disputes. The organization has its headquarters in El Paso, Texas, although it is considered a federal agency in the United States under the Department of State. In Mexico, the agency is headquartered in Ciudad Juarez. Each country has its own administrative and managerial bodies, with legal advisors, commissioners, and other staff.

During the negotiations on the 1944 agreement, several issues were encountered, including how the waters of the Tijuana River would be allocated, the quality of the water Mexico would receive, and how and where the water from each side would be delivered. President Franklin Roosevelt's Good Neighbor Policy, which focused on enhancing US relations with Latin America, along with the Second World War, positively influenced the US Senate's approval and ratification in April 1945. The treaty was believed to represent concessions on the part of all the entities involved, underscoring the importance of the Law of the River, and an institutionalization of international procedures that would later influence other transboundary agreements.

Another important section of the treaty deals with the postponement of deliveries during what is termed "extraordinary drought or serious accident," although there is no quantifiable definition of what constitutes an "extraordinary drought" or "serious accident." If such a condition occurs, for instance, and

Mexico is unable to fulfill its portion of the water-sharing agreement, it must repay the water it owes the United States during the next five-year cycle, and neither country can fail to pay its debt to the other for two cycles, putting some endpoint on water debt payments. However, not all conditions are equal. If the United States is unable to meet its water obligation from the Colorado River due to extreme drought, Article 10 of the treaty allows the United States to reduce the allotment to Mexico proportionally to reflect consumptive uses in the United States. There are no teeth in the agreement, however, for non-compliance, and disputes are to be decided by the IBCW's commissioners.

Mexico has defaulted on its water-sharing obligations several times since 1994, even though it previously was a good binational partner. In the period 1994–2003, drought conditions forced Mexico to incur two five-year cycles of water debt. Through a variety of negotiations and strategies, along with water from hurricanes, Mexico paid off its accumulated water debt in 2005. In 2013, Texas farmers were the ones facing drought conditions, and struggled when Mexico delayed its water deliveries to the United States. But in the 2015–2020 cycle, Mexico once again could not deliver a sufficient amount of water to meet its treaty obligations, but was able to do so in 2016.

On a more positive note, Minute 319 (2012) was a five-year agreement encompassing several cooperative actions: joint investment in water conservation and infrastructure projects; a pilot water-exchange program; proactive basin operations with water delivery from Lake Mead to Mexico depending on reservoir conditions; allowing Mexico to defer delivery of a portion of its allotment of Colorado River water due to the need to repair earthquake-damaged infrastructure; and creating a program of Intentionally Created Mexican Allocation where Mexico could temporarily reduce its allocation so that water could be stored and delivered to Mexico in the future. Senior officials from both countries lauded the first-time intentional release of water, called a pulse flow, from the Morelos Dam in March 2014. The experimental process, which ran for about eight weeks, involved opening control gates from the dam at various times and in various amounts, down the Colorado River's channel, as the water flows into the delta and its estuary to the Sea of Cortez. Ecosystem restoration in the Colorado River Delta, which covered 1.9 million acres of land a century ago, is needed because much of the river has been dammed and diverted to agriculture and cities.

When Minute 319 expired, it was continued with Minute 323 in another attempt at the two countries maintaining a constructive relationship. Signed in

2017, the agreement allowed Mexico to store water in Lake Mead, and required the United States to invest $31.5 million in Mexican water efficiency projects, along with creating a work group that explored a binational desalination project. The infrastructure project, when completed, will save about 200,000 acre-feet of water, with the project paid for by a combination of federal funds and money from US irrigation districts. The parties also agreed to provide a continuous flow of water to the delta, expanding restoration habitat from 1,700 acres to 4,300 acres. For its part, Mexico agreed to cut back its water consumption during times of shortage, but only after the US basin states implemented their own reduction protocols. As a result, Mexico took temporary conservation measures in the summers of 2021 and 2022 during the severe drought. The 2017 agreement is set to expire in 2026.

Despite these attempts at bilateral cooperation, the 2015–2020 water cycle again proved problematic for Mexico. *The New York Times* reported that activists had occupied the La Boquilla Dam in February 2020, protesting water deliveries, burning government buildings, destroying cars, blocking a major railroad line between the United States and Mexico, and briefly holding politicians hostage. Due to thirty years of drought, Mexico had delivered only 89 percent of the water that was due to the United States, and still owed the remainder of its delivery from the Rio Conchos and dams in the state of Chihuahua. As the October 24 deadline for the final delivery approached, Chihuahuan farmers wielding sticks, rocks, and homemade shields rallied at the dam in protest. In what was variously called a war, a rebellion, and a skirmish, they climbed over a hill and ambushed hundreds of soldiers guarding the facility, blocking local authorities from extracting the water that was to be delivered to Texas. The president of Mexico called out the Mexican National Guard to the area, and about 2,000 protesters closed the valves that then stopped the water flow, at which point the National Guard surrendered. The Texas governor then asked the US administration to become involved because the United States sends Mexico about four times what the United States receives. Later that day, protesters blocked the National Guard's route, the soldiers opened fire, and a woman was killed.

Three days before the deadline, a new agreement was reached, Minute 325, requiring Mexico to meet its water obligations by transferring all of the water it stored in the Amistad and Falcon reservoirs to the United States, depleting virtually all of northern Mexico's stored water. In exchange, the United States agreed to the terms of the 1944 treaty to provide humanitarian support by only providing water for domestic and municipal purposes to communities downstream from the Amistad reservoir, not for agricultural use. Mexico was also required to pay the United States in full for any water it used.

Salinity and Sanitation

Among Mexico's priorities in its continuing negotiations with the United States over water is its quality. As Stephen Mumme notes, the two factors that affected concerns about water quality post-1944 were rapid urbanization and the expansion of commercial agriculture, coupled with a rising environmental/public health movement in the 1960s and 1970s that led to important legislative efforts dealing with water pollution. In adjoining border communities like San Diego/Tijuana and Calexico/Mexicali, the discharge of raw sewage into rivers was commonplace and rarely dealt with effectively. Similarly, the amount of salt in the water Mexico received during the period 1961–1973 was part of a continuing dispute over the language in the 1944 treaty that Mexico would accept Colorado River water regardless of where it came from and Mexican interpretation that the water would be sufficient for ordinary irrigation.

These issues became part of subsequent bilateral negotiations, calls for technical studies to determine the effects of saline water on agriculture, and discussions on who would pay for any new infrastructural solutions. Both salinity and sanitation remained on the agenda as US companies moved their operations to Mexico, but Mexico's economic crash of the early 1980s, accompanied by spiraling migration and a burgeoning narcotics trade, made the disparity between what the two countries wanted, but could not equally afford economically or politically, even more acute. Even the 1983 La Paz Agreement, which had conservation of the environment as one of its stated objectives and highlighted the role of each nation's environmental agencies, was not specific enough to solve the border region's environmental problems. Most of the "fixes," including construction of expanded Mexican sewage treatment facilities, were unfixed due to equipment failures. The North American Free Trade Agreement (NAFTA), meanwhile, has been criticized for neglecting important water management issues and challenges along the Mexico–United States border.

What might have been a sanitation success, the completion of the South Bay International Water Treatment Project at the border between San Diego and Tijuana in 1997, was hampered by the failure of Congress to appropriate money for a secondary treatment facility that was to be completed by 2000. The plant was eventually opened in late 2010. Since that time, however, the population in the Tijuana corridor has grown far beyond either city's capacity to handle sanitary waste in a way that meets the requirements of US legislation and regulatory requirements.

Aside from some of the adjustments made through the Minutes, which are extensions of the treaty, up to now the two countries concur that there is a need to adjust the 1944 agreement to recognize how the world has changed in the last eighty years. Some observers point to the resource disparity between the nations, noting that Mexico does not have the same financial capacity as the United States. Can or will the United States channel public or private investment to finance the kind of infrastructure changes that are needed, especially in the Mexicali Valley where crops are irrigated with Colorado River water? Farmers have never had an incentive to deal with drought, or to upgrade their infrastructure to improve efficiency. Is it possible to transition to an agricultural economy where more is produced efficiently with less water? Can farmers shift away from crops like alfalfa to those that use less water?

Those on the Mexican side of the border have blamed NAFTA, the maquiladoras built along the northern border, and American consumer demands for agricultural products. Still others point to climate change and extreme weather for drying up the water Mexico and the border states have traditionally relied upon. Drought led to a 5 percent reduction in Mexico's share of water from the Colorado in 2022, and a 7 percent reduction in 2023 under the terms of the 1944 treaty. Some point to criminal groups in Mexico, referred to as the water mafia, who are accused of siphoning off or diverting water from local sources, then selling it at inflated prices, along with water theft and smuggling water. Others believe that conflicts arise because of the structural and political differences between the two countries when it comes to water policy.

In Mexico, all water is owned by the federal government and managed by one institution, Comisión Nacional del Agua (Conagua), a highly centralized administrative body. In the United States, however, individuals, state and local governments, and corporations can all own the country's surface and groundwater due to a complex system of water rights and jurisdictions. Almost everyone looks to the new Interim Guidelines for Lower Basin Shortages, waiting to see what the diminishing water resources that they always relied on in the past will be divided into even smaller portions.

Canadian and US Water Agreements

Along the total 4,800-mile length of the boundary between the United States and Canada are an estimated 300 lakes, rivers, and streams that flow along or cross the border. Unlike the situation with Mexico, there are no rivers that actually form the boundary between the United States and Canada. There are, however, ten Transboundary Aquifer Systems (TAS) along the border, identified as part of the Internationally Shared Aquifer Resources Management Initiative (ISARM) of UNESCO. About 55 percent of the ninety significant transboundary rivers flow from Canada to the United States. In one case the United States may be upstream, in another downstream.

Issues related to shared riverine resources between the United States and Canada date back to the turn of the nineteenth century, when settlers in Montana sought to divert water from the St. Mary and Milk rivers, building canals that would compete with those being built on the Alberta side.

Similar disputes along the Niagara River, where navigation and hydroelectric power were key issues, led to the signing of the 1909 Boundary Waters Treaty (BWT) and the establishment of the International Joint Commission (IJC). The six-member body held its first meeting in 1912, providing a framework for resolution. Key to the BWT are agreements that neither country will pollute their shared rivers; that water levels and flows will not be altered without agreement of the parties and the IJC.

Although most of the agreements do not specifically affect states in the western United States, the most important of them is the Columbia River Treaty. After the Second World War, both nations were faced with flooding throughout the Columbia Basin, and the need for additional sources of energy as the economy and population grew throughout the region. In 1961, both Canada and the United States agreed to the need for additional water storage capacity and flood control mediation, leading to the ratification of the Columbia River Treaty in 1964. The agreement has a minimum term of sixty years. Three dams were built on the Canadian side, and one in the United States. The US Army Corps of Engineers and the Bonneville Power Administration serve as the primary partners for the United States, and the British Columbia Hydro and Power Authority is their Canadian counterpart. In 2013, after an extensive review of the treaty, both nations recommended that the treaty be modified to consider environmental impacts and tribal concerns when its current term ends in 2024.

There have been differences between the two nations that affect the western states, but they have not been on the same scale as those with Mexico. For instance, traditionally, those on the US side have tended to view the boundary as part of the last frontier, whereas those on the Canadian side have seen those same lands and resources as part of a corridor for development. In the case of the Coal Creek open pit coal development in the upper Flathead Basin in British Columbia, for instance, the US position, endorsed by environmental groups, was that the project would negatively affect the water quality on the Montana side. It is there that the Flathead River was federally designated as "wild and scenic." Transnational coalitions have often formed to fight projects that change the character of a river or threaten it through pollution. The Canadian government has also had a different perspective on its water resources than the United States. The Canadian Parliament passed some of the world's most progressive water management legislation in 1987, but most of the measures were never implemented or enforced. It has been argued that Canadians, especially those in Parliament, believe that their country has an abundance of fresh water and therefore no real need to regulate it.

Proponents of bulk water transfers, such as shipping water in oil tankers from British Columbia along the Pacific Coast, resurrected the concept from the 1960s during the 1990s and the most recent droughts in the Southwest, but the idea has not had much traction in Canada, where bulk water transports are basically prohibited. This is not to say that Canada is taking water for granted. In 2023, Prime Minister Justin Trudeau announced the creation of the Winnipeg, Manitoba-based Canada Water Agency. The new administrative body is designed to work with the provinces and native people, as well as the nation's partners in research and development, to determine strategies for keeping the nation's water clean, safe, and well-managed.

Unresolved, however, are the two nations' differences in dealing with their indigenous peoples' water rights. In the United States, the creation of reservations for Native Americans has been recognized by the courts as including reserved water rights to meet tribal needs. Canada, in comparison, has established smaller reservations with limited water allotments. Ardith Walkem notes that Canada requires that its indigenous people either negotiate a succession treaty in exchange for limited land and water rights, or prove that they have aboriginal (original) title or rights to water, not only for drinking water but also for fishing and other uses. The latter is a costly and time-consuming process, not totally different from what US tribes experience.

In 2021, the Canadian government repealed a 2013 Act in a settlement agreement to engage First Nations in further discussion on water infrastructure, drinking water, and wastewater on First Nations lands. In addition to developing legislation to implement those discussions through 2023, Indigenous Services Canada (ISC) is mandated to gradually transfer responsibility for the care and control of water and wastewater services to First Nations bodies. The action, although somewhat vague at present, is being attempted to further self-determination and advance reconciliation.

The Dam Builders of the West: The Bureau of Reclamation

American geographer and explorer John Wesley Powell is credited by some as the reason why there is a Bureau of Reclamation today. Others point to the droughts that began in 1887 in the West and dried up the land and its people except for homesteads adjacent to rivers or streams that could easily be diverted. The hundreds of private irrigation companies that promised that the West would become an Eden were mostly gone by 1890. Several attempts at developing state-level irrigation programs were unsuccessful. California, for instance, enacted the Wright Act in 1887, creating irrigation districts that failed under the incompetence of their directors and internal squabbles. A similar system in Colorado led to the construction of five storage reservoirs, all of which foundered before they could deliver any water. Even the federal government's attempt to increase the amount of irrigated acreage in the West—the 1894 Carey Act—failed to work. But even as westerners lost confidence with Washington they expressed confidence they could reclaim the arid lands of the west on their own.

In 1901, Congressman Francis G. Newlands (profiled in Chapter 4), introduced a bill to create a nationalized irrigation program. It was soundly defeated, only to be resurrected by Theodore Roosevelt and Wyoming senator Francis Warren. When the revised measure became law as the Reclamation Act on June 17, 1902 (excerpted in Chapter 5), efforts had to be made to satisfy the diverse interests who had eventually decided to support the bill. There was also the task of setting up the administrative apparatus of the new United States Reclamation Service (USRS) within the Division of Hydrography in the US Geological Survey. The new director, Frederick Newell, was charged with not only hiring an engineering staff but also deciding where any new projects would be sited.

Newell decided to spread out the projects throughout the West in an attempt to curry favor with those whose support for the Reclamation Act had been lukewarm. Initially, projects were to be financed by a Reclamation Fund, whose revenue would come from the sale of land in the western states. The legislation also required users to repay the federal government for the water they purchased from various projects within ten years, although that time frame proved unrealistic and was extended to twenty years in 1914, and then to forty years, and then fifty.

Twenty years after the Reclamation Act was passed, only 10 percent of the Reclamation Fund loans had been repaid, and 60 percent of those receiving water were defaulting. With a 40 percent delinquency rate, there was vocal criticism of the agency. Calls were made for the Bureau to "lay down the law" to the farmers who had at least a moral obligation to make their payments on time. There was no interest charged on the payments water users owed—amounting to a substantial subsidy, thanks to taxpayers. In addition, there was no requirement that the money from the sale of land be spent in that state, allowing for considerable discretion on who would benefit from land sales.

In the 1912 annual report on the Reclamation Service, Newell admitted that the agency had made some mistakes in its first decade as a pioneering water management agency, noting that the organization operated under "fallacies" such as underestimating the costs of irrigation projects and that water alone would allow farmers to prosper. Admitting that not all of the landowners were competent to settle and farm their lands, Newlands identified the problems faced by poor soil conditions and the types of crops that could be grown on arid lands.

In 1907, the management of the USRS was switched to the Department of the Interior as an independent bureau. In 1923, the USRS changed its name to the Bureau of Reclamation (BOR). The infant agency was in a hurry to get going, with twenty-one projects completed or under construction within the first five years of its existence.

The keystone project of the newly named Bureau was the Boulder Canyon Dam, construction of which was authorized by Congress in 1928. There was a catch, however. Congress conditioned the building of the dam and the accompanying All-American Canal only if at least six of the seven states ratified the 1922 Colorado River Compact (discussed in Chapter 2 and excerpted in Chapter 5). There was an additional requirement that California's allotment of water from the Colorado River be limited to 4.4 million acre-feet per year, with 2.8 million for Arizona and 300,000 for Nevada. Arizona decided not to ratify the compact, but the other six states' votes were enough to get the Boulder Dam project started.

When Elwood Mead (profiled in Chapter 4) was named Commissioner of Reclamation by Calvin Coolidge in 1924, the Bureau focused almost entirely on building the Boulder Dam and other big projects that would serve to reclaim the West. The rains that fell on the western plains from about 1920 to 1930, generating bonanzas of wheat and other crops, provided no hint that the soils of that same region would dissolve into dust as winds and high temperatures blew through the prairie. Almost 250 million acres of land were destroyed, debilitated, or marginalized, by 1934, according to the National Resources Board.

With a change in leadership from Commissioner Elwood Mead to John Page in 1936, the Bureau's focus shifted to engineering rather than the social goal of reclaiming the arid lands of the West. Although Mead was a social idealist who wanted small farmers to benefit from the Bureau's activities, Page, an engineer who served as commissioner from 1936 to 1943, saw the benefits of the revenues that would accrue as hydroelectric power flourished.

In California's San Joaquin Valley, the BOR began building the Central Valley Project in 1933, including a series of dams on the state's major rivers. The Bureau also had its eyes on the country's fourth largest river, the Columbia, and what would become the Grand Coulee Dam in a region where few of the inhabitants had power, and there weren't very many people living there to begin with. Supported by President Roosevelt, the Columbia Basin Project was a huge endeavor that was part symbolism, part public works project. Critics argued that there was no real need for the Grand Coulee Dam to be built at that time, and that a surplus of electric power was unnecessary given the projected cost of the project.

The Bureau of Reclamation in the Post-Second World War Era

The vision of national reclamation in an agrarian society that had been the basis for the creation of the Bureau in the early twentieth century was replaced by one crafted to meet a new set of postwar (and post-Depression) challenges. Mead's successor in 1945, Michael Straus, elevated dam building to the top of the agenda within the agency, which immediately began to concentrate more on research, locating its primary laboratory in Denver. There was also a geographical shift as the potential benefits of reclamation in the Pacific Northwest began to be realized. The Columbia River Basin was perceived almost as an experiment in regional economic growth, especially as related to the basin's natural resources. Leland Olds, chairman of the Federal Power Commission, saw the potential for building a culture that was part spiritual, part economic. He envisioned the creation of a more diverse economy, less dependent on extractive industries like coal and oil because it would be powered by federally funded low-cost hydroelectric power.

As had been the case with the Second World War, the BOR experienced significant budget cuts during the Korean War from 1950 to 1953. After the conflict ended, Straus lobbied Congress to enact the Colorado River Storage Project. The project called for ten new dams with a storage capacity of 48.5 million acre-feet, and a planned 1,622,000 kilowatts of electricity. Of political importance was the fact that the project would subsidize agricultural irrigation in the Upper Basin states where the return on investment was marginal in the best of times. Despite opposition from early environmental leaders like the Sierra Club's David Brower, who was able to defeat the proposal for the Echo Park Dam, construction on the Glen Canyon Dam began shortly after the legislation was signed into law by President Dwight Eisenhower in April 1956.

A decade later, the Vietnam War brought an end to the Bureau's construction projects with only a few exceptions, mostly those already under development. As its budget shrank, the agency also faced the momentum of the environmental movement and a revived awareness of conservation of natural resources like water. The publication of books such as scientist Rachel Carson's *Silent Spring* (1962), which documented the awful impact of DDT and other widely used chemicals on wildlife and ecosystems, helped build public support for the passage of a series of important laws protecting the air, water, wild and scenic rivers, wildlife, and endangered species.

One piece of legislation that complicated the Bureau's attempts to build more dams was the 1970 National Environmental Policy Act (NEPA), signed by President Richard Nixon. The statute required that proposed federal building projects undergo and pass environmental impact statements before being greenlighted. This requirement created a new wrinkle in reclamation planning for an agency that had historically been managed by engineers rather than ecologists.

The Teton Dam Failure

Still another unexpected event, the failure of Idaho's Teton Dam on the Snake River on June 5, 1976, changed fortune into misfortune. The dam had been authorized by Congress in 1964 after persistent lobbying by the Idaho delegation, but construction did not begin until February 1972 due to Vietnam-related cuts to Reclamation's budget. Although critics openly questioned the costs versus benefits of despoiling a beautiful river that was favored by fly-fishers, and US Geological Survey warnings about siting the dam in an area of high seismic risk on a poor basaltic rock foundation, local support and key political figures remained strongly in favor of the $85 million project. While the Teton Dam was being constructed, cracks that would later be called fissures were detected in several areas of the abutments, and BOR officials met with contractors to discuss grouting them with liquid concrete under high pressure.

In May 1976, the heavy snowpack on the Teton mountains was melting and the water in the reservoir was filling much faster than had been expected. An emergency outlet works that had been built to allow the reservoir level to be drawn down was still not operational, and in early June, leaks began to appear. Construction officials then noticed that there was a torrent washing away the downstream face of the dam. On June 5, calls were made to local law enforcement telling them to evacuate 12,000 people from the towns of Teton, Wilford, and then Sugar City, not far from Rexburg, Idaho, with a population of 8,000. Later that morning, the dam collapsed into the reservoir, and a wall of water traveling at 15 miles per hour began flooding the Teton Canyon and the flat plain below. A seven-foot wave hit Rexburg, covering what was left of the burned town in topsoil, and made its way to Idaho Falls, where sandbagged levees helped to save the town from more severe damage. The end result of the dam's failure: 11 deaths, 4,000 homes damaged or destroyed, 350 businesses wiped out, and an estimated $2 billion in damage.

The Teton Dam disaster was seized on by dam-building opponents, who argued that they were not smart investments. After assuming office in January 1977, President Jimmy Carter developed a "hit list" of reputed pork barrel projects in order to shore up the president's credentials as both an environmentalist and a foe of wasteful government spending. Dam projects were among Carter's targets, with some canceled outright, others put on hold, and some scaled back. Even the agency's name came under fire, becoming the Water and Power Resources Service in 1979 but then reclaiming its title as the Bureau of Reclamation when Ronald Reagan became president in 1981.

The Bureau of Reclamation, 1982–2024

The signing of the Reclamation Reform Act of 1982 (RRA) marked a period of broad regulatory and bureaucratic changes as the government was tasked with economic recovery.

One of the biggest legislative changes involving agriculture, the RRA expanded the amount of acreage for which an individual could receive low-cost BOR water, a standard that would be applied throughout the West. Instead of the previous limit of 180 acres, the new law set the limitation for qualified recipients at 960 acres, with a number of special exemptions and circumstances. One of the requirements of the previous legislation from 1902, residency, was eliminated, marking what some considered to be the end of the family farm and the nation's focus on water for agricultural use.

In 1987, the change in the organizational mission of the Bureau became official; a report on the agency's future goals noted that in the era of shrinking resources, it would no longer construct large, federally financed water projects. Instead, the focus would be on efficiency, collaboration, smaller projects, and water conservation. Although there was over $2.4 billion for the agency's projects, there was an emphasis on fish and wildlife restoration that troubled many members of Congress, who felt the Bureau's record was not impressive in this area. Central to their unease was the salmon industry and environmental concerns that became the rallying cry of "fish versus dams."

The Grand Coulee Dam epitomized the struggle, and although the installation of fish ladders did help the migration of spawning salmon in smaller facilities, Grand Coulee was too big for ladders to be practical. Instead, the BOR began trapping the salmon and carrying them by truck to streams that were closer to the Pacific Ocean. Efforts such as these were only modestly successful. Debate over how to interpret and implement various fish and wildlife laws, especially the Endangered Species Act, emphasized the attempts to balance the environment and the economy, especially where water was concerned.

Under the presidency of Bill Clinton and his reinventing government directives, the Bureau of Reclamation's new mission in 1993 was "to manage, develop, and protect water and related resources in an environmentally and economically sound manner in the interest of the American public." This, too, was a continuation of the policy of moving the agency away from dam building and toward a more fiscally responsible, leaner, organization. One major change was a shift toward settlement agreements for disputes over tribal water rights. The focus during the tenure of the Obama administration, in contrast, was on infrastructure development. In 2011, in a Presidential Memorandum, the administration directed the BOR to expedite the permitting and environmental review process for the Navajo-Gallup Water Supply Project in New Mexico. Although the Trump administration can be credited with the naming of the first woman to head the BOR, and direction for the agency to modernize Central

Valley Projects operations, the biggest contemporary developments came under President Biden, when Congress passed the landmark Inflation Reduction Act. The measure included $4 billion for the BOR to respond to long-term drought conditions in the West. The legislation placed an emphasis on the Colorado River, adding $550 million to provide reliable drinking water for disadvantaged communities in the region, and building on an $8.3 billion allocation in a separate federal infrastructure bill for drought response. Critics called the funds a drop in the bucket for what was needed, but to the BOR, the newly found money was unheard of.

The Other Dam Builders: The United States Army Corps of Engineers

One of the oldest organizations within the US government, the Corps of Engineers started not as an entity but as an action during the Revolutionary War when a group of Continental Army engineers built a defensive breastwork (or parapet, as it is usually known) on Boston's Bunker Hill. After the war, its duties were formalized as the Army Corps of Engineers in 1794.

Although the vast majority of the Corps' projects are in the East, the agency has sometimes made its way west to carry out projects and operations in the traditional territory of the Bureau of Reclamation. In the mid-1930s, a bureaucratic and political race developed between the two organizations over who would develop the irrigation potential of the Kings and the Kern Rivers, which flow into California's Central Valley from the Sierra Nevada. The water projects were not exactly the same; the Corps said its design was for flood control rather than reclamation, so in 1940, Congress was given the opportunity to analyze and vote on both. President Franklin Roosevelt let known his preference for the Bureau's version that focused on irrigation; Congress sought to have the Corps work on the Kings River, and the agency did so in 1942, arguing that it was constructing an emergency flood diversion structure, which, perhaps coincidentally, would divert the river's water to four biggest agribusinesses. The duel was interrupted by the Second World War.

In 1945, as the country recovered from the government's war efforts and returned to rebuilding domestically, the battle between the two agencies began anew as the Corps announced that it would build dams on the two rivers, not flood control channels. Congress punted on making a decision, leaving it up to the House and Senate appropriations committees to decide which agency should be funded. Harry S. Truman, who became president after Roosevelt died, chose to support the Corps over the Bureau, as did corporate growers who contributed to the members of Congress who favored their needs. Not only did the Corps win the battle to dam the Kings and Kern Rivers, but they later got the nod over the Bureau to build dams over the other two rivers flowing out of the southern Sierra, the Tule and the Kaweah. Damming the Kings and Kern Rivers allowed the Corps to dry up the terminal but unpredictable Tulare Lake, part of the Tulare Basin hydrological area that was home to migrant bird species during wet winters. Drying up Tulare Lake meant that the large agricultural interests could plant crops on 80,000 acres of the shallow lakebed land they owned without worry about flooding. Dikes prevented water from intruding on the landowners' farmland so that their mega-farm business would continue without disruption.

Although the Corps' work might have been considered a success at the time, the four dam projects and the reservoirs they created—Pine Flat and Isabella–did not take into account the massive rainfall that resulted in flooding in 1983, or the same scenario when it was repeated nearly forty years later. In the first instance, the floodwaters that would have ended up naturally in Tulare Lake prior to the dams' construction began lapping at nearby towns in the Central Valley. In response, the Corps spent nearly $3 million to build levees to protect local residents and businesses. When one of the levees was breached in March 1983, 30,000 acres of farmland ended up under water. The local irrigation district then asked for a permit to begin pumping the water out so it could join the San Joaquin River and then into San Francisco Bay. The problem was that one or more of the reservoirs had been stocked with opportunistic white bass that had made their way into Tulare Lake, and if the fish were not stopped, the bass could eat young salmon and striped bass, destroying the region's commercial and sportfishing industry. Unable to stop the white bass, the California Department of Fish and Game decided to mass poison them (and everything else, including waterfowl) along six miles of the San Joaquin River while Tulare Lake dried up again.

The Corps' other duties include maintaining the National Inventory of Dams (NID), which documents all known dams in the United States and its territories. This database provides information about seventy different criteria including the dam's location, type, size, purpose, use, and benefits, along with date of the dam's most recent inspection, structural and geographical information.

Dams are regulated by a variety of agencies, the majority of them by states, with about 6 percent under federal regulation.

Removing the Dams and Restoring the Rivers

After more than twenty years of debate, the world's largest dam removal project along the Klamath River in northern California was completed in fall 2024, marking the most significant shift in the nation's policy of damming rivers. Dams have been an essential element of the country's growth, both for hydropower and to store water supplies in reservoirs, but removing them is a much more recent development, driven largely by tribes and environmental advocates to restore rivers and ecosystems, and concerns about the safety of the dams themselves. The Klamath project is one of many changes taking place on rivers in almost every state in the West in an effort to restore natural flows and open up fish and wildlife habitat.

The Klamath Basin covers 9.4 million acres, and is home to six tribal nations, six National Wildlife Refuges, family farms, agriculture industry, commercial salmon fisheries, and uncounted recreational opportunities. Between 1903 and 1962, PacifiCorp built seven dams along 400 miles of the Klamath River stretching along the border of southern Oregon and northern California. However, the water quality in the reservoirs created by the dams, along with the health of the river itself, deteriorated due to heat and the accumulation of farm runoff, leading to toxic algae blooms and disease outbreaks. In 2001, the federal government reduced the Klamath's water deliveries to farms to protect endangered fish, but it took a catastrophic fish kill in 2002 to focus attention on the damage being done to the salmon industry. Tribal leaders and environmental groups took their case to PacifiCorp, the utility company that owned four dams on the lower Klamath. The company's operating license for the dams was about to expire, and the four hydroelectric plants produced less than 2 percent of PacifiCorp's power. In 2010, after sustained lobbying and pressure by advocates for removing the dams, the company agreed to do so.

The dams' removal has been managed through development of a community-based proposal, a settlement agreement (the Klamath Hydroelectric Settlement Agreement, or KHSA), and creation of a non-profit organization to manage decommissioning, dismantling, restoration. and renewal (Klamath River Renewal Project). The $500 million project calls for KRRC (the Klamath River Renewal Corporation, the private, independent, non-profit organization made up of the signatories to the KHSA) to take ownership of the dams from PacifiCorp, remove the four dams, empty three reservoirs, restore 2,000 acres of previously inundated lands, and implement mitigation measures. The Yurok Tribe planted billions of seeds that nurseries have propagated. Once the infrastructure was removed, the Klamath began to flow freely again. Many believe the project has become an example of what could be done on a larger scale throughout the West.

Other Notable Dam Removal Projects

An earlier decommissioning project on a smaller scale had taken place on the Olympic Peninsula about 50 miles west of Seattle. In the early 1900s, the Elwha and Glines Canyon dams were built by the Olympic Power Company on the Elwha River to generate hydropower for Port Angeles, Washington and support the booming logging industry. The dams blocked the migration of salmon, whose populations plummeted, and damaged their habitat by preventing sediment from flowing downstream in the areas that were the ancestral lands of the Lower Elwha Klallam Tribe. After decades of lobbying, Congress enacted the Elwha River Ecosystem and Fisheries Restoration Act of 1992, authorizing the Department of the Interior to purchase the dams from the power company. Nearly two decades of planning later, the largest dam removal up to that time began at a cost of $350 million. The Elwha Dam was removed in 2012, with the Glines Canyon dam removed two years later. The National Park Service worked with the tribe on a massive habitat restoration project, and although salmon returned to the river almost immediately, it took years for the river's sediment to settle as the river's natural flow returned.

Also on the drawing board is a federal project to decommission four dams in eastern Washington along the Snake River, home to salmon and trout and an ecosystem that is critical to more than 100 species. The four hydroelectric dams on the lower Snake are of a much more recent vintage, built between 1961 and 1975, but they produce only 4.3 percent of the region's power. When they were built, the dams' reservoirs flooded valuable agricultural land and wildlife habitat, and changed the character of some rural communities. Pressure to dismantle the aging structures has come from political leaders, scientists, the Nez Perce, and other tribes. Another Washington state project on the Similkameen River has the support of the Colville Tribe, and supporters in Oregon are calling for a dam on the Willamette River to be dismantled.

There is even some support for the removal of dams on two of the most controversial projects in the country's history. In 1913 the Raker Act gave the city of San Francisco the right to take water from the Tuolumne River in California's Sierra Nevada through an aqueduct to the glacier-carved Hetch Hetchy Valley that had once been the homeland of a dozen indigenous tribes, and from there to the city. The need for more water had been intensified by the fires that followed the 1906 San Francisco earthquake, along with the growth of the city's population.

Naturalist John Muir, who led the campaign to have the area named a national park, called Hetch Hetchy one of nature's rarest and most precious mountain temples. Despite his appeal for preservation, the O'Shaughnessy Dam and a reservoir were built between 1919 and 1923, flooding Muir's beloved valley. Today, groups like Restore Hetch Hetchy are pursuing other storage options that would allow the valley to be drained and restored.

Near Page, Arizona, other groups have rallied against Glen Canyon Dam, built between 1956 and 1966 as a water storage facility for the Lower Colorado River Basin at a cost of $135 million. The dam, which created Lake Powell, and a similar proposed project, the Echo Park Dam on the Green River inside Dinosaur National Monument, became rallying points for the Sierra Club and its leader, David Brower. One of the most active groups seeking to have the dam removed, the Glen Canyon Institute, commissioned a study that showed that storing water in Lake Mead, rather than Lake Powell, would save 300,000-acre-feet of water per year, or about the same amount of Colorado River water allocated to the entire state of Nevada. Another activist group, the Grand Canyon Trust, notes that sending Lake Powell's water into Lake Mead would generate more power than trying to continue generating electricity from two existing power plants with low water levels at both sites.

Made of too much concrete that would be difficult to completely remove, some envision a reengineered facility that would drain most of the water from Lake Powell or some kind of bypass mechanism. The destruction of Glen Canyon was the subject of Edward Abbey's book *The Monkey Wrench Gang*.

Taking Stock of America's Dams

Although the US Army Corps of Engineers is one of the federal agencies tasked with keeping an inventory of the number of dams in the United States and its territories, the actual number of dams that exist is not known. The National Inventory of Dams (NID) does identify the largest structures, but some observers believe that the number—about 92,000 in 2023—is well below what actually exists. The American Society of Civil Engineers says that seven of ten of the country's dams are more than fifty years old, the point at which expensive repairs become more likely. The average age of dams in the United States is now sixty years. Some dams are in such a bad state of disrepair that the organization estimates it would cost $45 billion to upgrade them and make them safe. Many are obsolete due to the continued decline of manufacturing and a lower cost of renewable energy. The Corps has listed 76 percent of existing US dams as having "high hazard potential." This designation by the Federal Emergency Management Agency (FEMA) is applied to dams whose "failure or mis-operation will cause loss of human life and significant property destruction."

Since 1912, nearly 2,000 dams have been razed, nearly three-quarters of those since 1999 when the Edwards Dam in Maine was removed. The Klamath and Elwha projects are the two largest removal projects undertaken thus far as stakeholders take a closer look at the costs versus benefits of not only big dams but also smaller ones. However, the group American Rivers cautions that the number of dams that have been removed probably represents less than 2 percent of the total number of dams in the United States; less than 3 percent of the dams removed produced hydropower.

One alternative that is also under consideration is to raise the height of existing dams rather than building new ones. In California's Central Valley, the B.F. Sisk Dam and its San Luis Reservoir near Los Banos are most likely to be constructed. The 382-foot-high earthfill dam was completed in 1967 as part of the Central Valley Project. The project's latest plans were approved and funded in 2022 and 2023, and are expected to create an additional 130,000 acre-feet of water storage in the country's largest off-stream reservoir. Over $100 million had previously been appropriated under the Bipartisan Infrastructure Law to increase the dam's crest by 10 feet for seismic safety reasons; the 2023 funding would add 10 more feet to increase the reservoir's storage. The $1 billion project is expected to be completed by 2032.

Dams Are Expensive

One of the factors that has made dams less attractive as a way to deal with water scarcity in the West is simply the cost, whether building a new structure and a reservoir, or altering an existing facility. In 2023, the Association of State Dam Safety officials released a report estimating that the cost of upgrading the nation's nearly 90,000 non-federal dams (those not owned or operated by the federal government), which had been $75.7 billion in 2022, had jumped to $157.5 billion just a year later. For instance, the Santa Clara Valley Water District, which owns and operates the huge Anderson Dam south of San Jose, California, has suffered sticker shock while investigating the cost of bringing the dam up to modern earthquake standards. Federal safety officials had ordered the district to rebuild the dam and drain the reservoir in 2020, but the price tag tripled from $648 million in 2021, rose to $1.24 billion in 2022, climbing to an estimated $2.3 billion by 2023. Even thinking about a project, without turning over a single spade of dirt, is expensive. In Arizona, the Salt River Project (SRP) anticipates a cost of $28 million for a feasibility study that would review a proposal to expand Bartlett Dam along the Verde River. The concept would allow SRP to capture and store water from winter storms by raising the height of the existing dam by about 100 feet. The feasibility study could potentially be completed by 2026, at which point Congress could decide whether to move forward. If approved, the project would take at least ten to fifteen more years to complete.

Feasibility studies and construction costs are not the only figures under consideration, however. A 2022 report on the breaching of four hydroelectric dams on the lower Snake River in Washington noted that endangered salmon runs could be restored by removing the dams. But such a huge project would cost an additional $10.3 billion to more than $27.2 billion because of the need to find other sources of electricity, irrigation, and ways to enable commerce along the river that is now conducted by barges. Tribal leaders from the Yakima Nation support the hypothetical breaching project because of their economic and cultural reliance on salmon. Still, the removal of even the smaller dams on rivers in the Pacific Northwest have benefits that many believe outweigh whatever costs might accrue. Oregon, in particular, has made efforts to remove obsolete dams to improve fish habitat. In 2010, for instance, the removal of the Gold Ray Dam on the Rogue River opened up 333 miles of spawning ground. The dam, built to provide hydroelectric power, consisted of one wooden structure built in 1904 and a 38-foot-tall concrete structure built in 1941, but the facility had been taken off the grid in 1972, making the dam of little value. A similar situation took place on the Hood River, which flows into the Columbia. An obsolete hydro dam built in 1923 was removed in 2010, opening up untold miles of river for salmon passage.

For some species, however, the dam removals may have come too late. In California, Idaho, Oregon, and Washington, salmon have become extinct in about 40 percent of their historical range, with a population only 10 percent of what it had been in the early nineteenth century. In 1947, Secretary of the Interior Julius Krug announced that even though the decision to build dams on the Columbia River would result in the sacrifice of the salmon run, the development would have overall benefits to the Pacific Northwest.

The Other Water Agency: The United States Geological Survey

Not as well known as the two federal agencies, the United States Geological Survey (USGS) grew out of the vision of a changed nation at the end of the Civil War. The acrimony and battlefields gave way to exploration and the desire to assess the country's natural resources as the nation grew. In 1867, Congress authorized exploration of the West and studies of the geology along the fortieth parallel route of the Transcontinental Railroad that would be conducted by the Corps of Engineers (COE), and a General Land Office survey of the geology of Nebraska. The twenty-five-year-old geologist in charge of the COE exploration, Clarence King, in his first annual USGS report in 1880, would later call this time as a turning point when "... science ceased to be dragged in the dust of rapid exploration and took a commanding position in the professional work of the country."

Three important surveys were undertaken by 1874: the Hayden survey of Wyoming and Colorado under the Department of the Interior; the Powell survey of the Green River and the Grand Canyon; and the Wheeler exploration of the area west of the 100th meridian. Personal rivalries and a lack of uniform objectives among the surveys eventually led to the creation of the USGS in 1879 with Clarence King appointed as its first director. Initially, the new agency had two functions: to classify the public lands, and to examine geological structures and mineral resources. How did water resources become a part of the USGS portfolio?

That component can be traced to John Wesley Powell, the second director of the USGS, profiled in Chapter 4. Powell, who had published his findings about the reclamation of the arid West in the late 1870s, was charged by Congress in 1883 to make a topographic map of the United States as a basis for geological and economic maps. Powell inferred that this might also be useful in advancing his interest in irrigation, while Nevada's first senator, William Stewart, convinced other members of Congress that the USGS designate places appropriate for reservoirs, canals, "and other hydraulic works." By 1888, the USGS had been authorized to investigate "the extent to which the arid region of the United

States can be redeemed by irrigation" and the selection of sites to store water and prevent floods. The Irrigation Survey (1888–1890), as it became known, led to the development of systematic stream gaging and professional training for individuals investigating the country's water resources. These early historical accomplishments led to today's Water Resources Branch of the USGS within the United States Department of the Interior. The agency's headquarters are in Reston, Virginia, with operations in twelve regional areas of the United States. Water Resources (WMA) is now one of the agency's four science Mission Areas, with the tasks of water-resource monitoring, assessment, modeling, and research.

An overview of several 2023 projects conducted by the WMA in western states indicate how different the USGS's role is from the two water management agencies previously profiled. In June 2023, for instance, a USGS study examined arsenic levels at 230 groundwater sites sampled in the Grand Canyon region. In May 2023, the agency released new interactive maps dealing with groundwater availability in Arizona. And in a key partnership project in April 2023, USGS staff worked with the Idaho Department of Water Resources and the Bureau of Reclamation to measure groundwater levels in more than 1,400 private and public wells throughout southern Idaho's eastern Snake River, whose aquifer provides the area's primary source of drinking water. Although all three of these projects deal with groundwater, they involve different goals, skill sets, and equipment than might have been available to the BOR or the Army Corps.

The Role of Non-Governmental and Non-Profit Organizations

These two types of organizations, sometimes referred to as civil society organizations, special interest groups, or just interest groups, are not the same. The first term, sometimes abbreviated as NGO, refers to groups that are established and operate independently from any type of government. The second term refers to groups that have a special type of tax status under law.

However, sometimes the terms are used interchangeably or even incorrectly because groups may have some functions or a mission that seems similar, at least initially, or that might sound the same in even their name. Not all NGOs are non-profit, but all non-profit organizations could be classified as NGOs. There are an estimated 1.5 million NGOs in the United States.

When it comes to water issues in the West, every state has both NGOs and non-profit organizations, both operational and advocacy-oriented. One way of looking at how these groups work, and the interests they care about, is to break them down into the scale of their work. For instance, many of the national-level environmental organizations (ENGOs, for short) may be based in Washington, DC or nearby, but in addition to having a national focus, they might also operate satellite offices or branches, sometimes in every state. Although these large ENGOs have more members and resources than their local or regional counterparts, they sometimes are criticized for being top-heavy and administratively expensive compared to smaller groups with fewer members and leaner budgets.

For instance, the Environmental Defense Fund (EDF) has three main offices, with the main US office in New York, with operations in six other US cities. This large group (about 3 million members) has a broad domestic and a global agenda, which currently includes energy transition, healthy communities, and, under the banner "People and Nature" the group seeks to improve water supplies and reduce flood risk. To maintain a state or local presence as well as a national one, a large ENGO that lobbies Congress might sometimes focus on individual projects in a region. One of the oldest groups, the Sierra Club, founded in 1892 with naturalist John Muir as one of its members, includes the protection of lands, air, water, and wildlife under a single programmatic banner. In addition to state-level chapters, California has thirteen local chapters that focus on area-specific issues. Oregon's 73,000-member chapter has a Columbia Snake River Campaign that seeks to restore the salmon population, whereas the Rio Grande Chapter in New Mexico, which has about 10,000 members, has worked to oppose a proposed diversion of water from the Gila River that is believed to be too costly for the benefits the state would receive.

In more recent times, interest groups with a local or regional project or problem agenda have brought water scarcity issues to media and public attention, although some have been working to support or oppose an issue for decades. Here is a sampling of those working in the West on water-related problems.

When the environmental movement was just getting started, three women decided to mobilize their community to deal with an area of 75,000 square miles. Save the Bay, a regional non-profit organization in northern California, became one of the models of how an urban ENGO could function at a time when the concept was still new. The group's goal is to protect and restore San Francisco Bay for both people and wildlife, and more recently, to protect the region from the flooding caused by whiplash weather and rising sea levels. The area the group serves comprises over 100 cities and 7 million people, making for an extremely diverse membership base, but that also means that its leaders must listen to a wide range of viewpoints about how best to manage the bay's resources among so many jurisdictions.

More than twenty-five years after Save the Bay was founded, a small group of residents in Taos, New Mexico gathered to protect the Rio Grande River from a proposed mine tailings facility to be built bordering the river. They called themselves Amigos Bravos, which means Fierce (or Brave) Friends. They were successful in their opposition, and have evolved to become a statewide organization with a diverse constituency comprising local community members, Native Americans, and Hispanics. They are currently working on revitalizing and restoring the Rio Fernando, which flows through the center of Taos. They want officials to address contamination issues, improve the river's overall quality, restore the acequia functions, and connect people to the watershed.

In the early 1990s, public interest law became a subject of great debate in law schools across the country, not just as another field of law but also as a way of creating a voice for the public, especially in disputes involving the environment. Who, they asked, would speak for the public good when confronted by well-funded corporate interests, especially in the sometimes-arcane language of science and law?

The Seattle-based Center for Environmental Law and Policy was conceived by the University of Washington Law School in 1993 as a way to provide students with legal experience in dealing with causes that they cared about. One of the unique features of the program is its close relationship with the rights of Native American tribes, built on a series of cases to support voices that had often been silenced. The opportunity to work on water resource management and preservation of natural resources now includes projects that apply the public trust doctrine, the updating of state water laws, tribal treaty rights collaboration, legislative and agency advocacy, and the submission of comments on rulemaking and the issuance of water permits.

Utah's Friends of Great Salt Lake has taken on a substantial issue in both geographic size and complexity. The group, founded in 1994, seeks to preserve and protect the lake's ecosystem and increase the public's awareness of the Great Salt Lake as a resource. It has several smaller internal groups that, for example, monitor the water flows into the lake and its wetlands to make sure they are adequate. A smaller group also worked with a professional firm to conduct a conservation impact study to inform future water resource planning, and they have developed strategies to address declining lake levels. In its thirty-year history, the organization has become a well-respected presence in Utah's political scene, bringing in scientists, policymakers, and leaders from business to collaborate on solutions to the growing problems the lake faces.

There are other types of non-profit organizations and NGOs that fit slightly different niches in dealing with water in the West. Some might be called hybrids because they work primarily for a problem that rises up on the policy agenda, and then once solved, the groups disband or moves on to another issue. Others, such as the Colorado Water Congress (CWC), created in 1958, start out with one goal and then keep that goal but add others as time moves on. The CWC began its life long before today's ENGOs were founded and grew out of a hearing in Washington, DC in 1957. The state's governor and other officials testified in support of a large reclamation project, but were surprised to hear amendments presented that took a totally different approach. The governor then called for a meeting of all Colorado water users to help him decide what to do. At a coffee shop meeting that fall, several of the state's lawyers mentioned that there ought to be a way for them to meet and discuss water issues informally to better understand how others felt.

From there, the organization developed as an umbrella membership advocacy group, non-partisan in nature politically. Its 400 members not only share information, as was the original mission, but now have a mission with four pillars: inform, convene, train, act. They have provided leadership on key water issues, lent their expertise to meetings and hearings, mentored new members in the water resources profession, and acted on those issues that affect them.

There are also non-profit groups that might not initially seem to have a place in the water debate, but have found themselves actively involved. Both Trout Unlimited (TU) and Ducks Unlimited (DU), two organizations that would appear on the surface to be interested only in fishing and hunting wildlife, have prominently voiced their concerns on water issues. The national TU leadership, as part of its five-year strategic plan, has urged its chapters to focus on what they call the "Priority Waters Concept." The strategy calls for group members to realize their limitations when it comes to all the issues that affect trout species, and to focus instead on those that they see as their mission: the cold, fresh waters that sustain native and wild trout and salmon. For Arizona, that means eighty-five unique waters that the state's Game and Fish Department has identified as the species current or potential wild and native trout waters.

While the national group Ducks Unlimited might include commentary on how to choose the best hunting dog on its website, since 1937 the group has been steadfast in its mission of becoming the world's largest waterfowl and wetlands conservation organization. With a broad range of partners, DU's volunteers conduct their own fundraising activities while maintaining their status as a non-profit organization. Nationally, DU produces its own magazine, has its own television show and podcasts, an online merchandise store, and has established its place as a major NGO when it comes to water in the West. The group has worked tirelessly to restore wetlands and improve habitat around the Great Salt Lake, receiving $5 million in grants from the Great Salt Lake Watershed Enhancement Trust in 2023 to fix levees in need of repair, replacing a water delivery system at a waterfowl management area with state-of-the-art infrastructure, and replacing three aging dams on the Jordan River that feed the lake. Those types of activities go far beyond what outsiders might consider to be the things that duck hunters do. But they have earned its members a place at the table when it comes to decisions on the fate of the Great Salt Lake.

Droughts, Megadroughts, and Water Scarcity

Although there is no "official" definition of what constitutes a drought, the American Meteorological Society refers to a "period of abnormally dry weather sufficiently long enough to cause a serious hydrological imbalance." That requires a comparison of conditions between what has historically been considered "normal" and current conditions, but there is no easy answer as to what time period should be used as normal. Scientists look at factors such as the amount of precipitation, the condition of crops, and how much moisture is in the soil. They might also look at the amount of snowpack in the area, and levels of both surface water and groundwater. Droughts usually have two major characteristics: they are severe, and they are sustained. Another term that is often used to describe certain conditions is megadrought—an extreme or impactful drought event. Recently, studies of the last 2,000 years have examined other factors, such as tree rings and lake sediment to identify drought events. Some of the megadroughts are considered to be even more severe than what has been experienced in the last twenty years in the West. In the late 1500s CE, for instance, scientists like Benjamin Cook believe that much of the Southwest and the central regions of the United States experienced a megadrought that lasted over several decades. Using that period of time as a starting point, megadroughts are defined as multiyear drought events that stand out as especially extreme in terms of severity, duration, or spatial extent when compared to other droughts over the last 2,000 years.

One of the tools used in determining whether or not a drought exists is the US Drought Monitor (USDM), which indicates both the intensity of a drought in an area and where the drought is located. Like the definition of a megadrought, the USDM looks at historical trends and weather patterns, with attention to regional differences. It is a map of the United States, updated every Thursday, that indicates which parts of the country are experiencing drought, using five classifications:

DO: Abnormally dry, short-term dryness; a precursor to drought but not an actual drought
D1: Moderate, some damage to crops, pastures; streams low; some water shortages
D2: Severe, crop and pastures losses likely, water shortages likely, imposition of water restrictions
D3: Extreme, major crop and pasture losses, widespread water shortages and water restrictions
D4: Exceptional, exceptional losses; shortage of water in reservoirs and streams, water emergencies

The USDM is based at the University of Nebraska, Lincoln, as a cooperative effort of the National Drought Mitigation Center, the US Department of Agriculture (USDA), the National Oceanic and Atmospheric Administration (NOAA), the National Centers for Environmental Education, and the Western Regional Climate Center. About 495 observers across the United States supply information to the network, which includes scientists in multiple fields from climatologists and meteorologists to social scientists, biologists, and remote sensing specialists. Some work for federal agencies like NOAA, and others work at universities and state governments. They represent all fifty states and Puerto Rico, and they rely on local observers as well as their own expertise. They examine many factors such as temperature, soil moisture, the level of water in streams and lakes, snow cover, and meltwater runoff in making their assessment. In addition, they look at whether business operations are impacted by the drought, or whether water shortages or restrictions have occurred.

Another tool is the USDA's website, US Agricultural Commodities in Drought. It uses the USDM data and its maps of major and minor agricultural areas for several commodities (the National Agricultural Statistics Service Census of Agriculture), designated every five years based on the intensity of production, the livestock inventory, or the acres harvested in the case of alfalfa and hay. The combination of these two sources allows officials to determine whether the center point of a county is in a drought area.

Droughts may come and go, although there is agreement that the Southwest recently experienced its driest period in 1,200 years, making water conservation "a way of life" according to the *Los Angeles Times*. In California, for instance, the state experienced a three-year drought in 2007, and a five-year drought in 2012. In between, conditions improved, but then severe conditions reappeared in 2012. Droughts may occur, or become more severe, in some areas but not in others. When looking at a larger area, like the southwestern United States, the period between 2000 and 2021 was the driest twenty-two-year period since at least 800 CE. The period may, in fact, end up being as severe as the megadrought of the late 1500s. Scientists are now examining the impact of climate change in causing extreme events like droughts to determine whether changes are permanent or temporary anomalies from normal conditions.

Rainfall Trends in the Modern West

Why has the most recent drought in the Southwest that began in 2020 been considered exceptional? Over the period January 2020–August 2021, the Southwest had its lowest rainfall totals on record since at least 1895, as well as the third-highest daily average temperatures. These two factors reduced the levels of mountain snowpack and led to increased evaporation of soil moisture. The low precipitation appears to have been caused by natural variations in the atmosphere and oceans. However, the NOAA Drought Task Force concluded that the warm temperatures far exceeded what can be explained by random variations in climate alone, leading to the conclusion that the drought was due in large part to human-caused warming.

The effects of drought can be seen in numerous areas, from water shortages that affect the storage capacity of reservoirs that store water for municipal use, to impacts that affect entire ecosystems, to economic losses to agriculture and livestock production. The task force study also estimated an economic loss of between $11.4 and $23 billion, including impacts from associated wildfires, which in 2020 burned over 10 million acres, about three times what would have been expected during the comparison period of 2001–2018.

The intensity of a drought, and its length, may be among the factors that lead to policy changes. In 2021, for instance, California's governor Gavin Newsom issued the first of several proclamations designating the counties experiencing a regional drought as a state of emergency, until fifty of the state's fifty-eight counties were covered. He called upon Californians to support a Save Our Water campaign, implemented during the 2012–2016 drought, and signed an executive order calling for a 15 percent voluntary reduction in water use compared to 2020 levels. During the 2012–2016 drought, residents abided with voluntary measures, which led to a 21 percent decline in statewide per-capita residential water use. But a *Los Angeles Times* analysis of the reductions from the governor's call to action from July 2021 to when he rescinded his request in March 2022 found statewide savings were only about 7 percent. Perhaps, some wondered, is there such a thing as drought fatigue, when consumers get tired of the repetitive calls for action?

Public efforts to conserve may have wavered by late December 2022, when much of the Southwest experienced an abrupt change in weather, with well above normal precipitation due to an active storm track and a series of nine moisture-laden atmospheric rivers. An atmospheric river is a long, narrow band of moisture that typically forms in Hawaii, flows eastward, and then dumps its moisture on the West Coast, often accompanied by strong winds. They may lead to rockslides, flooding, toppled powerlines, and high waves along coastlines. Global climate change, and the resulting higher temperatures, may be the cause of the increase in the number of atmospheric rivers in 2023–2024. Warmer air—even one or two degrees warmer—holds more moisture, so storms become more intense, damaging, and wetter.

The weather patterns of both 2023 and 2024 were a meteorological wake-up call for the West, alerting policymakers and ordinary residents to the impact of climate change. For instance, in early 2023, San Francisco's hills were blanketed in snow, with California's snowpack topping 200 percent of normal. The southern Sierra Nevada, the source of nearly one-third of California's water supply, received the most snow in forty years, delaying the state's fire season and prolonging the state's ski season. A mild spring and weeks without major heatwaves allowed the early snow to melt at a moderate rate. The state's largest reservoir, Shasta, was 94 percent full by July, and Oroville, the second largest reservoir, was 99 percent full. Others in northern parts of California were also 95–97 percent full. The

Intermountain West states also faced unusual snowfall and subsequent canyon flooding in areas outside Salt Lake City.

Perhaps even more important than the precipitation was the resulting level of snowpack in western mountains, a sign of what would come in just a few months for many states. California, Nevada, Utah, and Arizona had well above normal snowpack levels, with most sites that were being monitored at more than 150 percent of normal snow water. As was the case with precipitation, Washington and Oregon reaches of the Cascades and the northern Rockies in Idaho and Montana had snowpack levels between 70 and 90 percent of normal.

This weather upheaval made a significant change in drought statistics. By the end of January 2023, 61 percent of the West was designated in drought, with 6 percent in level D3 (Extreme) or D4 (Exceptional) drought. The most widespread improvements over the previous year were in California; every state except Montana improved its drought status. Despite the storms, there were a few small areas in Oregon, Idaho, Montana, and New Mexico where the drought level increased by one level.

In the three weeks between late December 2022 and January 2023, storms dumped an estimated 32 trillion gallons of water on California. As the state's snowpack began to melt, the water began to scour rivers and streambeds, trees began to topple over, and hillsides that had burned in massive wildfires funneled water that turned into flash floods. The debris—boulders, shrubs, sediment, tree limbs, and anything else embedded in the ground—can be dislodged quickly and violently. The post-fire flooding along the California coast killed at least twenty-two people as the rain dumped over communities ill-prepared for the massive shift in the weather. The dramatic swing between periods of drought and flooding is called whiplash weather, and many areas were unprepared for those conditions in 2022–23. They also were unprepared for short-duration, high-intensity rainfall that kept coming and coming over that short period.

The atmospheric rivers that initially dumped rain on the coast then moved to the state's interior, much of which was, or still is, agricultural land without the urban infrastructure necessary to meet the demands of the recurring storms. In the area around Sacramento, for instance, the population growth has occurred in a natural floodplain—good for crops and bad for people. Houses have replaced barns as communities have spread out from the state's capitol.

Nowhere did the unprecedented storms have a more visible impact than in California's Central Valley. As the rain subsided, and warmer temperatures began melting the Sierra Nevada snow, the water flowed into the Tule River and the small agricultural communities of the San Joaquin Valley and the Tulare Lake Basin. The region has experienced similar flood episodes after snow fell heavily in the mountains. In both 1969 and 1983, major storms pounded the snowmelt and the Army Corps of Engineers built levees around towns like Corcoran to hold the waters back from the town of about 22,000. Over time, once the waters receded, some of the levees were removed. In other wet years, the levee was raised.

After the winter rain and snow, there were mixed messages about whether or not the West was done with the whiplash weather that changed from one week to the next and the need to conserve water. Citing a climatologist with the National Drought Mitigation Center, radio station KUNC in Greeley, Colorado, told its listeners on June 27, 2023, "A stretch of unusually wet months has erased drought across much of the Southwest." In summer of 2022, the Bureau of Reclamation's commissioner noted that the Colorado River was approaching a tipping point, calling upon the seven states within the basin to reduce their water use by 2–4 million acre-feet (maf) per year. But the agency appeared to change its position in October 2023 when it released a draft SEIS (Supplemental Environmental Impact Statement) for Colorado River operations through 2026 that indicated a preference for a no-action alternative as one of two remaining alternatives. To some, this meant the drought situation was now under control. The headlines in an article in the *Las Vegas Review-Journal* stated that the Colorado River System was safe, for now. By the end of the water year (September 30), California marked 2023 as its tenth wettest since record keeping began 128 years ago.

By mid-October 2023, the US Drought Monitor confirmed the abrupt changes in weather. The "drought-free" label had not been applied for brief periods except for a few months in 2019. Before that, the state had not been completely drought-free since December 2011. The National Weather Service's Climate Prediction Center said that the coastal areas of the Pacific Northwest would have a wet winter in 2024, although the downside was the threat of flooding and damage to levees. But predictions are simply that. In October 2023, the Bureau of Reclamation said that between October 2023 and September 2024, an estimated 9.4 maf of water would flow into Lake Powell. By January 2024, the estimate was revised to 7.6 maf, a figure that is just 79 percent of the historical average runoff during the 1991–2020 time frame. Another predictor, the January 2024 snow survey taken near Lake Tahoe, California, reported just 30 percent of the average measurement recorded at that location, with the statewide measure at 25 percent of average, a far cry from the 185 percent in January 2023.

But in February 2024, the weather pattern made earlier predictions seem unreliable. Tropical ocean surface temperatures that indicate the strength of the El Niño were 2° Celsius warmer than normal—or what some called a Super El Niño. California experienced a series of atmospheric rivers that pummeled coastal areas, with the downtown Los Angeles area receiving seven inches of rain in just two days, or half of its annual average. Overall, the statewide precipitation was 102 percent of average for the same date. But the rain came down so quickly that agencies were not able to capture much of the water in storage basins and instead had to focus on flood control. Many of the state's reservoirs were already near capacity when the back-to-back storms hit, and operators of the Oroville Dam, the state's second largest reservoir, actually began to release water to reduce volume and avoid floods.

The 2024 storms also failed to put much of a dent in snow drought conditions because of the warmer than normal water temperatures and rain-on-snow events. The worst conditions by February 2024, according to the National Integrated Drought Information System (NIDIS), were in the northern Rocky Mountains and the Missouri River headwaters. Western Montana, northern Wyoming, northern Idaho, western Washington, and the Rio Hondo Basin in southeastern New Mexico continued to have snow drought conditions, whereas the snowpack did improve somewhat in the Sierra Nevada, Great Basin, Colorado River Basin, and the Rio Grande Basin. Forecasters from NOAA's Climate Prediction center told CNN that the February storms meant that El Niño had peaked with possible cooler-than-average ocean temperatures in the eastern tropical Pacific that are more typical of La Niña arriving.

So, is the drought over? In one word, no. Although the moisture from the atmospheric rivers of 2023 and 2024 made a visible statement to many in the West, decades of low precipitation and snowmelt were too much to overcome in a single season, or even several seasons. The real answer to the question, however, is that it depends on what region, or even subregion, you are looking at. Regional differences can be significant, making broad statements about droughts unwise.

To prove that point, Tropical Storm Hilary, the first storm of its kind in California since 1997, dumped rain on several parts of the West in August 2023. Some parts of California's Coachella Valley and mountain communities near Lake Arrowhead, as well as those below the mountains around Las Vegas, received considerably more rain than would be expected in a drought year. Normally, California and Nevada are protected from tropical storms by three factors: the frigid Pacific Coast ocean current; the prevailing east to west wind pattern; and atmospheric subsidence and a downward flow of air. But the warmer than usual Pacific Ocean waters made what was normal for the region decidedly not normal at all. Even before the deluge, California was free of extreme drought for the first time in three years. Some analysts said that the storms would alleviate many concerns about wildfires that often occur in late summer and early fall.

In August 2023, the *San Francisco Chronicle* referred to the historic storms that bore down on California, covering the state's mountains as "The Big Melt," noting that the state had been "fundamentally changed" after years of drought. Forecasts at the beginning of spring 2023 were very conservative, but as the snow began to melt, those forecasts were revised. Most of the attention focused on the two largest reservoirs—Lake Powell and Lake Mead—but as the *Chronicle* reported, the Feather River, filled with snowmelt that flowed into the State Water Project's reservoir, Lake Oroville, filled the lake to capacity at 160 percent of average, boosting its hydroelectric output after years when California dealt with power outages.

By the end of water year 2023 (WY2023), analysts were mixed in how they looked at the future. Overall, winter snowmelt was at about 145 percent, helping to fill many of the region's smaller reservoirs. Some estimates of runoff, reservoir inflow, and increases in reservoir storage were very positive, but even the BOR's commissioner admitted that Lake Powell and Lake Mead remained at historically low levels at about 25 percent of capacity.

In late 2023, NOAA reported that strengthening El Niño conditions—causing the jet stream to shift southward and eastward—were in place for the first time in four years. The prediction for Winter 2024 in the West meant that the northern tier of the continental United States was likely to experience warmer-than-average temperatures, and wetter-than-average conditions from parts of California to the south-central Rocky Mountains. Drought conditions were expected to persist for the northern Rockies and portions of the desert Southwest, with drought development occurring in the interior Pacific Northwest. Brad Udall, Senior Water and Climate Scientist at Colorado State University's Colorado Water Center, predicted that it will take twenty-one more wet springs to fully restore the Colorado River watershed. That's what it would take to refill the basin's water infrastructure, including Lake Powell and Lake Mead. His prediction was based on the time it took Lake Powell to fill, between spring 1963 and 1983. After Hurricane Hilary, Udall told *USA Today* "This buys us a year. It doesn't remotely come close to solving the long-term problems." He characterized the winter's storms as an "aberration," with big snow years happening half as often as they used to, but dry years happening 2.5 times as often. Similar cautions were raised by the Central Sierra Snow Laboratory at the University of California, Berkeley, noting that 2023 was an exception. Others recalled that the last time similar conditions had occurred was in 1999, and that there has not been a string of high flow years during the twenty-first century, nor was such a pattern likely in the future.

Despite the cautions, some cities and water districts rolled back the water conservation policies that had been in place due to the severe drought. The Metropolitan Water District (MWD), which supplies water to 6 million residents in the Los Angeles area, had limited lawn watering in some areas to one day a week in 2022, but lifted restrictions in March 2023. The Los Angeles Department of Water and Power (DWP), which receives water from the MWD, informed its 4 million customers in July 2023 that the restrictions on watering lawns it announced in June 2022 would be loosened from two days a week to three days. Prior to the 2022 restrictions under the Emergency Water Conservation Ordinance, DWP customers had been subject to the three-day-a-week limitation since 2009. The time-of-day restriction due to evaporation remained in place, as did the time limit on outdoor watering and a ban on watering within forty-eight hours of a measurable rain event. But analysts said that the rollbacks should be considered as a short-term measure, implemented only because California had experienced an unusually wet winter. Predictions that 2023 would end up as one of the hottest years ever recorded were heightened by forecasts that 2024 would be even hotter due to El Niño and global warming.

In January 2024, however, the Bureau of Reclamation released its Colorado River Basin 24-Month Study, which determined the operating conditions for Lake Powell and Lake Mead for 2024. The BOR noted that Lake Mead's release in 2023 was projected to be the lowest in thirty years at about 1.5 maf lower than an average normal year, primarily because of the conservation efforts of the Lower Basin states and Mexico to conserve at least 3 maf through the end of 2026. Still, the two reservoirs had a combined storage of 36 percent—historically low levels and just 80 feet above the minimum power pool for Lake Powell.

The dueling predictions and what seemed like historic lows and highs in temperature, precipitation, snowpack, and snowmelt, combined to make climate-fueled whiplash weather the new normal throughout the West. They also forced the West's leaders to tackle water scarcity in new ways, as explored in more depth in Chapter 2.

Further Reading

Davis, Margaret Leslie. 1993. *Rivers in the Desert: William Mulholland and the Inventing of Los Angeles*. New York: HarperCollins.

Krist, Gary. 2018. *The Mirage Factory: Illusion, Imagination, and the Invention of Los Angeles*. New York: Crown.

Martin, Russell. 1989. *A Story that Stands Like a Dam: Glen Canyon and the Struggle for the Soul of the West*. New York: Henry Holt.

McCool, Daniel. 1987. *Command of the Waters: Iron Triangles, Federal Water Development, and Indian Water*. Berkeley: University of California Press.

Reisner, Marc. 1986. *Cadillac Desert: The West and Its Disappearing Water*. New York: Viking.

Rowley, William D. 2006. *The Bureau of Reclamation: Origins and Growth to 1945*. Washington, DC: U.S. Department of Interior, Bureau of Reclamation.

Stegner, Wallace. 1954. *Beyond the Hundredth Meridian: John Wesley Powell and the Second Opening of the West*. Boston: Houghton Mifflin.

Wilkinson, Charles F. 1992. *Crossing the Next Meridian: Land, Water, and the Future of the West*. Washington, DC: Island Press.

2

Moving toward Water Supply Resiliency: Western Water Demands and Coping Strategies

Introduction

The West's early settlers were almost crusade-like in their zeal to turn the barren lands into the same kind of garden as they did in the East. They listened to the words of climatologist Cyrus Thomas, who promised them, prophetically, that a long humid cycle that had turned the prairies green was, in fact, divine intervention, and that this was a permanent phenomenon. That conviction, shared by geographer Ferdinand V. Hayden, was encapsulated in the slogan "Rain follows the Plow." Combine the biblical scale of those promises with the promotional skills of William Gilpin, who described the North American continent as a "vast amphitheater, opening toward heaven …" ready "to receive and fuse harmoniously whatever enters within its rim" and you have the explanation why so many scrambled westwards.

Since their arrival, the challenge of finding sufficient water to quench the settlers' thirst has occupied the attention of public officials throughout the West. Today, the task of dividing up the Colorado River is at the top of the policy agenda, with a December 2026 deadline when current guidelines expire. All seven states that are signatories to the Colorado River Compact have approached water scarcity in different ways. Interstate cooperation rather than interstate discord has taken on new meaning, and there is an international element involved for those states who adjoin Canada and Mexico.

Spawning Chinook salmon in the Pacific Northwest. Four dams along the Klamath River in California and Oregon were removed between 2023 and 2024. The dam removal reopened 400 miles of habitat for Chinook salmon, coho salmon, steelhead trout, and other threatened native fish and marks a shift in the nation's damming policy. (Ryan Hagerty/U.S. Fish and Wildlife Service.)

Dividing Up the Colorado River

At the center of much of the controversy involving water in the West is the Colorado River, winding 1,450 miles from the Colorado Rockies to Mexico's Sea of Cortez, serving over 40 million people, or about one in ten Americans. The river provides water for an estimated 5 million acres of agricultural lands, along with providing critical habitat. For years, scientists have warned that the initial estimates of the river's flow were never accurate, warned that the resources of the Colorado are declining. With drought lasting more than twenty years, reducing the levels of reservoirs, coupled with changing hydrological conditions and climate change, there is little argument about whether the existing way the Colorado's water is divided needs to be changed. The debate is over how those changes might look. There have been congressional hearings, public meetings, contingency plans drawn up, and arguments whether the winter rains and snow in 2022–24 ended the drought, making immediate action unnecessary. But now a years-long process is underway that guarantees that guidelines to protect the Colorado River System will be changed and implemented before the end of the decade.

The agreement on how to divide up the Colorado River, called a compact, was led by Secretary of Commerce Herbert Hoover and held in Santa Fe, New Mexico in 1922. One question that was raised almost immediately was how much water actually flowed down the river. The instruments used to measure stream flow at that time were somewhat primitive, varying considerably from 10 million-acre-feet (maf) during droughts to twice that much or more during wet years when precipitation was heavy. The delegates decided that an average flow between 1905 and 1922, a short and especially wet time frame, or about 17.5 maf measured at Lee's Ferry, Arizona, would become the basis of the negotiations. One arbitrary decision was made to divide the Colorado among the Upper Basin states (Colorado, New Mexico, Utah, and Wyoming) and Lower Basin states (Arizona, Nevada, and California), splitting the estimated flow in half. By agreement, 7.5 maf would go to each basin, and 1.5 maf would be set aside for Mexico, even though that nation was excluded from the negotiations. The remaining 1.5 maf was added to the total the Lower Basin states would receive in a deal made to keep those states' delegates from walking out of the negotiations. Left up in the air was how the states in each basin would divide the water up among themselves. Participants representing the seven states and the Bureau of Reclamation (BOR) took eleven months to finalize the 1922 compact (excerpted in Chapter 5) prior to it being signed, then taken back to the states for ratification. The Lower Basin states divided up their share in 1928 as part of the agreements to build the Boulder Canyon Project (excerpted in Chapter 5), and the Upper Basin states agreed how to split their share in the Upper Colorado River Basin Compact of 1948.

The 17.5 maf believed to flow along the Colorado when the 1922 agreement was reached was not just conservative, as some officials believed. It would trigger a numbers game that would lead to controversy for decades. One hydrological engineer told a conference in 1953 that the average discharge at Lee's Ferry was 11.7 maf, whereas another hydrologist told a meeting in 1965 that the flow was actually 15 maf, not counting 1.5 million lost to evaporation. Since that time, some tree ring studies have pegged the average flow at between 13 maf and 14.3 maf. The Water Education Foundation has estimated that the Colorado River's flow in the Upper Basin has dropped by 20 percent over the last 100 years. The 17.5 maf figure in the 1922 agreement has been reached just four times at Lee's Ferry since 1991, and the average flow since 2000 has been 12.3 maf. The difference in that number and the Compact has been made up by the reservoirs that supplement the river itself, and levels have continued to decline except for parts of 2023.

The implications are clear: how would the basins deal with the fact that there was not enough water to fulfill the Upper Basin's obligation of 7.5 maf and the 1.5 maf owed to Mexico? How would the deficit be explained to the farmers and customers counting on their share, and who would bear the brunt of the deficit? As temperatures in the Upper Basin grow even hotter, how will the aridification trend affect the Lower Basin? These questions continued to plague the Bureau of Reclamation's planning as climate change gained a place on the policy agenda, and greenhouse gas emissions, warming temperatures, and changes in weather patterns were considered as factors impacting the Colorado River's flows. Colorado State University climate researcher Brad Udall has noted that a 1°C warming of temperatures or more by 2050 could reduce the Lee's Ferry flow to as little as 9 maf, about half of the basis for the 1922 agreement.

Driven by five years of drought, at a time when both Lake Mead and Lake Powell lost nearly half of their combined storage, coupled with increasing demands for water, in 2005 federal agencies started the process of examining the operating guidelines for both reservoirs and ways to deal with the shortage in the Lower Basin. This process took more than two years, during which various compliance requirements were developed under the National Environmental Policy Act (NEPA). Each year, the Secretary of the Interior reports on the water supply conditions for the Lower Basin states, categorized as Normal, Surplus, or Shortage. As part of the 2007 Interim Guidelines, the Lower Basin states agreed to reduce their annual allocations based on the water elevation level in Lake

Mead, agreeing that if Lake Mead reached 1,075 feet, the states' allocation would be reduced to 7.167 maf; at 1,050, the allocation would be 7.083 maf; and at 1,025 feet, the allocation would be reduced to 7.0 maf.

The Interim Guidelines were finalized in December 2007, considered "interim" because they were to be implemented until new guidelines could be adopted and the parties could develop operating experience, but no later than December 2026. The guidelines are important because they are designed to provide better guidance to users who are exceedingly worried that their allocations of Colorado River water will be reduced, and a need for predictability in knowing how much water they would receive as the drought conditions worsen.

Contingencies and Conservation of the Colorado River

The Department of the Interior (DOI) took another step to respond to historic drought in December 2017 when the agency called on each of the seven Colorado River Basin states to develop drought contingency plans (DCPs) that would be in place before the end of 2018. The goal was to ensure compliance with the 1922 Compact and to maintain a minimum power pool at Lake Powell. Those plans were not submitted to Congress until March 2019, with implementing legislation signed a month later. As drought conditions worsened in 2020, states began contributing thousands of acre-feet of water savings to Lake Mead, followed by supplemental releases of water from several reservoirs in July 2021 and the first reduction in historical water release from Glen Canyon Dam in January 2002, from 7.48 maf to 7.0 maf.

This led the DOI to take unprecedented actions between 2021 and 2023 to respond to the drought, low-runoff conditions, and dramatic changes in weather beyond the release of additional water from upstream reservoirs in order to stabilize the water level at Lake Powell. By June 2022, the Basin's two reservoirs reached the crisis stage, with water levels dropping below 30 percent, marking the period 2000 through 2022 as the driest twenty-three-year period in more than a century. In August 2022, the DOI called on all seven states to voluntarily reduce their water use, setting a goal of a 2–4 maf total reduction in 2023, depending on basin conditions. The states could not, however, meet the August 15 deadline to reach an agreement on a reduction plan.

The federal government originally proposed three options that would respond to the water shortage in the three Lower Basin states of Arizona, California, and Nevada. The states responded by proposing their own alternative in May 2023, agreeing to conserve an additional 3 maf to protect Lake Mead's water levels through 2026. The proposed voluntary cuts amount to a 13 percent reduction in consumption, or avoided water use. In return, the three states wanted the federal government to pay $1.2 billion from the Inflation Reduction Act to compensate irrigation districts, cities, and tribes for conserving 2.3 maf of water. The remaining 0.7 maf in conservation reductions would have to be uncompensated or paid by other entities in the Lower Basin.

In August 2023, the Bureau announced that the previous wet winter meant that projected cuts in water allotments would not be as harsh as had been expected. Arizona would face only an 18 percent cut, Nevada 7 percent, and Mexico 5 percent, with no reduction in water consumption required for California, the largest user of Colorado River water. But just four months later, the Bureau announced that several California water agencies had agreed to conserve up to 643,000 acre-feet of water in Lake Mead through 2025 in exchange for $295 million. This funding, like the money for Arizona and Nevada in the earlier agreement, also came from the Inflation Reduction Act, and included an agreement with one tribe and several water and irrigation districts in Southern California. These short-term solutions covered the river's allotments for the time being, and avoided more serious cuts that might have been imposed by the federal government. However, critics argued that paying people to conserve water was an unsustainable fix that was not sustainable, especially because the federal money would run out eventually.

Negotiations, both informal and formal, to decide what to do when the 2007 guidelines and related documents expire have been ongoing for years, but became more critical as the West faced more long-term drought and the aptly named whiplash weather conditions. Changes to the 2007 guidelines require a lengthy, multiyear, complex and complicated process of public notices, analyses, and meetings required by the NEPA process. Early on, the federal government acknowledged that circumstances had changed since the adoption of the document. First, the Colorado River's hydrology had changed, with a dramatic reduction in the annual natural flow due to significantly drier conditions. Even actions taken after the 2007 guidelines were adopted were deemed demonstrably insufficient to address the ongoing drought and low-runoff conditions. The BOR noted that with projections related to climate change, it would be best to start consideration of changes in light of deep uncertainty. Second, the BOR acknowledged the need to more deeply engage a broader range of stakeholders that would be more inclusive, transparent, and encourage meaningful engagement. Third, the BOR recognized that in addition to post-2026 planning, the agency might need to prioritize the implementation of near-term actions to stabilize the decline in reservoir storage.

In June 2023, the BOR announced that it was initiating the formal steps to develop the public process for the next set of operating guidelines, including consideration of the current and projected hydrology of the Colorado River Basin. The process would provide an opportunity for stakeholders to comment about the scope of analysis, potential alternatives, and relevant information the Bureau should consider. Among the issues raised was the role of the thirty tribal nations that account for 3.4 maf of the Colorado River, which could be as high as 26 percent of the river's yearly flow. To put that number in perspective, that would amount to the third-largest share of the river's water behind California and Colorado. Tribal leaders have repeatedly attempted to have a seat at the table when the Colorado's allocations have been discussed, almost always unsuccessfully.

The formal process undertaken by the DOI continued in October 2023 with the issuance of a draft Supplemental Environmental Impact Statement (EIS), with a completed draft EIS anticipated to be available by the end of 2024, a final EIS by late 2025, and a Record of Decision (ROD) that would replace the 2007 document available in early 2026 before the 2007 guidelines expire. The draft EIS was important to the process because it included updated modeling analyses that indicated that there had been a substantial reduction in the risk that Lake Powell and Lake Mead would reach critical elevations through 2026.

The next two to three years of negotiations to develop the post-2026 guidelines are likely to be among the most contentious in US water policy, because the implications for social and economic development in the West are so critical. Every stakeholder has something to lose, with untold dollars at risk depending on an uncertain outcome. Litigation is virtually guaranteed, as it is likely that there will be interim agreements made until some compromises are made among the states.

Arizona: Agriculture and Growth

Arizona's climate and water policies are confusing to many people unfamiliar with the state, in part because its landscape consists of desert to the south, and the largest tract of Ponderosa pine forest in the contiguous United States in the north. Arizona's approach to managing water also varies from one part of the state to another, sometimes inexplicitly. A study of municipal landscaping ordinances in two dozen municipalities in the greater Phoenix area found that 68 percent stress water conservation, compared to 87 percent in the Los Angeles area. How did these inconsistent water policies develop in a state usually thought of as arid?

In central Arizona, where much of the state's population resides, the native Hohokam people developed a complex system of about 150 miles of ditches around 200 BCE that they dug with simple tools to control the Salt River and irrigate their farms. Over the centuries, other tribes settled throughout the lands as well. Miners came to the state in search of copper, ranchers brought their cattle, and the third letter C—citrus—became the mainstay of the economy, as long as there was water and a way to control it. In 1891, the city of Phoenix was devastated by floodwaters, and it became apparent that the region's settlers needed to do something to both store water for times of drought, and then control it and move it to where it was needed.

With passage of the Reclamation Act of 1902, Arizona geared up for an era of flood control projects. In Phoenix, the city's leaders formed the Salt River Valley Water Users Association to obtain a loan to build the Theodore Roosevelt Dam, a six-year-long project that was completed in 1911. Although the dam, and others that followed along the Salt River, helped bring water to the central part of the new state of Arizona, farmers in outlying areas relied on wells and irrigation to build the agriculture industry. For much of the state's early history, groundwater was the primary source of the state's water supply—an estimated four out of every five acre-feet by the 1960s.

The Central Arizona Project

If it were not for Arizona Senator Carl T. Hayden (profiled in Chapter 4), it is doubtful that Arizona would have become the driving force in agriculture when it did. A longtime supporter of the BOR and the Colorado River Compact (which Arizona did not ratify until 1944), Hayden began introducing congressional legislation to create the Central Arizona Project (CAP) in 1947. Hayden wanted the BOR to build a large dam on the Colorado, and a pumping plant and canals that would transport water to the rapidly growing metropolitan area of Phoenix—a plan that California officials vehemently opposed. Stewart Udall, an Arizona native who served as Secretary of the Interior from 1961 to 1968, had his own ideas about what the state needed, and in 1963, he and the BOR offered Congress a different proposal, the Pacific Southwest Water Plan (PSWP). Although it went through several incarnations, the $2 billion project had something for everyone in the Colorado Basin, and was much more ambitious than what Hayden had envisioned.

After considerable political maneuvering, mostly between members of the California and Arizona congressional delegations, a deal was struck in 1965 that protected California's historic appropriation of Colorado River water, so the state dropped its opposition to the CAP. Arizona, in exchange, would agree to regulate its diversions so that California never got less than a promised appropriation, forcing the PSWP out of contention. In its place was a different legislative proposal, the Lower Colorado River Basin Project Act, which met both California's and Arizona's needs. In typical logrolling strategy, where everyone insists upon getting their way, Colorado congressman Wayne Aspinall introduced amendments to the legislation that added five projects in Colorado at a cost of $360 million, bringing the total cost to $1.3 billion. After years of contentious negotiations, court cases, and stalemate, President Lyndon B. Johnson signed the Colorado River Basin Project Act of 1968, which included not only the CAP and the five Colorado projects but also the Dixie Project and a unit of the Central Utah Project in Utah, and the Hooker Dam project in New Mexico. At the time, it was the most expensive single congressional authorization for reclamation in history.

The Central Arizona Water Conservation District (CAWCD), created in 1971, has two functions. First, it serves as a special taxing district that serves as the mechanism to repay the federal government for the cost of constructing the CAP, although the project itself did not get underway until 1973. Second, under a general manager and a fifteen-member board, the CAWCD contracts with the Secretary of the Interior to operate, maintain, and manage the CAP. The project took twenty years to complete at a cost of more than $4.7 billion, and now provides water to three counties, with about 46 percent of the CAP water allocated to the state's Native American tribes.

Designed and built by the BOR, the CAP begins at the pumping plant on the shores of Lake Havasu named for Mark Wilmer, profiled in Chapter 4. The facility lifts water 824 feet, high enough that gravity pulls the water along its journey south. From there, three aqueducts send the 1.5 maf of water per year 336 miles through tunnels, gates, and pipelines to reservoirs; two dams store water and help provide flood protection.

The 1980 Groundwater Management Act and Active Management Areas

Concerned about the state's exploding population, the Arizona legislature enacted a ground-breaking 1980 statute requiring developers in designated Active Management Areas (AMA) to demonstrate that there is an assured water supply that will last at least 100 years. The law was designed to provide some degree of certainty to residents that there would be a sustainable supply of water. Negotiated primarily by water interests rather than by political party leaders, the bill passed the legislature in a special session in a single day without any amendments and virtually no debate. The statute basically ignores Arizona's rural counties, focusing instead on the three where most of the state's irrigated agriculture (and groundwater basins) are located. The AMAs are required to diminish their reliance on groundwater so that the amount they take out is equal to the amount of recharge of the groundwater source by the year 2025. The state's five active management areas represent only about a quarter of Arizona's land mass, but over 75 percent of its population, primarily in the urban areas of Phoenix, Tucson, and Prescott.

The problem with the 1980 law, political leaders in Arizona now admit, is that the statute was predicated on the belief that Arizona's major urban areas and agricultural interests would move from using groundwater to using what was thought to be a sufficient supply of Colorado River water—a prediction that failed to take into account the droughts that would follow and changes in the West's political climate when it came to allocating the river's water.

Arizona's diminishing groundwater has plagued the state since just about forever, compounded by the reduced allocation of Colorado River water that began in 2022 because of widespread western drought. Although it is not the state with the driest weather, Arizona gets only about 13 inches of precipitation each year. The problem of finding sufficient water for the state's agricultural lands, as well as its population, showed up on everyone's radar. The Colorado River and other sources of surface water provide 54 percent of the state's water supply, and Arizona is one of the major beneficiaries of the Colorado River Compact. About 3 percent of the state's water supply now comes from reclaimed wastewater.

The 2023 Housing Moratorium

Arizona's governor announced on June 1, 2023 that the state had approved more housing construction than it could serve with the existing water supply. An analysis of the state's water supplies found that there was a 4 percent shortfall, or 39 maf, in Arizona's groundwater supply from what was needed over the next 100 years if nothing changed. Unlike other western states that rely heavily on water from the Colorado River to serve their population, Maricopa County—home to Phoenix and most of the state's residents—now relies on groundwater for more than half its users' needs. Water use in the desert city is about 2.2 billion gallons of water per day—twice as much as is used in New York City, even though Phoenix has half as many people. The governor abruptly called for a moratorium on future housing development in some areas of the state, including the metro Phoenix area, while allowing construction to continue on an estimated 80,000 unbuilt lots for housing where building permits had already been approved and issued.

How did such a miscalculation happen? According to a study conducted by the Kyl Center for Water Policy at Arizona State University, Arizona has been pumping out too much groundwater, mostly to meet the needs of industrial projects that do not operate under the same restrictions as home developers. Commercial buildings and industrial sites were not affected by the governor's action. In early 2024, the governor seemed to change her mind a bit when she announced what was termed a path to construction—the Alternative Designation of Assured Water Supply—that would allow some communities to continue building if they found water from other sources.

One of the places the governor was thinking about in potentially easing the building moratorium is the town of Queen Creek, a high-growth area on the perimeter of Phoenix that was traditionally an agricultural community. In 2010, the population was about 26,000, but a decade later it was almost 60,000. To meet its needs, Queen Creek agreed to pay about $21 million to a local farm for its water rights in perpetuity, about 2,033 acre-feet per year, that was previously used for growing alfalfa. The property is in a different county in an unincorporated area alongside the Colorado River. The agreement is called a water transfer, a process that involves a significant level of public outreach prior to approval. The transfer was proposed in August 2019, followed by a public comment period and meetings that resulted in a decision in September 2020 by the Arizona Department of Water Resources (ADWR) recommending the transfer be approved. The process continued in January 2021 with the Bureau of Reclamation reviewing the agreement with specific attention paid to any environmental impacts due to the transfer, followed by more public participation. In 2022, the BOR issued a ruling that would allow the town to enter into agreements that would provide alternative sources of water for use by its residents. This gives Queen Creek access to a water supply that does not involve groundwater pumping while continuing to grow, precisely what the governor eventually suggested.

The Saudi Deal

In 2014, a series of state land lease agreements between the Arizona State Land Department and Saudi Arabia's agribusiness firm Fondomonte became so controversial that, once exposed by a local newspaper, it became an issue in the 2022 elections. The leases were only a small part of a bigger controversy that has yet to be resolved—the unregulated use of groundwater in the rural parts of the state.

Fondomonte Arizona is a subsidiary of the Saudi company Almarai, a huge dairy/agribusiness firm outside Riyadh. The larger firm holds numerous international land holdings, many of which are used to grow crops for the country's massive dairy herds. The Saudis have exhausted most of their own aquifers, and have even banned the growing of some crops in their country.

Agriculture accounts for about 90 percent of Saudi Arabia's water consumption, making food security a critical concern. Fondomonte Arizona spent $47.5 million to purchase nearly 10,000 acres in one of the poorest and least-populated parts of Arizona. A year later, the state leased 3,520 acres of state trust land in a largely undeveloped area for Fondomonte to grow alfalfa, a water-intensive crop that can be harvested several times a year, at what was estimated to be one-sixth the market rate, in violation of state law. The agreement also allowed the company to draw unlimited amounts of Arizona's groundwater from a nearby basin to irrigate the alfalfa, which is then shipped back to Saudi Arabia. Arizona's new governor terminated one of the leases in 2023, and announced that three more leases would not be renewed upon expiration in February 2024.

The agreement is not the only one of its kind. Fondomonte also grows crops on land in California's Imperial County near Blythe, and Almarai purchased 14,000 acres of land in the Palo Verde Valley that draws water from the Colorado River. Bakersfield, California hay exporter Al Dahra ACX Global Inc. is owned by the Al Dahra Agriculture Company, based in the United Arab Emirates. It farms not only in California but also in Arizona and Washington, utilizing the limited water resources from the three states. Despite criticism that foreign interests are buying up land for their own needs despite the impacts on the West's depleting water supply, in Arizona, the practice is completely legal.

Voluntary Water Reductions

Arizona is one of the Lower Basin states that agreed to a plan to reduce their dependence on Colorado River water in 2023 as part of the federal Inflation Reduction Act and Bipartisan Infrastructure Law. The carrot that incentivized the states to participate was simple—money–with the rate ranging from $330 to $400 per acre-foot of water. Arizona provided its cities with an additional incentive: a one-year agreement with the ADWR's Intentionally Created Surplus program to reduce water use in exchange for a payment of $330 per acre-foot with nearly twenty local entities participating. The water-use reduction amounts to nearly 900,000 acre-feet of water, half of which comes from two Arizona tribes, the Gila River Indian Community and the Fort McDowell Yavapai Nation, for which they will receive $167 million.

Another type of agreement involves private companies that agree to reduce their water use. California-based Limoneira, an international agribusiness firm, produces lemons, avocados, and other crops, and owns 1,300 acres of farmland in Yuma, Arizona. In 2023, the company announced it had entered into a fallowing agreement with the Yuma Mesa Irrigation and Drainage District and the BOR to refrain from diverting Colorado River water that would otherwise go to irrigate 581 acres of its farm acreage. In exchange, the company will receive $1.32 million annually through at least calendar year 2025 and the water will remain in Lake Mead.

California: Thinking Big, Really Big

In his acclaimed book *Cadillac Desert*, author Marc Reisner (profiled in Chapter 4) noted, "No other state has done as much to fructify its deserts, make over its flora and fauna, and rearrange the hydrology God gave it. No other place as put as many people where they probably have no business being."

California is different from the other states in the West. Reisner may have been referring to the disparities in water resources, precipitation, politics, and population growth that further complicate California's efforts. If recent climate extremes weren't enough, water management in California is a complex tapestry of large and small agencies ranging from the mammoth bureaucracy of the federal government to the smallest community and its irrigation district. In addition to the federal agencies discussed in Chapter 1, the state has its own Department of Water Resources (DWR), an agency that evolved out of fifty-two smaller ones. One of the department's primary tasks deals with the management of the California State Water Project (SWP), the water storage and delivery system that extends more than 705 miles and most of the length of the state. It is the nation's largest state-owned water and power generator and user-financed water system; canals, pipelines, reservoirs, and hydroelectric power facilities deliver water to 27 million Californians, 750,000 acres of farmland, and untold businesses. The nine-member California Water Commission advises the director of the DWR on water rules and regulations and the operation of the SWP.

The five members of the State Water Resources Control Board have responsibility for allocating water rights for the state's surface water. The Board also regulates the state's water quality in conjunction with nine regional boards. Water rights in California are based on the doctrine that those who claimed water rights prior to 1914 have "senior rights" that allow them to have a virtually unlimited supply of water, even during times of drought when other users must cut back.

California's local drinking water system is extremely diverse, and one of the largest. According to a study conducted by the California WaterBlog in 2022, there are about 8,000 Public Water Systems (PWS) in the state, and about 3,000 Community Water Systems (CWS), defined as systems that serve a residential population year-round. The remaining 5,000 are considered non-community systems that serve sites such as schools, businesses, and campgrounds that serve at least twenty-five people but have a transient or non-residential population. Added to those numbers are an unknown number of unregulated systems that do not serve at least twenty-five persons or fifteen connections.

Historically, California has a reputation for thinking big when it comes to water, from passage of the Central Valley Project (CVP) in 1933, a partnership of sorts with the Bureau of Reclamation, to the voter-approved California Water Project (1960) providing water to the San Joaquin Valley and Southern California, and the Feather River Project that Governor Pat Brown saw "as a monument to me," when the state legislature authorized it in 1959. There have been huge projects that failed to win voter support, such as Governor Jerry Brown's (Pat Brown's son) campaign to build the Peripheral Canal, originally proposed in 1965. His canal proposal, a part of the California Water Project, would have diverted water from the Sacramento River through three counties across the eastern and southern edges of the Sacramento–San Joaquin Delta. A 1982 voter referendum on the project, which included language that the construction costs alone would be in excess of $3.1 billion "plus unknown additional costs, plus interest" was approved by Southern California's voters by two to one, but in the northern Bay area counties, it lost nine to one. The governor's Peripheral Canal idea lost by garnering just 40 percent of the statewide vote.

California's Central Valley Project

The CVP evolved from the Reclamation Act of 1902, and is now a system of twenty dams and reservoirs, plus hydroelectric plants, canals, and facilities that convey water about 400 miles to the Sacramento, San Joaquin, and Tulare water basins. The federal government built the CVP with the goal of bringing water for irrigating small farms. The project has come under scrutiny and criticism in recent years as land consolidation, primarily by growers, thwarted the original goal. Industrial agriculture, critics say, especially the subsidization of water-intensive crops with high returns like alfalfa and almonds, allow contractors to get federal water without paying the costs of the federal investment in providing that water. Environmental damage caused by the CVP, they argue, including the destruction of habitats and overdrafting of valuable aquifers, are externalized costs borne by taxpayers.

At the center of the controversy over the CVP is the Westlands Water District, the largest agricultural water district in the state. The politically powerful agency delivers water to 600,000 acres of almonds, pistachios, tomatoes, and other water-intensive crops in two counties covering 1,100 miles in the San Joaquin Valley. Using a 2016 law that allowed districts to change the terms of their contract if they repaid the federal government what they owed for construction of the CVP, the district paid about $210 million to convert its contract with the BOR to an agreement that it would have a permanent water entitlement. In this instance, the 2020 agreement gave the Westlands district permanent access to up to 1.15 maf of water per year. To put that number in perspective, that is more than double the amount of water that the 4 million residents of Los Angeles use in a year.

The 2012–2016 drought, combined with record-breaking high temperatures, along with a well-below-average snowpack, resulted in less water captured in California's reservoirs and an increased reliance on groundwater. In 2014, the governor declared a state of emergency, mandating a 25 percent reduction in water use compared to 2013 by March 2016. By August 2015, nearly three-quarters of the state was experiencing extreme drought. The 2014 Sustainable Groundwater Management Act (SGMA, pronounced sigma) required local entities to form groundwater sustainability agencies (GSAs) by June 30, 2017. Each GSA, consisting of a single local agency or a combination of agencies, was required to develop a plan for its overdrafted basin(s) based upon the importance of groundwater to the location, how much agriculture and domestic wells are supported by groundwater, and the location's population, among other factors. Basins were divided into categories of medium and high priority and required to submit a plan for protecting groundwater supplies. Initially, over 260 GSAs covering the state's 515 basins were formed by the initial planning milestone, and since then, some have been reorganized, formed, or consolidated as conditions changed and information about overlap situations was found, and as institutional knowledge about the implementation of SGMA was developed.

The underlying principle behind the legislation is that groundwater is to be managed locally, with the state's role being one of support. The goal is to have steady progress in eliminating undesirable results by 2040 or 2042, depending upon the severity of the overdraft. The DWR implements the SGMA, evaluating the Groundwater Sustainability Plans (GSPs) and providing guidance documents. The first batch of documents were submitted in 2020, and by January 2024, 119 GSAs had been submitted. At the same time, the DWR announced that it had completed the review process and issued determinations for all the GSPs in high and medium groundwater basins in the state.

The process of developing the GSP is grueling; many of the plans are over 1,000 pages in length. Most of those pages include information about hydrology, projections of water demands and potential supplies, with only a tiny portion of the plan actually detailing what the GSA plans to accomplish. If deficiencies are found after the DWR completes its review, the GSA has 180 days to revise and resubmit its plan. If a plan is found to be inadequate, consultation initiated by the State Water Resources Control Board can determine whether intervention is warranted. Other procedures include the prioritization and scheduling of probationary hearings with at least ninety days' notice to the parties, followed by public comments and outreach to stakeholders. While on probation, the GSAs must correct the deficiencies that have been identified, and if not addressed in a timely manner, the Board can implement an interim plan. The procedures are designed to be open and transparent, but the time allowed at each step is also aggressive.

It is too early in the GSP process for there to be many data about how well the program is functioning, as many of the plans include items that are contingent upon obtaining funding, require lengthy studies to be completed prior to implementation, or involve projects that are still in the early planning stages. Hurdles like land acquisition, permitting, and data acquisition hinder some plans that are under development, along with the challenges that face small, low-financed water districts.

Despite the fact that the GSAs are supposed to be self-sufficient, in 2022, twenty GSAs were awarded $150 million for planning and projects as part of the implementation of the SGMA. GSAs are also expected to develop fee structures to pay for the projects they develop locally, but there has been backlash from those who have historically pumped groundwater for free. In the Chowchilla subbasin, voters rejected a measure that would require a fee to pay for their region's projects.

The six San Joaquin Valley GSPs that were rejected by the DWR in an initial evaluation had already received tens of millions of dollars in state funds for studies and data management systems. In September 2023, another $187 million in SGMA grant funds were awarded to thirty-two groundwater subbasins to support 103 projects.

In addition to the actions being taken through the SGMA, at the beginning of the historic drought that began in 2020, Governor Gavin Newsom directed state agencies to create a portfolio of actions California could take to develop long-term water resilience including clean, dependable water supplies. The resulting suite of actions, released in July 2020, has become the state's blueprint for coping with the myriad problems related to water scarcity, climate change, and long-standing issues related to the ecosystem and water quality. A report on the state's progress was released in January 2022. The initial document included 142 actions to be taken by state agencies as a way of supporting local efforts, led by the state's Secretary for Natural Resources, the Secretary for Environmental Protection, and the Secretary of the Department of Food and Agriculture. It consists of four major sections: developing new water supplies through investments in wastewater recycling and desalination technology; expanding water storage capacity above and below ground; reducing demand; and improving forecasting, data, and management, including water rights modernization.

Thinking Big: The Delta Conveyance Project

Conceptualized and proposed since the 1960s, California has grappled with ways to bring water from the Sacramento River to the Sacramento–San Joaquin Delta, the estuary that supplies water to 27 million people and 700 million acres of farmland. The Sacramento is the state's largest river, and its 400 miles starts with the snowy slopes of Mt. Shasta, eventually passing through the city that is its namesake and on to the Pacific Ocean. The inland water body, about 1,300 miles in size, is where the ocean and fresh water meet. Various plans have included one or more tunnels that would be built under the estuary; the 2016 version lost even the governor's support due to the projected high cost. The most recent proposal, the 36-foot-wide, 45-mile-long Delta Conveyance Project, commonly called the Delta Tunnel or the Bethany Reservoir Alignment, is potentially on track to begin construction in 2028, taking fifteen to twenty years to be completed at a cost of at least $16 billion. The DWR released the final environmental documents for the project in December 2023, but despite a public outcry, refused to allow a sixty-day comment period on the 27,000-page document.

The acrimonious debate has been multifaceted, with concerns about the scope and cost of the project, its impact on the environment and local communities, the threats of damaging earthquakes, and questions about whether the tunnel could withstand the effects of global climate change such as rising sea levels and catastrophic storms. The most recent proposals have been mired in the state's budget debates. When the final environmental report was released, criticism focused on the agency's lack of responses to new scientific research dealing with climate change and hydrology. Some critics wanted the state to rein in what they termed water abuses by big agribusiness and fossil fuel corporations, an attitude characterized as distrust of politicians who put Southern California's interests ahead of those of one of the state's poorest regions. Supporters argue the need to move forward as quickly as possible to secure a reliable water supply that would serve two-thirds of the state's population, arguing the aging water infrastructure system was broken. Modernizing that system, they said, would create tens of thousands of jobs while shoring up water resiliency. Although the governor noted that the project had been redesigned and rightsized following public input, it was not enough to satisfy several groups of litigants who strongly opposed the project. Just before the deadline in January 2024, eight lawsuits opposing the project were filed against the DWR, ranging from a coalition of environmental groups, several city and county entities, water agencies, and a tribal organization. Most of the suits alleged the agency had violated the California Environmental Quality Act (CEQA) by approving the project, with one attorney calling the department's environmental impact report profoundly deficient. Others noted the agency's failure to analyze the impacts of the project and its failure to respond to the public's comments.

The mammoth project has been referred to as a "two governor project" that would need to be set up by the state's current governor for his successor. The next step, regardless of the ongoing litigation, will involve engineering, design, and permitting by the Delta Conveyance Design and Construction Authority, along with the further development of what DWR calls a comprehensive Community Benefits Program. An updated May 2024 cost estimate that accounted for inflation to 2023 dollars was $20.1 billion, similar in cost to the earlier estimates.

Thinking Big: The Sites Reservoir

California's water supply and storage issues are not limited to a single region—they are statewide. But in such a big state, water scarcity requires planners and officials to think really big, as is the case with the proposed $4.5 billion Sites

Reservoir in northern California. Money for the project was approved by voters a decade ago. The project would pump water from the Sacramento River when the stream flow was high, but only after all other water rights were met and state regulators approved. The reservoir has recently been fast-tracked by state and federal agencies; when completed, it will be the second largest off-stream reservoir in the country, and the state's eighth-biggest storage facility, with a capacity of 1.5 maf. That represents water for 3 million households for a year, or a 15 percent increase in northern California's water storage capacity. Currently there are more than two dozen local and regional water delivery agencies that have partnered with the project, serving 24.5 million people and 500,000 acres of farmland.

Although California's governor lauded the state's ability to cut red tape so the project could be built more quickly to capture water during wet seasons, the Sierra Club, among others, called the project environmentally destructive. The group noted that existing diversions had caused a decline in the San Francisco Bay/Delta area, and that building new dams and reservoirs was an idea of the past. The last reservoir of this size was New Melones Lake, built in the late 1970s. In late December 2023, five other environmental organizations filed suit against the project, arguing that the environmental impact report for the reservoir was insufficient because it failed to address the harm to fish and the impact of greenhouse gas emissions. Despite the suit, the Sites Project Authority plans to break ground in 2026, with completion slated for 2032.

Thinking Big: Restoring the Salton Sea

Along southern Riverside and part of Imperial County, almost the entire desert is below sea level, reaching 235 feet below at the edge of the Salton Sea, California's largest lake, spanning 370 square miles. Millions of years ago, the area was entirely submerged, with its sediment eventually turning the valley into prime agricultural land and home to the native Cahuilla people, about 700 of whom now live on tribal lands near the area. Over time, the lake went through a cycle of expansion and shrinkage, from wetlands to dry desert. In 1900, an irrigation canal was created to bring water from the Colorado to an old river channel, but in 1905, spring flooding broke through a canal and the dry lakebed became today's lake until the breach was repaired.

In 1930, the US Fish and Wildlife Service established part of the area, which is 40 miles north of the Mexican border and part of the Pacific Flyway for birds, as a national wildlife refuge. The site attracted birdwatchers from all over the world who came to see over 400 native species.

Dozens of resort hotels and other accommodations were built along the edges of the lake, hosting celebrities and tourists, and at its peak, more than 1.5 million visitors a year. In the 1970s and 1980s, a combination of agricultural runoff and flood irrigation poisoned the lake, resulting in massive fish and wildlife die offs. Heavy precipitation from tropical storms caused the water to flood the resort communities, many of which became submerged. As the lake began to dry up, and fertilizer and chemicals became more desiccated, the odors and animal carcasses kept tourists away. Congressman/celebrity Sonny Bono advocated for a solution to the dying Salton Sea, which was in his district, and in 1998, the 35,000-acre wildlife refuge at the south end was renamed in his honor for his efforts to conserve the Salton Sea.

The 2003 Quantification Settlement Agreement transferred water from the Imperial Irrigation District to California's coastal communities, including San Diego. The water transfer limited the amount of water going into the Salton Sea and the reduced inflows exposed the lakebed (known as the playa), degraded the aquatic habitat, and increased the salinity of the water so it is now about twice that of the ocean. Toxic dust released as the lake dries up has caused the region to have some of the worst air quality in the country, with one in five residents diagnosed with asthma. The Salton Sea Restoration Act was signed into law in 2003, but the level of the sea has dropped 10 feet since then with the surface area shrinking by about 38 square miles, reducing valuable fish and bird habitat. Most of the plans to restore the lake and wetlands have never been implemented due to the costs involved. Similarly, projects and proposals to increase water flow have been deemed too expensive.

California's Salton Sea Management Program is now being implemented by three state agencies over a ten-year period. Critics say it took too long to get the program off the ground with few results other than studies and meetings. The goal is to restore habitat and suppress dust on 30,000 acres of the playa by 2028, with specific acreage targets each year. The largest project, a 4,100-acre Species Conservation Habitat Project along the shallow southern edge of the Salton Sea, was finished at the end of 2023. But it falls short of 11,500 acres that should have been completed by the five-year mark, especially when it comes to controlling dust. A pilot program at the northern end began in late 2023 to create a 156-acre lake with both habitat and recreational features. Although there have been some vegetation projects completed to control dust, other projects are still in the design and permitting stage, with no comprehensive schedule for 2026 through 2028 developed. The federal government joined the restoration efforts with a $72 million package in December 2023, almost all of which would be spent to expand the Species Conservation Habitat Project.

Thinking Big: The Lithium Valley

The Salton Sea region is also a geothermally active, mineral-rich trough on top of the San Andreas Fault and other geological features. More recently, it has attracted energy companies seeking to mine the mineral that is used in making electric vehicle batteries. A 2023 study for the Department of Energy estimated that there was enough lithium at the site to make 375 million electric vehicle batteries, enough to allow the United States to be an exporter rather than an importer of the mineral, enough lithium that it would take 100 years to extract what is known to be there. The California Energy Commission reported in 2020 that the lithium is so abundant that companies could produce more than $7 billion worth of the mineral per year, based on current prices. As much as the 180,000 residents in local communities in Imperial County, which are predominantly home to minorities and immigrants, welcome the potential economic boost, they also worry about the loss of groundwater that is used in the mining process. There is also uneasiness that the companies who are investing heavily in the area will threaten vegetation, wildlife habitat, and air quality. The promises of job creation ring hollow for those still living in poverty in Imperial County. A new group, the Lithium Valley Commission, began working with local residents in 2023 to provide information and hear residents' concerns, and in early 2024, a group of Latino legislators toured the area to witness problems for themselves. Three companies are actively involved in the area, called "the Saudi Arabia of lithium," driven by tax breaks and federal dollars, with actual delivery of the product tentatively scheduled for 2025.

Thinking Big: Some New Approaches

McKuin and Bales report on another promising technology called solar canopies that has replaced the often talked about but rarely implemented idea of covering the network of about 4,000 miles of irrigation canals that are blamed for the evaporation of the state's valuable water. India has used the concept through steel-truss systems that could not easily be adapted to California. However, researchers at the University of California Merced have developed cable suspension designs that are more flexible, lighter-weight, and less expensive that could potentially save 63 billion gallons of water annually. In 2022, they joined in a public–private partnership funded by the state to build solar panels over nearly 2 miles of canals in the San Joaquin Valley by 2024. The pilot project would reduce evaporation while providing renewable energy to meet California's goal of generating 60 percent of its power from renewable resources by 2030.

Alternative sources of water, discussed later in this chapter, have been a staple of California's water portfolio for years, but in July 2023, the state went a step further when the State Water Resources Control Board (SWRCB) proposed regulations for direct potable reuse. This process would allow water agencies to add wastewater that has been treated to drinking water standards to be added to their potable supply, a procedure that takes just a few hours. The benefits are twofold: increasing drinking water sources while also reducing the amount of wastewater that is released into surface waters and the ocean. A panel of researchers and engineers evaluated the proposed regulations and declared them to be protective of public health, thus opening the proposals to public comment and revision.

Like Arizona and Nevada, California has implemented conservation strategies, but in some ways, has gone a step further to squeeze out as much water as possible. Some efforts have focused on providing funding for cities to implement conservation. The state gave the city of Modesto a $3.2 million grant from the Urban Community Drought Relief Grant Program in 2023 to replace turf at twenty-one parks and supplement a rebate program to replace lawns at $2 per foot with water-saving surfaces. Instead of limiting turf uses, the governor signed legislation in 2023 that bans the use of potable water for irrigation on non-functional turf. The law requires new and renovated commercial and industrial areas, including parking lots, to use 25 percent local native plants beginning in 2026, increasing that to at least 75 percent in 2035. In addition to the reduction in water use, the bill is designed to support biodiversity. The legislation does not affect residences, edible gardens, cemeteries, lawns used for recreation such as sports fields and school fields, or lawns used for civic functions. In May 2023, the SWRCB readopted a regulation it had initially adopted in May 2022 that bans the use of drinking water for watering decorative grass, but it does not ban the use of recycled water for irrigating non-functional turf.

When the proverbial carrot has not been enough, the state has also begun to implement two controversial laws signed by Governor Jerry Brown in 2018 that will require permanent water conservation strategies starting in 2025. The "Making Conservation a California Way of Life" program establishes how urban water-use objectives will be determined, and which of the state's 405 urban retail water suppliers will be affected. The California State Water Board is responsible for drafting the implementing regulations, with a goal of reducing urban water consumption by 400,000 acre-feet per year by 2030, just a tiny fraction of the state's overall use. Critics argue that the regulations will amount to water rationing for urban residents when other methods of conserving water or other ways of increasing the water supply are readily available. In January 2024, a state Legislative Analyst's Office report questioned whether the benefits of the rules would outweigh the costs, which likely would be borne by customers. In a series of recommendations, the SWRCB was warned that several of the proposed regulations should be made less stringent and less expensive, especially for low-income households that would bear most of the rate increases likely to be needed to pay for the program. One critic asked, "Is this juice worth the squeeze?"

California's sheer size and resources make any comparison with the other western states inappropriate. For example, in fiscal year 2022–2023, the SWRCB continued to augment local resources and advance the governor's agenda by distributing nearly $1.2 billion to water systems and communities. Half of that amount went to grants and principal forgiveness—funding and loans that do not have to be repaid—most of which went to fund drinking water and wastewater projects in small or disadvantaged communities. Another $560 million for major resilience and drinking water projects was targeted toward federal–state partnerships with low-cost financing for water quality infrastructure. The federal government smiled favorably on the state, making $2.8 billion for water projects available until 2026 under the Bipartisan Infrastructure Law. Other federal grants were made available from the Environmental Protection Agency for drinking water and clean water projects.

These numbers are unfathomable in scale to the other states in the West, as are many of the problems California faces. But the numbers also point to the strengths of the state's congressional delegation as they lobby for federal dollars, and to representatives of the agriculture industry and other groups that lobby the state legislature and Congress. Smaller states, more rural states, and states whose voices are less likely to be heard in Washington are simply unable to compete with California.

Nevada: Conservation and the Southern Nevada Water Authority

Nevada faces challenges that are somewhat unique to the state, some political, some economic, some geographic, some statutory, but many affect the state's demand for water and how it can be met. Of particular importance is southern Nevada and Clark County, where Las Vegas is the dominant player in all of the region's decision-making. Nevada is dependent, to a large extent, on the Colorado River and other surface water, which provide about 70 percent of the state's water supply (in Southern Nevada, the figure is closer to 90 percent), with the other 30 percent sourced from groundwater. It is the driest state in the United States, with southern Nevada receiving only about 7 inches of rain each year.

Of the state's 3.2 million people, 2.3 million live in Clark County, home to the city of Las Vegas. The population of the region has grown dramatically since 1931, when construction began on the Hoover Dam and the state legalized gambling, and again after the Second World War, when major casino hotels and resorts began being built on the Las Vegas Strip. Water resources, which had historically been controlled by the railroads, became more important as Las Vegas expanded. In 1944, a Union Pacific Railroad geologist reported that the Las Vegas groundwater basin was a closed basin, meaning that its aquifer could only be replenished by snowmelt from the Spring and Sheep mountains. The limitation on the area's groundwater led Nevada's state water engineer to urge Las Vegas' leaders to take immediate steps to acquire a supplemental supply of water in order to allow for the continued growth of the metropolitan area.

Las Vegas hasn't always been such an arid place. Perhaps just 10,000 years ago, the Las Vegas Valley looked attractive to the early people who came there to hunt. They would have found springs, creeks, and streams flowing from the snowmelt of the Spring Mountain Range rising about 12,000 feet above the valley floor at its highest point. As other hunting peoples visited the Colorado Plateau, some decided to stay and began to cultivate crops like corn. They would have seen the Colorado River as it snaked its way through canyons to the east, and they found the seeds of the mesquite to their taste. By the mid-1800s European settlers had arrived, as had Mormon missionaries in 1855 and others who used the water for their own crops. The Las Vegas mission of the Mormons failed after two years, in part due to internal dissension but also due to disputes with the Paiute tribe. Mormon leader Brigham Young recalled all settlers to Utah in case there was to be warfare with the government. The Las Vegas Valley remained mostly pastoral until the railroads appeared just after the turn of the century. Their presence changed the region dramatically, as the railroads promoted settlement, and the Nevada State Engineer granted the railroad groundwater rights beneath the valley. This meant that the local settlers no longer controlled their own water sources, and officials began looking elsewhere for water to soothe the parched throats of the growing population, which had reached over 8,500 people by 1920.

Las Vegas was key to Nevada's growth, and the city's leaders convinced the state legislature to establish a special service district in 1947, the Las Vegas Valley Water District (LVVWD). The agency gained control over not only the city's groundwater supplies but also its allotment of Colorado River water under the 1922 Colorado River Compact. The district bought out the Union Pacific Railroad's water infrastructure in 1954, and constructed a pipeline from Lake Mead to bring water to the city. For once, the city controlled its own water future, even though its allotment from the Colorado—stored in Lake Mead—was only 300,000 acre-feet. That allotment, however, led to disputes with the unincorporated municipalities in the Las Vegas Valley, who sought their own allocation of the river's water. The legislature responded by designating the Colorado River Commission (CRC) as the manager of the state's water. By the late 1980s, however, the relationship between the two water entities soured, coupled with both a casino and housing construction boom that increased population growth but threatened to deplete the state's Colorado River allotment. These factors opened the door for the Clark County Commission to usher in a new management style with a new general manager of the LVVWD, Pat Mulroy, profiled in Chapter 4.

Mulroy inherited a system that allowed developers to get building permits without the agency knowing whether there was sufficient water to service the development. In 1991, she issued a temporary moratorium on building permits in Las Vegas, although other cities continued to approve them. Realizing that this disjointed approach to water use was not sustainable, the parties eventually, with spurts of contentious opposition, formed the South Nevada Water Authority (SNWA) in 1991. The new agency was tasked with representing the metro Las Vegas area in discussions over additional Colorado River water for Nevada, speaking as one voice rather than as individual members representing their own interests. The SNWA became one of the most politically powerful voices within the state.

Between 1995 and 1997, officials also began looking at ways of paying for the need for additional water delivery infrastructure, seeking an increase in the state sales tax to pay for projects estimated to cost about $2 billion. There was an additional proposal for a local quarter-cent sales tax increase, with the expectation that tourist dollars would offset about 30 percent of the overall tax burden. Putting the matter to voters was risky, but in June 1998, the measure won by 70 percent of the vote.

The SNWA predicted that southern Nevada would have sufficient water resources to last until 2010 while still supporting development. The agency's leaders also realized that they would need to be creative in finding new sources of water. One by one, the agency purchased water rights from various sources, looking at the Virgin River and east-central Nevada, knowing they needed to put together a portfolio of strategies.

Dealing with Drought

When the federal government issued its first-ever official water shortage declaration in August 2022, Nevada's allotment from Lake Mead was cut by 7 percent, or about 21,000 acre-feet from what it would ordinarily get, starting in 2023. Although that number may have sounded alarms, it made some decisions easier to make than others. In Las Vegas, an estimated 99 percent of the indoor water that is used, or about 1 maf, can be treated and returned to Lake Mead for what is called a return-flow credit. The actual net cost of water use is less than 100,000 acre-feet. That meant outdoor use would become the target for sizable restrictions.

Nevada's current allocation is not enough to match population growth. According to long-term projections from the University of Las Vegas Center for Business and Economic Research (CBER), Clark County's population will reach about 2.94 million by 2035 and nearly 3.39 million by 2060. The non-profit group ProPublica has noted that to meet the demands of that type of growth, water use must be reduced by more than 100,000 acre-feet. To reach that goal, Nevada has implemented a variety of strategies ranging from practical and obvious to politically unlikely and voluntary.

Conservation Efforts

The SNWA has used a carrot-and-stick approach that looks at every potential conservation tactic. Around 1997, the SNWA targeted outdoor water use as nearly three-fourths of the water used in the metro area went to watering lawns, washing cars, and swimming pools. The strategy has recently been applied to businesses, many of them from California, seeking to move or enhance their presence in Nevada. Economic development and water officials are now taking a second look at the level of tax incentives traditionally offered to companies as the carrot for relocating or developing in the state. Using a type of water-investment tool that analyzes a project's water use and scores it alongside factors such as job creation, average pay, and tax revenue, local and state officials can work with the company to balance their water score against other measures.

Nevada has also engaged in adaptive management through water banking agreements with Arizona and California, "saving water," to use the banking metaphor, by storing water for use when needed. The SNWA has agreed to pay other Colorado River water rights users to store unused water, in times when there is a surplus, by injecting it into aquifers. The state receives "credits" for storing water, and if the water is then needed, it draws from Lake Mead, and the "banker" takes a similar amount out of the aquifer. The SNWA considers water banking a type of temporary resource in its portfolio, with most of the agreements occurring since the 1990s to meet short-term gaps between supply and demand. According to the SNWA's figures for 2021, the agency had stored about 345,000 acre-feet in the Southern Nevada Water Bank, 330,000 in the California Water Bank, and 614,000 in the Arizona Water Bank.

The broad conservation campaign has definitely been successful, and the state has done better than projected. In 2024, the valley's water use was 89 gallons per capita, down from 104 in 2022, and 235 in 1990. The current goal is to reduce use to 86 gallons per person, which would extend the existing water supply for the next fifty years without bringing in additional water.

Turf Battles

The image of water being used to irrigate grass, which then evaporates, has been an easy visual target for the state, and a problem that has garnered national publicity. Again, the carrot-and-stick approach has been used to find ways to rid communities and commercial sites of water-guzzling turf where it could be eliminated. Cities throughout the Las Vegas Valley have adopted ordinances that bar owners of new homes from planting grass lawns in the front of their homes, restricting their backyard lawns by half. Commercial developers are no longer allowed to plant grass around their buildings—policies that were considered draconian at one time. In addition, several communities offer incentives if the existing turf is ripped out, thus reducing the amount of water used. The SNWA has paid homeowners, businesses, and multifamily properties for every square foot of existing grass replaced with landscaping that uses little or no water. The SNWA says that since its Water Smart Landscapes rebate program began in 1999, over 210 million square feet of lawn has been transformed into water-efficient landscaping, resulting in a savings of 170 billion gallons of water. For homeowners taking part in the program in 2024, the rebate program was increased from $3 to $5 per square foot, with the rate going back to $3 in 2025 as an incentive to participate earlier rather than delay.

The next target was non-functional or decorative turf, a somewhat nuanced term that can be used to describe unused grass under trees, medians, sports fields, some areas on golf courses, and parks. A 2021 state law prohibited the use of Colorado River water to irrigate this type of turf, supported by almost every interest group except homeowners' associations (HOA). The "stick" part of the equation is controlling water waste. Lawns still exist, but there is a complex seasonal schedule for when they can be watered, and the restrictions are enforced. There are three distinct seasonal watering periods; there is no watering on Sundays; and it makes a difference where in the area you live. Witnesses to broken sprinklers, excessive watering, and watering outside of prescribed days or hours are asked to report to their water service provider. Depending upon the provider, a city's ordinance, and their rules, fines can range from $40 to $5,000 for repeat offenders.

Increasing the Cost of Water

One of the more controversial strategies that Las Vegas has implemented is actually one of the most obvious and on the face of it, the simplest. In 2023, the Las Vegas Valley Water District began charging customers based on "excessive use," a monthly fee structure that assesses a $9 charge for every 1,000 gallons used, based on the season. The fee targets the top 10 percent of the water users within the district—one out of six homes—homeowners who use more than the bottom 60 percent of water users. In the first six months the new assessment was in force, nearly 60,000 single-family homes in Las Vegas and the unincorporated areas of Clark County saw their water bills increase—some of them dramatically. During those same six months, the district generated more than $12 million in new revenue from the assessment.

Sometimes there are factors that affect water use that are out of the control of policymakers. During the first five months of 2023, for instance, southern

Nevada consumed 25 percent less water from the Colorado River than it had in the previous three years. Officials noted that the reduced amount was due to conservation efforts that had been implemented. But they also stated that the weather during the period was both cooler and wetter than usual, reducing the state's consumptive use from the river by about 82,000 acre-feet in 2022, 84,500 acre-feet in 2021, and 80,900 acre-feet in 2020.

Although Nevada has been proactive and successful in many of its efforts to deal with water demands, some of its proposals just did not work out. The SNWA had concluded that Nevada was highly unlikely to obtain more than its current allocation of Colorado River water, and the state was going to have to look closer at in-state options. One of those options, initially explored in the late 1980s, involved the Las Vegas Valley Water District's application for water rights in the rural northeastern part of the state. The 2004 version of the plan was to pipe the water about 250 miles to Las Vegas, adding those acre-feet to the metropolitan area's resources, and thus indirectly supporting more growth. The opposition to what became known as the SNWA pipeline was fierce, with the proposal framed as a rural versus urban battle involving legal challenges and public relations imagery. Ranchers viewed the plan as a land grab that would destroy their culture. Environmentalists said the pipeline would destroy biodiversity. Native American communities argued their lives would be damaged. After more than a decade of dueling court cases, appeals of court cases, and appeals to the public's conscience, the Seventh Judicial District Court of Nevada ruled against SNWA in March 2020. The court's ruling focused on procedural elements, rather than on environmental or humanitarian ones or a western ethos argument. The SNWA had failed to follow the proper legal protocols, the court said. A month later, the SNWA voted to discontinue the project.

New Mexico: Planning beyond the Acequia

In Truth or Consequences, New Mexico, a community of 6,000 on the bank of the Rio Grande about three hours south of Albuquerque, the city made over 400 repairs on its water supply lines in 2022. Some of those lines date to the 1930s—well beyond their expected useful life. That same year, over 200 million gallons of water was lost to leakage, or about 43 percent of the water in the system, with line breaks a daily occurrence. The cost of replacement of the lines and the other improvements that are needed in the city is estimated to cost Truth or Consequences an estimated $150 million, and it might as well be $150 gazillion.

Unlike cities where finding a reliable water source is of critical importance, in this instance, the problem is keeping the little water that exists *in* the pipeline. And Truth or Consequences is not the exception. In New Mexico, two-thirds of the state's water systems serve 500 people or less, making them exceptionally vulnerable to infrastructure breakdowns. Is it any wonder that the state's population base is shifting from rural communities to urban ones?

New Mexico struggles with problems that are both the same and yet different from the rest of the West. Like most of the others, New Mexico's arid climate makes water policies of prime importance, as most of the state receives less than 10 inches of precipitation each year.

Groundwater is one of the major sources of water for the state, with the exception of Albuquerque, and most communities are not located near a surface water source. New Mexico's population is unlike others in the region—states like Utah, Idaho, Texas, and Nevada—that increased their population by double-digit percentages between 2010 and 2023. Eight of the twelve fastest-growing states in the United States are located in the West, but New Mexico is not among them. Like most of the western states, irrigated agriculture accounts for the bulk of water use consumption. Unlike other more urbanized states, New Mexico has a poor track record when it comes to water and planning, although leaders have been drafting a water planning document for the next fifty years. These factors, both old and new, make water resources and consumption extremely complex problems to which the state historically has not paid much attention. Until now.

When Spanish explorers reached what is now New Mexico in the mid-1500s, some of the land was home to the Pueblo people who irrigated their field with water from the Rio Grande. In 1848, the United States acquired New Mexico, and along with the territory, the Pueblo water rights that had been given to the people, although never quantified. From a historical perspective, New Mexico is unique in the importance of *acequias*, the community ditches or water courses that often date back to colonial times, which are recognized as political subdivisions under state law. The acequias are used to irrigate fields, with acequia associations that maintain and improve the ditches with the cost borne by the irrigation system users.

Water Supply Management Today

The New Mexico Environment Department (NMED) is responsible for protecting the state's water quality, overseeing state and federal regulations, and water infrastructure. The basis of the agency's work are the groundwater laws enacted in 1931. About 80 percent of the state's residents rely on groundwater as their drinking water source, with most of that water supplied by public systems. Due to the largely rural nature of much of the state, another 170,000 residents rely on private wells, making an adequate supply of uncontaminated groundwater crucial.

Groundwater makes up about half of the water withdrawn for not only drinking water but also for industrial use and agriculture, which accounts for about three-fourths of New Mexico's water use. No other state in the Southwest relies on groundwater for domestic use as New Mexico.

Albuquerque, the state's largest city with a population of about half a million, has its own water utility, the Albuquerque Bernalillo County Water Utility Authority, and its own conservation program, with water sourced from both the Rio Grande and the Santa Fe Group aquifer. The city's residents have reduced their water use by over 150 gallons per person per year, and the county has offered toilet retrofits, rain barrel systems, and other projects under its conservation program. Despite those efforts at conservation, Albuquerque still uses 15 billion gallons of water annually.

The primary sources of surface water are the 1,900-mile-long Rio Grande, the fifth-longest river in North America, and New Mexico's allocation of Colorado River water based on the Colorado River Compact of 1922. Under that agreement, New Mexico is entitled to 11.25 percent of the Upper Basin's share, pending the next round of discussions when the compact expires at the end of 2026. The Rio Grande's water management stems from the Rio Grande Compact, an interstate agreement between Colorado, New Mexico and Texas, signed in 1938. The compact allocated the river's waters from its headwaters in Colorado to El Paso, Texas. There is also a Pecos River Compact that requires New Mexico to limit the state's water use to make sure that Texas receives its share of water. The agreement resulted from a suit brought in 1974 by Texas in which New Mexico was accused of failing to deliver Texas' share of Pecos River water. Texas won the suit, and was awarded $14 million in damages, with New Mexico ordered to meet its required delivery without any exceptions. In addition, New Mexico has twenty-two Native American Pueblos and tribes with senior water rights, and some settlement agreements have been reached to settle tribal water claims. Attempts at storing water in reservoirs have been unsuccessful during the decades-long drought. At Elephant Butte, the largest reservoir, water levels reached only 4 percent capacity in 2022, one of the lowest levels in fifty years. As negotiations over these agreements continue, New Mexico's water future looks especially precarious.

Putting the Blame on Agriculture

As in many other western states, agricultural water use is blamed for New Mexico's water woes, especially industrial-scale agriculture like dairies, the state's largest agricultural sector. The group Food and Water Watch notes that industrial agriculture uses more than 774 billion gallons of water each year, representing over 80 percent of the state's fresh water, compared to the 10 percent used by public water supplies and domestic wells. Farms producing alfalfa and pecans, the state's two most dominant crops, have historically relied on flood irrigation. As is the case in Arizona, alfalfa is exported to other countries like Saudi Arabia. New Mexico also produces one-third of the country's pecans, another water-intensive crop that is not only thirsty but also profitable. As consumer demand for pecans has grown, production of the crop has increased by about one-third to accommodate export of the nuts. Both of these components of agriculture rely heavily on groundwater, potentially threatening domestic water wells in counties where both crops are dominant.

Dealing with Drought and Climate Change

Although New Mexico has been affected by changing weather conditions like most of the Southwest, the state has not, until the early 1990s, had to face severe drought. Water abundance on the Rio Grande was sufficient for most years except in Texas, with little attention paid to changes in the river's hydrological cycles, climate impacts, and changes in water demand. In 2022, however, more than 90 percent of the state experienced severe drought conditions, coupled with the largest wildfire in the state's history.

There has been considerable criticism that the state has fallen short over the years in water-resource planning, failing to devote sufficient funding and expertise to problems as they arose. Beginning in 1987, the Interstate Stream Commission prepared a state water plan to determine the state's water resources, monitoring groundwater levels, and measuring stream flow. At that same time, the state legislature established sixteen water regions, with each region expected to complete its own water plan that could be merged into a statewide one. Because of the drought that began in the early 2000s, the State Engineer developed an Active Water Resource Management action plan to manage water resources during periods of drought. The State Engineer and the Interstate Stream Commission prepared two state water plans (one in 2003 and another in 2018), and various reports, followed by the governor's request that the Interstate Stream Commission prepare a scientific report, the *Leap Ahead Analysis Assessment*. The actual report was prepared by the New Mexico Bureau of Geology & Mineral Resources. The State Engineer's office was tasked with preparing a fifty-year water plan, but he noted that his office did not have sufficient capacity to do so.

The assignment he was given is a lofty one—prepare a state water plan (with only two staff) that will adapt to climate change, water bankruptcy that occurred because the state has been barred from storing water upstream since June 2020, changing snowpack levels, the limited capacity of other state agencies to assist in preparation of the plan, the Endangered Species Act's protection of the silvery minnow, the inclusion of traditional ecological knowledge and expertise, and a budget that was less than half what the State Engineer had requested. Those challenges, along with the perceived lack of inclusion of key stakeholders, led one observer to comment that "really all we have will be a plan to plan." Critics also complain that New Mexico lacks adequate data to help leaders make informed decisions. As Food and Water Watch reported in July 2023, "It is extremely difficult to prepare for a disaster if you have no idea when it is coming or how much time you have to prepare." Because of a lack of centralized tracking, many key variables, such as the amount of water left in the state's aquifers or how many wells have gone dry, may not be available. New Mexico's 2019 Water Data Act was expected to help planners work together to close gaps in information, but insufficient legislative appropriations have hindered implementation.

Compounding the problems, the state faces its reliance on so few sources of water, and the expectation that in the future New Mexico's weather will be hotter and drier. Scientists believe that snow will turn into rain causing spring runoff to start earlier, affecting fish spawning and other environmental processes. That pattern was observed in July 2022 when the Rio Grande dried up in the Albuquerque area for the first time in forty years. Calls to prioritize residential users over industrial agriculture are unlikely to be heard in a state that is the third-poorest in the country, losing rural population to urban centers like Albuquerque, and where there is a history of inaction on environmental issues like water scarcity.

Some state leaders believe that this is the time to move forward in water planning because of a single change in the political environment—the availability of federal funds. Under the Bipartisan Infrastructure Law, New Mexico is poised to receive about $3.8 billion for projects ranging from roads to dams to bridges and rural water systems. Two of the projects for which funding is designated from the Infrastructure Investment and Jobs Act will benefit the state's rural communities. The Eastern New Mexico Rural Water System will receive $7 million for a 39-inch pipeline that will transport water from the Ute Reservoir to about 75,000 people who face water uncertainty due to a rapidly declining aquifer. The Bureau of Reclamation will provide 75 percent of the project's funding, with 15 percent provided by the state and the remaining 10 percent contributed by the four small communities that will be served by the project. Another $10 million will go to the Jicarilla Apache Rural Water System to pay for the completion of various components of an existing project. Those numbers pale in comparison to the $235 million that comes from the Infrastructure Law and the Reclamation Water Settlements Fund. Those dollars go to the Navajo-Gallup Water Project and four Pueblos under the Aamodt Water Rights Settlement. Without the federal funding, there is doubt whether any of these projects would be moving forward. Although it might seem as if the infrastructure measures doled out something for every state and every interest, New Mexico, given its lack of political support for water programming in the past, will reap the benefits of the government's largesse more than other states.

The Pacific Northwest: Challenges to Managing Water in Oregon, Idaho, Montana, and Washington

The Pacific Northwest is not as monolithic a region as some might think when it comes to water. Oregon and Washington are considered "wet" states in most accounts, even though desert-like conditions might be present in some areas. Montana and Idaho, in comparison, are the "dry" states despite the fact that they both have wet parts as well. Political pundits and scholars may consider Oregon and Washington more progressive when it comes to protecting natural resources like water than their neighbors, whereas Idaho and Montana have a smaller economic base. All four have dealt with population growth; all four face challenges in dealing with tribal agreements.

Legal experts Caccese and Fowler have found four themes that are common to the region: (1) they are affected by claims to water that were established prior to the development of water codes; (2) they face tribal claims to water;

(3) they must deal with the Columbia River Treaty with Canada; and (4) they are affected by the federal Endangered Species Act. In 2016 the National Ocean and Atmospheric Administration (NOAA) launched a Drought Early Warning System for the Pacific Northwest (including Washington, Oregon, Idaho, and western Montana) to help its partners share information and coordinate responses as widespread climate change affected the region more severely, something the state shared.

Oregon

It is easy to associate Oregon with water. It is, after all, nicknamed the Webfoot State, with a college football team called the Ducks. But the water references challenge the facts; parts of Oregon are frequently listed in extreme drought conditions. "We need a damn water plan," Oregon's Secretary of State said in early 2023 after an audit of the state's handling of water issues. The audit found an uncoordinated regulatory environment, lack of a water conservation plan, competition among state agencies for limited state funding, and a lack of collaboration with each other and with the state's tribes. The audit determined that the state lacks a central natural resources department, or a formal interagency system that can identify problems or guide the state's water policy.

Like most other western states, Oregon's water policies evolved from a frontier character and culture that revealed a preference for limited government involvement. Originally part of the Office of the State Engineer, the day-to-day management of surface water in Oregon is conducted under the 1909 Water Code, which like that of other western states says that all water in the state belongs to the public, and that the waters of the state may be appropriated for beneficial use.

Prior to the development of the code, water claims were like mining claims—staked out and recorded at the county courthouse. Later, claims were formalized, requiring the issuance of a permit from the state. That process is now managed by the Oregon Water Resources Department (OWRD), which began issuing permits for groundwater in 1927 for the eastern part of the state, and for western Oregon in 1955. In 1975, the legislature created the Water Policy Review Board, and then merged the State Engineer's Office and the State Water Resources Board to create the present OWRD. A different organization, the Oregon Water Resources Commission, is a state policymaking body, with oversight of the OWRD. Its members are appointed by the governor.

The problems cited in the audit are not new. The state developed its first water plan in 1955 when the State Water Resources Board was created. In 2003, the legislature recommended the creation of a long-term water supply plan, noting the lack of one that considered Oregon's reliance on its surface water for almost 70 percent of its fresh water, a growing population, and a growing economy. Similar plans were issued in 2012 and updated in 2017, but without funding, noting the agency lacked the authority or staff to implement ways the state could use to improve the water situation. Still another plan, the 100-Year Water Vision, was initiated by state agencies in 2018, and three years later, the state legislature enacted a $538 million package to carry out the initial steps for water infrastructure and planning. But the 2023 audit criticized the Vision document, noting that it repeated the work of the 2012 and 2017 plans with the same suggestions but insufficient funding or staff to implement the plans' recommendations.

Ascertaining potential solutions and then finding the money to fund them took on special meaning during the recent drought. In its 2023 session, two state legislators attempted to put pressure on the OWRD by introducing a measure that would order the department to stop approving new applications for water rights permits until it completed an inventory of existing water resources. The most recent water supply analysis was done in the 1980s; the 2023 proposal would require the agency to report on how much groundwater exists in the state's twenty basins, and how much was being used by the estimated 90,000 water rights holders. The OWRD would then need to update its rules so that water supplies were not overdrawn. Recently, 80 percent of water rights that were approved were in areas where groundwater levels are declining. Oregon is also actively courting more semiconductor companies and expansion plans by data centers, sectors that are heavy water users which consume millions of gallons a day. Despite being called one of the best bills of the session, the proposal died.

There are nine federally recognized tribes within Oregon, all of whom have reserved water rights, with adjudication of those rights granted to the director of the OWRD who has responsibility for negotiating settlement agreements. The process of getting OWRD approval is not an easy one. For instance, it has already taken more than thirty-five years for an agreement over the quantification of those rights to be hammered out between the Klamath Tribes and the OWRD. One agreement was reached in June 2023 when the county circuit court ruled that the water claimed by the Klamath Tribes was the amount necessary to establish and maintain a productive habitat for treaty species that would enable them to exercise their protected hunting, fishing, trapping, and gathering rights. Those rights may include, the court ruled, off-reservation water sources to support the tribes' on-reservation treaty harvest rights.

Although the OWRD is specifically tasked with dealing with water quantity, rather than quality, the state's approach to drought has been more near-term than long-term. Half the state has recently been classified as being in severe to exceptional drought, affecting levels in the state's reservoirs and subsequent effects on local water supplies. In 2023, the state legislature passed the $143 million Drought Resilience and Water Security package that focuses on seven areas ranging from water for fish, farms, and families, to data and analysis.

Washington

Washington state has actually codified its definition of what constitutes a drought in its state law. Conditions are analyzed by geographic area, with a drought projected to be below 75 percent of normal, and likely to create undue hardships for water users or the environment. The term normal applies to the median amount of water available for the most recent climate period. There is usually more precipitation on the western side of the state, home to Seattle and Olympia and urban users, compared to water for agricultural use and the need for irrigation on the eastern side. The state is dependent on hydroelectric power (Washington is the leading hydroelectric power producer in the country) from the Grand Coulee Dam and other smaller facilities. Surface water is also the source of drinking water on the western side, dependent on melting snowpack, whereas on the eastern side, users are dependent on aquifers.

By 2050, Washington is expected to experience a quadrupling of the severity of widespread summer drought—the single greatest increase among all US states—with conditions varying considerably from one county to another. That pattern is already being investigated. Washington is heavily reliant upon snowpack from the Cascade Range, but there are differences between coastal areas that might get 80 inches of precipitation a year and areas east of the Cascade that get less than 10 inches. Since detailed record keeping began in 2000, the Evergreen State had never seen an exceptional drought; in 2015, when the governor declared a statewide drought emergency, the conditions in 85 percent of the state were declared as extreme but not exceptional. That emergency affected 6.6 million people in forty-eight of the state's sixty-two river basins. In 2021, fewer areas were designated in drought conditions, but in those that were, the drought reached more severe levels.

Surface water is especially important to the state. Under a landmark 1971 law, the Washington Department of Ecology measures the water supply and levels of the state's rivers, establishing minimum flows to balance the needs of people and environmental concerns like wildlife. Consumer practices have been changing since 2003 when the state's legislature enacted water efficiency requirements. There has been some support for the use of reclaimed water, along with the more traditional efforts to provide rebates for the use of water-efficient products. In 2000, Seattle Public Utilities joined with eighteen other water providers in the Saving Water Partnership, with promotions like The Great Flush-Off to show the capacity of water-efficient toilets. In addition, the state has undertaken efforts to compensate farmers for leased water rights, promoting a pause in irrigation during the dry summer months.

The Pacific Northwest Salmon Controversy

Washington faces similar problems as other western states when dealing with groundwater and overpumping, but in the Pacific Northwest, there is a different issue that distinguishes their water policy. The states are home to numerous dams that interfere, some believe, with the commercial fishing industry that is the livelihood of generations of fishers and at the cultural heart of numerous tribes. The species that is at the center of the controversy is the salmon—all of whom belong to the Salmonidae family, although not all Salmonidae family are salmon. The fish's complicated life cycle is because it is anadromous, spending part of its life at sea and another part in rivers, streams, and lakes. That life cycle calls for complex management of both marine and terrestrial waters, and includes corollary issues related to the protection of endangered and threatened species, the logging industry, recreational use of waters, energy production, tribal customs, food production, pollution, and climate change.

Oregon's primary policy for protecting its fish and wildlife is the Oregon Conservation Strategy, which serves as the federally required State Wildlife Action Plan. State law includes a unique Sensitive Species Rule classification, defined as species that need conservation attention because they have small or declining populations or are at risk. Within the list are two additional categories: Sensitive and Sensitive-Critical. Basically, these policies go a step further than federally-defined threatened or endangered species under the Endangered Species Act (ESA). The federal and state lists are separate; the Sensitive Species List is also updated every five years. Under the 2021 state list for Oregon—the most recent one—152 species (or taxa) of wildlife are listed and 58 fish. It is the latter category which has led to most of the controversies and legal proceedings.

Both states have faced decades of disputes and litigation over multiple species of salmon, many of which are on the Oregon Sensitive Species List or the ESA. Complicating the issue even more is the fact that several rivers and basins are involved, with differing circumstances and stakeholders. In the Columbia River Basin, for instance, salmon protection has affected surface water policy for more than forty-five years. ESA consideration began in 1978 but was suspended just a few years later, when Congress authorized the Northwest Power Act and mitigation strategies related to hydropower development within the basin. Petitions for salmon protection were made to the National Marine Fisheries Service by various groups beginning in 1990, followed by petitions for additional species and runs through the 1990s until twelve were eventually listed. According to the Northwest Power and Conservation Council, the ESA has become full-employment legislation for many lawyers.

On the Snake River, salmon protection has affected the full spectrum of economic activities, from resource extraction and agriculture to recreation and the fisheries industry. There is considerable evidence that human activities have affected the salmon population, which in the 1800s meant an estimated 1.5 million salmon and steelhead came back to the Snake River annually to spawn. The numbers declined sharply after the 1960s; the number of Chinook was just seventy-eight in 1990. At Redfish Lake at the headwaters of the Salmon River, which is a tributary of the Snake, there were an estimated several thousand fish in the 1950s, eight fish in 1993 and only one for several succeeding years. Recovery plans to increase salmon populations have included dozens of recommendations, ranging from better fish hatchery practices to managing and, if necessary, increasing river flows to benefit the salmon. Reducing reservoir levels (called drawdowns) and even removing the dams on the Snake (called breaching) were mentioned, but had less support than transporting fish on barges. Biological opinions (directing agencies to take specific actions, sometimes called BiOp) were issued numerous times, and then challenged in court by almost every conceivable interest group with opinions that were in total opposition to one another. The judicial decisions were then appealed by various defendants. Further south, in the Willamette River Basin, three fish listed under the ESA have held up the continued operation of the Willamette Valley Flood Control Project because its thirteen dams would jeopardize the species. Nine of the dams, eight of which are operated by the Army Corps of Engineers, generate hydroelectricity, and as a whole, the project protects against massive flooding throughout the basin and its tributaries.

In the Columbia Basin, which spans Washington, Oregon, and Idaho, agricultural practices in both the ranching and farming industries have damaged salmon habitat. The development of the hydroelectric industry, and the jobs that were created as dams and reservoirs were built during the Depression years, was considered vitally important to the economy of the Northwest. The destruction of salmon runs began with the building of the Grand Coulee Dam and Bonneville Dam; the Columbia Basin is now blocked by 211 dams, with 905 smaller dams built in Oregon, and 842 in Washington, according to Mark Kurlansky, who has written extensively about the salmon's plight.

Montana

Although one might not think of Montana as a dry state, drought is actually a significant element in its water sources and management planning. As is the case throughout much of the Missouri River Basin, droughts are common. Although locals might refer to wet or dry years, the state consistently gets only about 18.65 inches of rain each year. Most of the precipitation comes in the form of rain or snow in the mountainous parts of the state at higher elevations, with about 80 percent of the water derived within Montana's own boundaries, making it a "headwaters state." The snowpack itself has steadily declined since the 1930s. Temperatures have been rising since the 1970s, accompanied by a dramatic increase in wildfire activity. In 2021, Montana had its worst drought since the US Drought Monitor's period of record in 2000. In late October 2021, 100 percent of the state was classified as in severe drought, with 70 percent in the category of extreme drought.

When Montana's Constitution was ratified in 1889, like other western states, the law stated that all water within state boundaries belonged to the state as its property for the use of its people. No individual can own water, but Montana's citizens have a right to use it. That means two things: using the water beneficially, and since 1900, filing a water-use claim with the court. Of equal importance is historic consumption. When a water right changes owners, for instance, the change cannot increase the amount of water that has historically been put to beneficial use.

The state compiled a Drought Management Plan in 1995, developed a state water plan in 2015, experienced a severe drought in 2017, and began a three-year-long period of updating the Drought Management Plan in 2020. NOAA established a second Drought Early Warning System (DEWS) for the Missouri Basin in 2014.

Idaho

Of the Pacific Northwest states, Idaho has perhaps been least affected by the water wars and drought. A quick look at the organizational management of its water policy might make it look as if the state has mostly been active in changing agency names and logos. Water resources were first managed in 1895 by the Office of the State Engineer, which became the Department of Reclamation in 1919. Voters approved a state constitutional amendment in 1964 that created the Idaho Water Resource Board, whose eight members were tasked with state water planning. In 1970, the agency underwent another name change, becoming the Department of Water Administration, and four years later, the two groups were combined, becoming the currently named Idaho Department of Water Resources (IDWR). The eight members of the board, appointed by the governor, are responsible for the development of the state water plan and for financing water projects. Under state law, the IDWR can declare drought emergencies for designated counties with the governor's approval. This designation allows temporary changes in water rights to lessen the impacts of drought.

Most of the time, the state is in moderate drought conditions, although in 2021 the drought was compared to that of 1924. In Idaho, droughts are almost predictable, based on data from the NOAA Regional Climate Center. They indicate that exceptional droughts occur about once every fifty to one hundred years, causing extreme and widespread crop and pasture losses. Severe droughts, in contrast, happen more frequently, about every ten to twenty-five years, with minor crop and pasture losses and water shortages. In some cases, water use fees have been imposed. Precipitation falls during a short period (November to May), leading Idaho's agriculture department to propose a cover crop grazing program. Farmers impacted by drought would plant forage cover crops that would then be made available to ranchers for grazing livestock when forage was in short supply, especially in years when the state has suffered through damaging range fires.

The IDWR is also responsible for monitoring over 1,100 wells in the state in conjunction with the Bureau of Reclamation, which monitors levels in an additional 1,200 wells. That information goes into a database used for groundwater planning, including recharge efforts within the Eastern Snake Plan Aquifer and the designation of groundwater management areas. Agricultural users and dairies are the prime consumers of the state's water. In 2021, the Idaho Farm Bureau estimated that 97 percent of the water withdrawn from surface waterways went toward irrigation—a staggering 17 maf.

There are four major projects that are being implemented by the IDWR: the state Water Plan, Comprehensive Basin Plans, Comprehensive Aquifer Plans, and State Protected River Plans. The Idaho Water Plan has been revised numerous times since 1974, when the document's objectives were outlined, with the initial policy itself set forth in 1976. The plan was revised and readopted in 1982, and then updated periodically from then on, followed by sections related to sustainability that were included in 2016. The state also prepares strategic planning documents, the most recent of which focuses on water rights, adjudication, managed recharge, and agency operations.

Adjudication

All four states in this region have dealt with the consequences of their frontier history. Because mining claims and water claims were dealt with in a somewhat informal fashion during prior to statehood, with no one's approval needed to use resources (legal or otherwise), it took decades before permit systems were codified. Oregon was the first to do so in 1909, followed by Washington in 1917, Idaho in 1971, and Montana in 1973. From a practical standpoint, this has meant decades of dispute settlements as claimants and the states try to determine which claims have priority over others, and how much water is being claimed. Three of the states have faced lengthy adjudication accompanied by litigation. In Idaho, the Snake River Adjudication took place from 1987 to 2014; in Washington, the Yakima Basin case started in the 1970s but was not finalized until 2019; and Oregon's Klamath Basin adjudication started in 1975 with an initial decree in 2013. But as Caccese and Fowler note, many cases involving significant watersheds in the Pacific Northwest are not yet completed.

An administrative process that sets Montana apart from all the others is its unique way of dealing with conflicts related to tribal water rights. The *World Population Review* ranked Montana fifth in the United States in the percent of its population that is Native American (7.68 percent) in 2023, living on seven tribal reservations. Most western states have dealt with tribal water rights incrementally under the concept of federal reserved rights, a topic explained in Chapter 1. In many other conflicts, the tribes and government have gone through protracted litigation for years, a process that is both expensive and which often fails to give either party what they are seeking. Montana, however, has a mechanism for dealing with tribal water rights agreements that is unlike any other in the country. The concept evolved in 1979 from a measure that would create a system of state water courts that would adjudicate all water rights claims, but tribes opposed the bill because they felt the state did not have jurisdiction over tribal water rights. Instead, the state legislature created the Reserved Rights Water Compact Commission, a nine-member body specifically tasked to deal with the negotiation of reserved rights. During the negotiation process, the parties cannot seek adjudication.

One of the most difficult aspects of the process is the quantification of water rights, as water may have symbolic or cultural value that cannot be measured. Negotiation, however, is seen as a more flexible option, taking into account the nuances of individual situations, including multijurisdiction and public participation in the process. Between 1979 and 2015, when the Commission became inactive, the body negotiated eighteen water rights compacts involving the tribes, the federal government, and the state that were then approved by the state legislature, by Congress with the president's signature, by the tribal council or other body, and finally by the Secretary of the Interior or Agriculture, depending on the kind of agreement.

One of the most recent actions of the Commission dealt with the CSKT-MT Compact, an important water rights agreement that began with negotiations in the 1980s, and enacted by the Department of the Interior in September 2021. The Compact was the outgrowth of a lack of administrative authority and several Montana Supreme Court cases over the Montana Department of Natural Resources and Conservation's (DNRC) handling of water rights on tribal reservations. In 1996, the court ruled in favor of the Confederated Salish & Kootenai Tribes (CSKT) that the DNRC could not issue water-use permits on the Flathead Indian Reservation, established in 1855 and home to the CSKT, until the Tribe's reserved and aboriginal rights were quantified. The tribe sought to do its own inventory, and the state of Montana sought a joint inventory process. The enactment of the compact and its accompanying administration and management ordinance codified the process, giving the Flathead Reservation Water Management Board exclusive regulatory authority for issuing new water rights and changes in existing and new uses of water. The board is assisted by a water engineer and a technical staff—the operating arm of the board—to oversee the distribution of water with the tribe's irrigation project.

All four states, however, regardless of their administrative approaches to managing water or their historical attitudes about natural resources, or even demographic and political differences, are more alike the other states in the West than they are different. They face the same challenges of population growth as big cities like Los Angeles. They have strong ties to agriculture like Arizona. They face the unknown impacts of climate change, of whiplash weather, and drought, over which none of them have much control.

The Rocky Mountain West: How Colorado, Utah, and Wyoming Manage Water

The three states known collectively as the Rocky Mountain West face somewhat different water resource issues than neighboring states and regions. They do not have the precipitation that characterizes the Pacific Northwest, nor the scale of water scarcity that typifies the Southwest. Some of the states have issues related to the Colorado River because they are part of the Upper Basin as defined in the Colorado River Compact. At least two states in this region have been crucial in the development of water policy because of the role they played historically in western expansion. And yet they have unique challenges and histories that make their state distinct from the others.

One factor that sets these three states apart from others profiled in this chapter is that only the Lower Basin states—Arizona, California, and Nevada—have been directly affected by recent agreements requiring them to reduce the amount of water they use. This difference is due to the Law of the River and a series of legal agreements like the Colorado River Compact that require the Upper Basin states to deliver 7.5 million acre-feet of water to the Lower Basin states that have senior water rights *before* they can use the 7.5 million acre-feet they have been allotted. The Secretary of the Interior has the authority to require the Lower Basin states to make cuts but does not have a similar authority over the Upper Basin. Still, the Upper Basin states are affected because when there are shortages in the Lower Basin or in Lake Mead, the Upper Basin must release water out of Lake Powell to make sure the other three downstream states get what they are allotted as senior water rights holders.

Utah

Mormon pioneers who came from states with abundant water arrived in the Salt Lake Valley in 1847. They are credited with establishing the first agricultural water diversions when they built a dam and diverted water from City Creek to irrigate their fields to plant potatoes. One early pioneer cited by Hooton noted

"Streams from the mountains and streams were abundant, the water excellent and generally with gravel bottoms," whereas another referred to "a seemingly interminable waste of sagebrush bespangled with sunflowers." As the Mormons began to settle in the new territory, they chose sites near or on waterways such as the Provo, Weber, and Logan rivers. Perhaps even more importantly, Brigham Young, the leader of the Latter-Day Saints, established the doctrine of prior appropriation that was applied at over 365 communities throughout the Great Basin, directing the West away from common-law riparian rights that were used in the East.

Artificial irrigation had been practiced for centuries by indigenous people before Utahans claimed to have been the first irrigation-based economy in the Western Hemisphere in modern times. But as Marc Reisner noted, the Mormons were unique because they were a close-knit society that was linked by a common faith and a history of persecution that made their irrigation efforts successful. The fact that the Mormon pioneers were attempting to develop permanent community settlements distinguishes their efforts from those of the Spanish at Santa Cruz, California or the more primitive irrigation practices of the native inhabitants. The twelve ecclesiastical wards established in Salt Lake City became the basis for the city's decision to make the supervision and management of the irrigation facilities the responsibility of the bishops in those wards.

Other Mormon leaders would direct the construction of major hand-hewn canals, and during the first fifty years of Mormon settlement, the pioneers dug an estimated 1,000 miles of ditches, irrigating 500,000 acres or 1 percent of the state's land. Although still a territory, settlers acquired water rights by physically diverting water from streams, and putting them to beneficial use, or by a grant from the legislature. A county courts water allocation system was enacted in 1852 and was in effect until 1880, when it was replaced by a statute providing for county water commissioners.

In 1897, a year after statehood, a state engineer was appointed as the individual who served as Utah's primary water rights administrator. The state legislature then enacted a water code in 1903, which was revised and reenacted in 1919. In keeping with many of the movements toward professionalizing civil service positions, the position of Chief Engineer remained but the administrative agency became the Division of Water Rights. In 1902, after several years of drought, Utah State Engineer Abraham Fairbanks Doremus proposed bringing water from the Uintah Mountains to the rapidly growing Wasatch Front. But unlike a similar scenario in California, Utah did not have the capacity and resources to undertake such a massive project, or the political will to do so; in 1902, when the concept was suggested, the entire population was less than 300,000.

Utah is different from other Rocky Mountain region states from one unique perspective: the Great Salt Lake, the largest saline lake in the Western Hemisphere. It is a terminal lake, which means it has no outlet to the sea, but its salt level is about eight times higher than ocean water. The lake's size averages about 1,700 square miles, but it is extremely shallow, averaging a depth of 14 feet and at its deepest point, just 35 feet. In addition to being an important water resource, this body of water is a keystone ecosystem that supports biodiversity, and a link in the Pacific Flyway, providing food and habitat for more than 10 million migratory birds and wildlife along the Wasatch Front. It also provides about $2.5 billion in economic productivity each year and supports about 9,000 local jobs, along with serving as part of Salt Lake City's cultural identity.

The water level of the lake is always changing, primarily due to climate and factors such as evaporation. The US Geological Survey has been collecting data since 1875, although there is some information that has been gathered since the Mormons arrived in 1847. There were changes in the lake's levels from 1847 to 1982, but there was no net change overall until the lake rose about 5 feet in 1982–83 due to greater than average precipitation. It reached a record high level in 1987, then a record historic low in July 2021 when the lake continued to recede until its lowest point was reached in November 2022. That drop between 1987 and 2022 is more than 20 feet.

The snowpack from the storms of the 2022–23 winter was 270 percent above average, a good thing for states suffering from drought but a not-so-good thing for states like Colorado and Utah that experienced flooding as the snow melted. But that same snowmelt that flooded the western side of the Wasatch Range gradually made its way to the Great Salt Lake, which has risen more than 4 feet since it was at its lowest point. Some Utah reservoirs and the Central Utah Water Conservancy District that would normally divert water to Utah Lake began diverting excess water to the Great Salt Lake in late April 2023. Just a few weeks later, the water level was still 6 feet below what is required to support a healthy ecosystem. At that point, the lake was at the verge of ecological collapse, one Utah State University researcher noted. Researchers at Brigham Young University (BYU), however, were even more pessimistic, reporting in January 2023 that "Great Salt Lake is facing unprecedented danger." Although the BYU report was written prior to the winter 2023 storms, the authors of the study warned that "excessive water use is destroying the Great Salt Lake, desiccating habitat, exposing toxic dust, and driving salinity to levels incompatible with the lake's food webs." The warning included the prediction that if the lake's drop in elevation continues as it has since 2020, "the lake as we know it is on track to disappear in five years."

Utah has become the country's fastest-growing state, projected to grow by 2.2 million people by 2060, all of whom are thirsty, and one-third of whom rely on the Colorado River as the source of their drinking water. Utah also has one of the nation's highest per-capita rates of water use, and some of the country's lowest water rates. The Greater Salt Lake Collaborative's Great Salt Lake Strike Team released a report in February 2023 with six specific recommendations that focus on human water use, including agriculture, municipal and industrial consumption, and extractive industries adjacent to the lake. Conservation, the group said, would increase the lake's level by only three feet in five years, whereas changes to mineral extraction industries would jeopardize a $1.1 billion industry.

As a whole, however, Utah's stance on water is perhaps as conservative as the state itself. The state legislature approved a seven-member Colorado River Authority of Utah in 2021, years after most other western states had developed a mechanism or individual to negotiate on their behalf. Given the state's population growth and dependence on the Colorado River, it may be more surprising that it took Utah so long to create such an official body. There was general agreement that the initial administrative focus on water rights and irrigation in the existing Division of Water Rights was insufficient to deal with issues related specifically to the river. The new Authority's mission is to protect, conserve, use, and develop the state's interests in the Colorado River. Currently, that includes the negotiations over the post-2026 operations guidelines, and the addition of a board seat for a tribal member. However, Utah is also one of the states that has taken the step of enacting legislation in 2020 that promotes voluntary, temporary, hyper-local water transfers. Its water banking program allows a user with "extra" water to lease it to another user in the same area without triggering the "use it or lose it" aspect of their water allocation. Four pilot programs are underway, including one in the Price River region that allows an agricultural user to rest their fields, for instance, and lease that water to an environmental organization. From there, a group like The Nature Conservancy or even the state of Utah can use the water to benefit an ecosystem.

One of Utah's most controversial undertakings is the Lake Powell Pipeline Development Act, enacted by the state legislature in 2006. It authorized the state's Board of Water Resources to plan and construct a 143-mile-long buried pipeline that would divert 86,000 acre-feet of water per year, using the state's existing water rights to the Green River, a Colorado River tributary. Water would be transported to southwestern Utah and growth areas like Washington County and St. George which are single-source, dependent on the Virgin River. Cost estimates ranged from $1.3 billion to $2.2 billion, depending on how the pipeline was routed and its final design, to be paid for by the state and participating water districts. Initially, the plan was to generate electricity from four hydroelectric generating stations, but questions arose over the role of the Federal Energy Regulatory Commission (FERC) because the project involved both water delivery and licensed hydro facilities. In 2018, FERC determined it had jurisdiction over only the hydro station part, which would require Utah to go through the permitting process with three other agencies: the Bureau of Land Management, the Bureau of Reclamation, and the National Park Service. A year later, Utah decided to scrub the hydroelectric power portion (eliminating FERC) to focus on water delivery with the Bureau of Reclamation taking the lead on preparing an environmental impact statement (EIS) in 2019. Over the next year, one county pulled out of the project, and the six other Colorado River Basin states asked the Department of the Interior not to move forward until all seven states reached a consensus on the project. Utah asked for more time to review the EIS, but by the end of 2023, no analysis had been completed and no design or construction had begun. Several non-profit groups, including the organization No Lake Powell Pipeline, argued that the project was unnecessary, expensive, and destructive. Other groups asked that the project be tabled from the permitting process, citing the lack of available water resources in the Colorado River, a lack of demonstrated need from Washington County, and unresolved tribal water rights. By 2024, it looked as though the pipeline project might be on permanent hold, especially considering the negotiations in place over the post-2026 operating guidelines for the river.

Colorado

Like the other western states, Colorado's water heritage can be traced back to the early native people who built earthen reservoirs to store storm runoff, and to the early Spanish settlers from northern New Mexico who built acequias in the San Luis Valley. In 1861, when Colorado became a territory, its leaders took a similar view of water and land rights, adopting prior appropriation as its legal doctrine. When Colorado became a state in 1876, the Constitution provided that all state waters belonged to the public, and in times of water shortages, domestic use took priority over any other use, followed by agriculture and then manufacturing. The Constitution also provided that water rights are a usufructuary, a special kind of property right that allows someone to use a resource without actually owning it.

Colorado has a self-described complex water system, partly due to the fact that 80 percent of the state's water falls west of the Continental Divide, whereas 90 percent of its people live on the Front Range on the east side. More than half of Colorado's water flows downstream to other states in the Southwest. The water that remains from rainfall and snowmelt requires an infrastructure of twenty-seven tunnels and ditches that move 500,000 acre-feet of water from the west side to the Front Range each year. By sector, 90 percent of its water is used for agriculture and 7 percent goes to municipal water uses (83 percent of which is supplied by surface water), and just 3 percent to large industry. Surface water sources include 90,000 miles of rivers and streams flowing through eight major river basins with smaller watersheds and tributary streams, 480 lakes, and wetlands. Unlike some of the conflicts in Arizona and California that involve tribal access to water, Colorado has only two federally recognized tribes despite a history of having forty-three tribes call the state their home.

From a day-to-day operations perspective, the Division of Water Resources (DWR) is responsible for dealing with water rights that are under the jurisdiction of the water courts, issuing permits for wells and licenses for well drillers, construction and repair of the state's dams, and compiling and maintaining water information. From an administrative perspective, water planning is under the jurisdiction of the Colorado Water Conservation Board (CWCB), created in 1937. The fifteen members of its board are responsible for protecting the state's surface water resources, planning for flood mitigation, and stream restoration. In 2004, the state legislature, through the Statewide Water Supply Initiative, or SWSI, began an intensive planning process to project Colorado's future water needs through the year 2030. The SWSI was updated in 2010 to project water needs to 2050, followed by an executive order from the governor in 2013 for the CWCB to create a state water plan by 2015. That version was replaced in 2023 by a new water plan that takes into account Colorado's responses to climate change, massive wildfires and post-fire flooding, and long-term drought, while including input and more participation by a more diverse set of stakeholders.

One of the key elements of Colorado's plan is water conservation, implemented through a four-year multistate System Conservation Pilot Program (SCPP) launched in 2015. Between 2015 and 2018, Colorado paid farmers and ranchers $8.5 million to use less water to address declining water levels in Lake Mead and Lake Powell. The program was subsequently discontinued in 2018. In 2022, when water levels reached historic lows, the four Upper Basin states put together their own conservation plan, calling for the SCPP to be reauthorized. The federal government agreed, allocating expenditures of up to $125 million for the SCPP from 2023 to 2026. There are, however, no target levels of the amount of water to be conserved, and participation by users is considered both voluntary and temporary.

The state's largest public utility, Denver Water, supplies about 1.5 million people, with about half of the water sourced from the Colorado River. Recent wildfires have greatly impacted the utility, causing changes in both its operations and the quality of the water it provides its customers as ash and debris have clogged nearby reservoirs. Although there are divisions within the state over potential mitigation steps to combat climate change by reducing carbon emissions, not everyone is on board with proposed changes to fossil fuel use. Instead, Denver Water has taken more conservative approaches to water sustainability, such as raising the height of the dam at the Gross Reservoir west of Boulder by 130 feet to increase the storage capacity of the reservoir threefold; assisting in the development of a more sustainable university campus; and the reduction of non-functional turf grass by 30 percent. The state's political climate, however, is more of a policy driver than climate change.

In a somewhat surprising marriage of interests, Colorado voters approved a state proposition in 2019 that legalized sports betting, with much of the tax revenue directed toward implementation of the water plan. More funding comes from the Colorado Recovery Act and from the state general fund, and local ballot measures have been approved that benefit specific water districts. But even if all the money from sports betting materializes, additional revenues will be needed beyond legislative appropriations to fund the grant programs that have already been identified in the state.

Another strategy has been Colorado's efforts to purchase existing water rights from other sources. In 2023, the Colorado River District joined a coalition of nineteen environmental groups, utility providers, and local governments to purchase some of the state's oldest water rights directly on the Colorado River from the Shoshone Power Plant, owned by Xcel Energy. The facility, located in Glenwood Canyon, has senior water rights, and agreed to sell those rights to the district for $98.5 million. The agreement would be that the district would lease the water rights back to Xcel for continued power plant operations. If those operations cease, the water would revert to instream flows, benefitting both the environment and water users downstream. By late 2024, the river district had raised $55 million of the purchase; the group planned to request the remainder from the federal government. If fully funded, the purchase would provide more stability to the state's water supply, and would protect critical habitat for endangered species of fish. Supporters have also focused on how important the plan would be to supporting tourism, recreation, and the region's agricultural users once approved.

Wyoming

Wyoming's water management issues are closely tied to two key incidents, both of which relate to the state's territorial history. In 1887, pioneer William McCrea developed an irrigation project on the Little Powder River in northeast Wyoming; three years later, Charles Moyer developed a spring he used for irrigation that also supplied some of the water for McCrea's ditch. Moyer's use of the spring meant that McCrea's ditch was often short of water, and the battle between the two men found its way to the Wyoming State Supreme Court. The court ruled against Moyer, siding with McCrea and the adage "First in time is first in right." Somewhat coincidentally, the man who affirmed that doctrine was Wyoming's Territorial Engineer, and later, its first State Engineer, Elwood Mead (profiled in Chapter 4). Although he was new to the state, Mead understood that in a region where water was in short supply, the person who had been the first to put the water to beneficial use has the first use of that water. Mead also believed that the amount of water to which an individual had a right could not be infinite, but must be based on the amount that could be put to beneficial use. Unlike some other states, Wyoming considers water rights as property rights, attached to the land and subject to transfer or modification only after consideration by a Board of Control, rather than by water courts used elsewhere. Under the Wyoming Constitution, the Board of Control consists of the four water division superintendents within the state and the State Engineer, who serves as the chief administrator of the state's waters. The Board, which meets quarterly, primarily deals with amendments or corrections to water rights.

Wyoming was known at the turn of the twentieth century for its legendary promoter, William F. Cody, better known as Buffalo Bill. He and other investors formed the Shoshone Land and Irrigation Company, founded the town of Cody, and planned a 150,000-acre irrigation project that they believed would "make the desert bloom." Initially, Cody irrigated 60,000 acres of land by acquiring water rights to the Shoshone River, with canals built to divert water from the river. He and his associates could not afford to build a storage reservoir, however, so Cody transferred his water rights to the Secretary of the Interior in 1904. Drilling subsequently began on the Shoshone Dam in 1905, which was completed in 1910 and later renamed Buffalo Bill Dam.

Although not nearly as well known today as its namesake, the 325-foot concrete arch dam was the highest dam in the world, part of the Shoshone Project that included a reservoir, tunnels, and canals. In 1922, the Shoshone Powerplant was completed, and in 1993, the dam was raised to 350 feet, adding more than 260,000 acre-feet of storage capacity to the reservoir. Today, the project irrigates 93,000 acres of crops, supplies four irrigation districts with water, and hosts a state park, visitor center, and multiple recreation sites.

The management of the state's water is under the direction of the State Engineer, with the state divided into four water divisions, each with its own superintendent, and those four plus the engineer make up the State Board of Control. The board is responsible for adjudicating water rights. Receiving less than 16 inches of precipitation per year, Wyoming is the fifth-driest state in the country, although it is not usually thought of in the same way as the more desert-like states. The lack of rainfall was one reason why Wyoming was one of the last parts of the United States to be settled by non-native people. Unlike some of the western states, Wyoming has the second highest mean elevation in the country, meaning that melting snowpack levels are essential to the runoff into the three major river systems (the Missouri, the Colorado, and the California), along with the Bighorn, Green, North Platte, Snake, and Yellowstone. Snowmelt also helps recharge aquifer systems, although less effectively than in some other states.

After a major drought in 2000, the state developed the Wyoming Drought Plan, which borrowed heavily from one drawn up by the state of New Mexico. The 2003 plan noted that because drought is a natural climatic condition, the government can do very little to alleviate the effects of drought. Instead, the government can be prepared and have mitigation plans already in place to lessen drought's consequences. The Wyoming Drought

Task Force is tasked with plan implementation, with technical assistance from the Climatic Monitoring subgroup, along with five other subgroups focused on Agriculture and Natural Resources; Drinking Water, Health, and Energy Implementation; Wildfire; Tourism and Economic Implementation; and Communication.

Since 1979, state water planning has been the responsibility of the Wyoming Water Development Commission. The group completed river basin planning studies through 1995. In 1996, the state's legislature sought recommendations for updating the 1973 Framework Water Plan from the State Engineer's Office and the Wyoming Water Development Office, which were presented in October 1996. The governor asked a new group to revisit the 1996 recommendations to include grassroots efforts, and a consulting firm was asked to assist in that project.

Several state water plans have been developed, including the 2007 Wyoming State Water Plan; the 2012 Wyoming State Water Plan—Statewide Products; and the 2015 Wyoming Water Strategy—Leading the Charge. Generally, the plans deal with themes including water management; water development; water conservation and protection; and water and watershed restoration. The 2015 plan included ten initiatives, ranging from the development of credible climate, weather, and stream flow data; to development of a uniform hydrographers operations manual; to completion of several water development projects.

In 2023, Wyoming's population was 584,000, compared to Utah's 3,456,000, and Colorado, with a population of 5,878,000. Those numbers are important in understanding why two of the Rocky Mountain states have developed an extensive administrative and planning history, while another has not done so. Although it might be possible to put water resource management in some political context, the more likely explanation would be each of the states' capacity, a term often used to describe how well the government is able to accomplish a specific policy goal. Although the concept is often applied on an international or global level, on a micro level, it can be used to explain why some states seem to accomplish a great deal while others do not. Certainly, there is an element of perception, such as how seriously the state's leaders consider drought, flooding, or climate change affects their constituents. Even the most serious policy issues must scratch and claw their way on to the policy agenda, skipping ahead of other problems at that moment in time. And as always, there is the financial ability of the government to pay for a desired solution among the crowded field of problems. In this region of the West, where does water scarcity fit in?

Traditional vs. Alternative Water Management Strategies

It seems simple enough. If there isn't enough water available in our present sources, then we need to find some other ones, right? But what might at first glance look easy is much more complicated, and in some cases, scientifically impossible to pull off. Developing water resilience is essential—no one disagrees with that. But the discussion on potential solutions must begin with knowing what sources are available, currently or even hypothetically, and how those sources might be harvested and used.

Around 1960 or so, the Ralph M. Parsons Company, which had been actively involved in water projects in several other countries, began development of the North American Water and Power Alliance (NAWAPA). After engineering studies and field investigation, the company released its plans for public comment in 1963. The concept behind the NAWAPA consisted of 369 projects, costing an estimated \$80–\$100 billion, that would provide more than 78 maf of water to the United States, 40 maf to Mexico, and 58 maf to Canada. In addition, NAWAPA would increase irrigable land by 20 million acres, provide 38 million kilowatts of power to the United States, and would potentially create a navigable waterway in Canada—the Transcontinental Canal. Water would be diverted and redistributed from undeveloped wilderness areas in Alaska and the Canadian Yukon, channeled into a modified reservoir in British Columbia's Rocky Mountain Trench, then lifted into the Sawtooth Reservoir in southwestern Montana. Using gravity, the water would then flow to various western states, the Rio Grande River Basin, and three states in Mexico. Leaders claimed it would reverse the depletion of the Ogallala Aquifer, provide a mechanism for reversing the salinity of irrigated land, create substantial numbers of productive jobs, provide new markets for American agriculture and industry, and increase the national income by about \$30 billion. The Parsons Company estimated that the project would take twenty years to complete, and could assure water supplies for the next 100 years.

Parsons Company officials actively lobbied Congress, the Western Governors' Association, the National Water Alliance, and other potential stakeholders for support. Senator Frank Moss of Utah, Texas Representative Jim Wright, and other officials actively backed the plan, with Senator Moss calling upon President Lyndon Johnson to invite Canada to develop an economic and engineering feasibility study. Although the US Army Corps of Engineers had studied the project previously, no official proposal was ever developed. Still, there was, at least initially, a diverse group of backers for the NAWAPA project. Opposition from environmental leaders just as the movement was gaining momentum was credited with convincing mainstream political officials that the plan was worthless. The NAWAPA Foundation, a subsidiary of the Parsons Company, was dissolved in 1990.

Today, a proposal of this magnitude would be a non-starter among policymakers. The complexity of the engineering involved, the myriad agencies with cross-cutting missions and jurisdictions, the transnational agreements and compacts, the enormous cost in today's dollars, and the political risk—any one of these factors, among others, would have killed NAWAPA on arrival. But the fact remains that there is also an urgent need for policymakers to continue to build a toolbox of options for meeting the needs of a thirsty people that demands a sustainable water supply and resilience in times of drought.

The emphasis among policymakers appears to be focusing on freshwater sources that can be used for drinking and other household uses where the quality of the water is vitally important. This is where the debate over water security has been heading for decades. In cases where there is a disruption, such as a breakdown at a water treatment plant or a broken water main, or when usage becomes exceptionally high, a redundant water source reduces the risk to our daily life.

Phrases like "drought-proof" have been applied to some alternatives, even though it is unlikely such a resource or technique actually exists. Water that is clean enough for humans to drink is termed potable, and there just isn't enough of it to go around, no matter what we do to make it safe. As humans cannot get by without water, researchers keep attempting to find ways to make more of it.

Desalination

Throughout human history, and especially in arid places like deserts, the need for water has fostered a relentless quest for solutions to scarcity. The water in the world's oceans has long been viewed as one potentially accessible source. Legislatively recognizing the shortage of both groundwater and usable surface water, and the need to find more sources of supply, the federal Saline Water Act was enacted in 1952. Congress appropriated $2 million to establish the Saline Water Conversion Program to research and develop practical, low-cost methods of converting saline water, including seawater into useful water, over a five-year period.

Although the cost of desalination was not competitive with natural freshwater, in 1964 the Office of Science and Technology pushed forward a plan to develop nuclear energy–saltwater conversion plants by 1975. President Lyndon Johnson called for an "aggressive and imaginative program" to develop desalination on a large scale, predicting that in ten years, desalted water would be the cheapest, and in some cases the only way to obtain new water supplies in some areas. Progress continued in 1965 when the world's first commercial reverse osmosis plant was built in Coalinga, California. From that point on, reverse osmosis has been one of the most promising methods of converting seawater, and the scale of water produced has increased dramatically. However, the process requires a great deal of energy to produce freshwater, making desalination more costly than other sources (sometimes as much as double the cost), and contributing to global warming due to the greenhouse gas emissions produced through power generation.

As was the case with many policies and programs, desalination fell victim to politics and events that researchers and politicians could never foresee. During the late 1950s, the drought that had plagued the Southwest when demonstration plants were being considered and built ended, and rain refilled reservoirs. The energy crisis of the 1970s also pushed some programs off the public and governmental radar. Simply put, water lost out to energy. About the same time, President Ronald Reagan's plans to eliminate non-defense government spending on science programs led to consolidation and elimination. The environmental movement, although still in its infancy at this time, still brought attention to issues like protecting marine life, coastline conservation, and residential water use—all hot button topics that made desalination a less than ideal option for many communities.

Santa Barbara, California is a good example of the fortunes of desalination projects in the United States. In the 1980s, when the state experienced historic drought conditions, the city made the decision to construct a seawater desalination plant. The $34 million facility, built in 1991 and 1992, was designed to produce 7,500-acre-feet of water per year, with the neighboring cities of Goleta and Montecito negotiating a five-year contract that would provide water for their residents as well. The plant operated successfully for four months in 1992. But the area's abundant winter rains and subsequent winters helped reduce drought conditions, so the facility was placed in long-term standby mode. This allowed the city flexibility for changing weather conditions, as the plant could be reactivated whenever its other water sources were insufficient. In 2015, when drought conditions became exceptional once again, the city council voted to reactivate the desalination plant, and after more than a year of testing, desalinated water became available again in 2017.

The capital costs for reactivation were $72 million, but the plant represented a more energy-efficient design that reduced its carbon footprint. Today, the facility produces 3 million gallons of drinking water per day, equal to about 30 percent of Santa Barbara's demand, or 3,125 acre-feet per year.

Another successful example of a city that uses desalination in its water-resource portfolio is the Carlsbad Desalination Plant in north San Diego County that went online in December 2015. This facility was built as a public–private partnership between the San Diego County Water Authority and Poseidon Water. The company constructed and presently operates the plant, whereas the county's water authority buys the water produced by the facility. Poseidon is required to comply with various state regulations designed to protect the adjacent marine environment, as well as other federal operating regulations. About 100 million gallons of seawater are used to produce 50 million gallons of water per day, about 10 percent of the region's water supply. The desalinated water is combined with water from other sources including conserved water, groundwater, and recycled water, and then piped to municipal users. There are, however, environmental consequences to the process, because in reverse osmosis, half the water taken in at a facility is still briny and it must go somewhere. In coastal plants like the one in Carlsbad, the water is returned to the ocean. Unless that water, called brine waste, is redistributed properly, there can be negative impacts on sea life.

Recycled Water

California's Water Code defines recycled water as "water which, as a result of treatment of waste, is suitable for a direct beneficial use or a controlled use that would not otherwise occur and is therefore considered a valuable resource." Another way of thinking about recycled water is that it is treated municipal sewage, although the use of this type of potable water varies considerably. Recycled wastewater has been used since the 1950s for crop irrigation, but droughts and water scarcity have led researchers to consider direct potable reuse, another phrase for adding wastewater that has been treated to levels meeting or exceeding drinking water standards. There are numerous ways the water can be cleaned to make it potable, from advanced water filtration systems, to disinfection that removes organic particles after water is filtered, to more exotic and experimental technologies. Once consumers trust the science of the process and get past the "ick" factor, this strategy is one way to generate a climate-resilient source of potable water and at the same time, reduce the amount of wastewater that is currently released into rivers, streams, and the ocean. In January 2023, Colorado became the first state (followed in December 2023 by California) to consider regulations for the use of treated recycled water as a source of potable water. California's State Water Resources Control Board voted to accept sixty-three pages of recycled water regulations that took more than a decade to produce. The complex "toilet-to-tap" process also requires extensive monitoring to ensure standards are met. Texas, Florida, and Arizona are also investigating how to regulate this type of potable water use.

The oldest (1962) potable reuse water groundwater project in California is located in southeastern Los Angeles County, designed to recharge the Central Basin underlying the metropolitan area. The project uses disinfected activated sludge effluent that is treated through filtration and nitrification and discharged into a local creek, along with stormwater runoff and some imported surface water for recharging the groundwater basin. Another pioneer in developing methods of turning sewage into drinking water is Orange County, California, which began research into various processes in the 1970s. The research was conducted out of necessity because the region's primary aquifer had become so overdrawn that saltwater was seeping into the basin. Because allocations from the Colorado River for drinking water were preset by the Colorado River Compact, local officials began scrambling for alternatives that the public would accept. A collaboration between the Orange County Water District and the Orange County Sanitation District built the world's largest wastewater-to-drinking-water plant, GWRS, or the Groundwater Replenishment System, which came online in January 2008. The facility initially produced 70 million gallons of drinking water per day, and when it expanded in May 2015, it could produce 100 million gallons per day. In 2023, a third expansion increased capacity to 130 million gallons per day, with the total costs to date at about $900 million. This brought the cost of an acre-foot of water to about $800, about one-third the cost of desalinated water. The expansions allowed the county to decrease its dependency on imported water while maintaining local control, replenishing its groundwater basin, and reducing the amount of wastewater that would have been discharged into the ocean.

In what officials called a "hydrological Hail Mary," Arizona's new Water Infrastructure Finance Authority (WIFA) considered getting into the desalination game with an Israeli company in December 2022 to build a $5.5 billion desalination plant in Puerto Penasco, Mexico, also known as Rocky Point. IDE Technologies, one of the world's largest desalination companies, said it had worked with state officials for four years on their ideas. Their proposal called for a 200-mile-long pipeline from the Mexican coast to the Central Arizona Project's canals, with delivery of desalinated water to cities like Tucson and Phoenix. The agreement with WIFA invoked considerable controversy from all sides, in part because critics felt the deal had been hastily decided before contract policies and procedures were in place with the new agency. In 2023, WIFA changed its mind, saying Arizona would seek competitive bids in 2024, but an unsupportive governor sought to cut the program's budget to one-tenth of the previous year. The move was viewed by some as pushback for what was considered too ambitious a project at a time of fiscal uncertainty.

It appears that the pendulum is swinging toward more research and development and smaller plants rather than huge ones. In May 2023, Secretary of the Interior Deb Haaland and New Mexico Congressman Gabe Vasquez announced that $12.6 million from the Bipartisan Infrastructure Law would be allocated to the Brackish Groundwater National Desalination Research Facility in Alamogordo, New Mexico. The facility is owned and operated by the Bureau of Reclamation, and used for small- and pilot-scale demonstration projects and research studies. The funding is just a small part of the $8.3 billion for reclamation water infrastructure projects appropriated over five years, with the goal of revitalizing water delivery systems, advancing drought resilience, and expanding water storage and completing rural water projects.

When treated municipal wastewater does not meet certain standards for potable use, that does not mean that it is not valuable. Instead, non-potable reuse applications include disinfected or undisinfected irrigation, industrial and commercial cooling, or planned placement into a raw (untreated) surface water reservoir. Many states are now considering regulations for non-potable water, including sources such as graywater, rainwater, stormwater, and blackwater that can be used in a variety of end uses.

Due to technological breakthroughs such as those developed by the National Alliance for Water Innovation at the Lawrence Berkeley National Laboratory in Berkeley, California, non-potable water can be treated with processes such as membrane filtration, ultraviolet light, and chlorine, so it can be used repeatedly.

San Francisco has already taken a step forward in using non-potable water with a 2015 requirement that all new buildings of 100,000 square feet or more to have on-site water recycling programs. The process for treating what was once sewage varies as researchers look at not only how the water can be treated effectively but also how to make using it palatable to the end user.

Another way recycled water can be applied is through agricultural reuse on food and non-food or garden crops. The water must be treated appropriately for its end use according to state and federal regulations, but can offset the amount of imported water used for irrigation or other purposes. For instance, the city of John Day, in eastern Oregon, replaced its aging wastewater treatment plant with a totally different facility, piping wastewater to a greenhouse the city owned where vegetables are grown hydroponically instead of in soil. The produce is sold at a local farmers market, generating revenue that helps pay for the greenhouse, with a production goal of over 4,000 pounds of fresh produce per month for the rural food desert. In Hayden, Idaho, 1.2 million gallons of wastewater is treated each day and recycled to irrigate alfalfa and poplar trees growing on farmland owned by the city. In addition to irrigating beneficial crops, the reuse of the water keeps it from being released into waterways and groundwater. And in Monterey, California, where severe groundwater overdrafting began occurring in the 1940s, the local utility treats and recycles a variety of sources, including stormwater, wastewater, and food industry processing water to irrigate both conventional and organic food crops. In an eleven-year-long, $7 million study that began in 1976, vegetable crops that could be eaten raw, such as lettuce, celery, and broccoli, were treated with well water and two types of recycled water, looking at food safety and the effect on soil. The study also included a marketing analysis. After obtaining favorable results, a full-scale facility was built next to a regional treatment plant in 1998.

Industrial reuse refers to situations where water is used repeatedly, either on-site by the same facility that captures, treats, and then uses it, or through a partnership where, for example, a municipal treatment plant treats water and then provides it to an industrial user. This form of reuse may include cooling, toilet flushing, dust suppression on roads or building sites, laundries, and car wash operations. By developing treatment approaches through a fit-for-purpose system, a business, for instance, can avoid overtreating water that would be used for a specific use, such as an industrial process. In 1984, chip maker Frito-Lay built a 283-acre processing plant in Casa Grande, Arizona that employed strategies ranging from landfill waste reduction to energy efficiency.

Then in 2010, it became the first United States-based food processing plant to produce water up to drinking water standards for reuse in food production by building a 650,000 gallon per day water treatment and recovery system, recycling 75 percent of its process water that previously had been used to irrigate crops on its property. Through the use of a membrane bioreactor and a low-pressure reverse osmosis system, the filtration system can reclaim all but the sanitary stream at the plant. Although the environmental benefit is substantial, the company has received numerous awards like LEED Gold Certification, and the prestige that comes from being named Sustainable Plant of the Year in 2011.

Cloud Seeding

One approach that is not new is making something of a comeback as planners attempt to add options to their toolbox. Commonly called cloud seeding, rain enhancement, and fog collection, this relatively simple process improves the conditions inside a cloud by introducing naturally existing (and safe) silver iodide compound, which helps to create ice crystals. Researchers believe that this process produces about 10 percent more snowfall than if they did not use the seeding procedure. In some studies, precipitation in the seeded area increased precipitation by 14 percent.

In Nevada, cloud seeding efforts date back to the 1960s at the Desert Research Institute (DRI), which has been conducting research across six mountain regions to improve snow totals for the nation's driest state. The cost per acre-foot is about $10, compared to about $2,000 per acre-foot for alternatives like desalination. Nevada's governor signed legislation in June 2023 granting the DRI $1.2 million to fund two more years of cloud seeding research.

Unconventional and Futuristic Strategies

Unlike cloud seeding, atmospheric water generation, also known as air water harvesting, requires a device to extract water from the air. The device captures the condensation from cooling surfaces (called captured condensate), such as the air handling units of mechanical equipment, typically located on a building's rooftop. In areas where humidity levels are high, such as the southeastern United States during the summer, that water is drained away to prevent damage to the equipment or to the building where the cooling equipment is located. In cooler climates, the cost and energy requirements of this method may preclude its use, however. The Federal Energy Management Program within the US Department of Energy has promoted a variety of ways this condensate can be safely collected to prevent bacterial contamination while offsetting the demand for freshwater in non-potable uses. Similarly, in the process of draining blowdown water from cooling equipment, evaporative coolers, condensers, and central boilers to remove mineral buildup, the water usually ends up in the sewer system but can be recovered. Blowdown water, however, typically contains a high mineral content and may need to be diluted before it can be reused for something like irrigation.

Physically moving water such as Antarctic icebergs or diverting water from rivers such as the Mississippi, the Missouri, and Utah's Bear River is still on the table as an option for securing more fresh water. The iceberg idea is not new; between 1890 and 1900, small icebergs were towed to Chile and Peru. Although the number of icebergs makes the endeavor feasible, there is only one geographic location where tabular icebergs (vertical sides with a flat top) are found, and this is the Antarctic, where they form when they break off from an ice shelf, called calving.

Studies have shown that there is an abundance of Antarctic icebergs available that could potentially be moved as far as Australia, the west coast of South America, and the southwest coast of Africa. Polar orbiting satellites can track their location, movement, and dimensions. By adding information on sea currents, winds, temperatures, and developing methods to reduce the melting of the ice, models show it might be possible to create what is known as a train configuration. The longer and wider the train icebergs are, the more it would cost to insulate them with a plastic film to protect them from wave action and sun. In one scenario, the train convoy could be operated using electrically driven propellers that are harnessed to the convoy. Another method being studied is the use of conventional tugs to push them to their eventual destination. Regardless of the logistics involved, which do not appear to be insurmountable according to one study, there are environmental and political issues that would need to be resolved. For instance, how would an iceberg terminal be integrated with a conventional water delivery infrastructure system? How would the "ownership" of icebergs be resolved among international stakeholders? Could icebergs be used for storing water, like a reservoir, or shared among different entities? How could marine animals be protected from mechanically moved icebergs?

Although moving icebergs might seem like a big unconventional alternative, there have been suggestions that policymakers should think even bigger. In 2012, the Bureau of Reclamation published a study that examined potential options for increasing freshwater imports in the Colorado River Basin that were then organized into groups by location. For the Colorado Front Range, the study looked at both the Missouri and the Mississippi River. For the Green River, the options were the Bear River, Snake River, and the Yellowstone River. And for Southern California, the options included the Columbia River, Alaskan icebergs, hauling water in tankers, and hauling water in giant bags from Alaskan rivers. The BOR said the Mississippi River cost was estimated to be $14 billion; the Missouri project cost would be $14.6 billion. In each case, feasibility studies would take five years, permits would take fifteen years, and construction would take ten more years. The estimates were considered to be more like guesses. The projects did not move forward. Arizona, which had spent forty years in an attempt to get Congress to approve the $4 billion Central Arizona Project, discussed earlier in this chapter, was considered by some to have built the country's last big water project. Still, in 2021 its state legislature asked Congress to pay for a feasibility study of a 1,000-mile-long pipeline from Davenport, Iowa to Rock Springs, Wyoming, where Mississippi River water would be pumped into the Green River, a tributary of the Colorado.

The Mississippi pipeline concept gained traction among policymakers again in 2022 from an unlikely source—a letter to the editor from a retired engineer to *The Desert Sun*. Don Siefkes wrote a letter to the Palm Springs, California newspaper suggesting that the United States build an aqueduct that would cut across four states to divert the Mississippi River from the system of giant levees and locks built in Louisiana by the Army Corps of Engineers in 1963 to Lake Powell. His letter went viral, reaching 3.2 million people on Google, and grabbed the interest of readers across the country and set off a debate about the technical feasibility of such a mammoth project. In response, the newspaper asked experts, attorneys, and researchers whether Siefkes' idea would work. Although engineers said building the pipeline would be feasible, most of those commenting were skeptical, just as they had been with the Parsons project.

Further Reading

Harrison, Christian S. 2023. *All the Water the Law Allows*. Norman: University of Oklahoma Press.
Hundley, Norris, Jr. 2009. *The Colorado River Compact and the Politics of Water in the West*. 2nd ed. Berkeley: University of California Press.
Kuhn, Eric, and John Fleck. 2021. *Science Be Dammed: How Ignoring Inconvenient Science Drained the Colorado River*. Tucson: University of Arizona Press.
Mumme, Steven P. 2023. *Border Water: The Politics of US–Mexico Transboundary Water Management, 1945–2015*. Tucson: University of Arizona Press.
Pearkes, Eileen Delehanty. 2023. *A River Captured: The Columbia River Treaty and Catastrophic Change*. Revised 2nd ed. Victoria, BC: Rocky Mountain Books.
Qadir, Manzoor, Vladimir Smakhtin, Sasha Koo-Oshima, and Edeltraud Guenther, eds. 2022. *Unconventional Water Resources*. Cham: Springer International.
Robison, Jason Anthony, ed. 2022. *Cornerstone at the Confluence: Navigating the Colorado River Compact's Next Century*. Tucson: University of Arizona Press.

3

Perspectives

Water Use and Distribution for Agricultural Food Production in California

Dr. Amrith Gunasekara

Water use and distribution in California is complex, dependent on annual rainfall, steeped in history, and often political. The lack of easily accessible and transparent data has only complicated the understanding of how water is distributed. This, in turn, has led to misinformed reporting. The result is a misinformed public, a lack of appreciation for agriculture and food production, increased risks associated with food security, an agricultural community that does not feel appreciated, and short-term political agendas that lack transparency.

Water for agriculture in California competes with two other sectors: the urban sector and environmental allocations to meet federal and state endangered species requirements. Water allocations for the environment take precedence over water allocations for agricultural food production. This essay provides an overview of California agriculture and how water is moved, captured, and distributed in the state, including water allocations to agriculture and other sectors.

To understand water distribution in California agriculture, it is essential first to understand agricultural food crop production in the state. California agricultural food production and food security are inherently connected within the state, the nation, and the world. Its Mediterranean climate provides a unique

---

The Owens Valley was home to the Indigenous Paiute and Shoshone people, who called it the Land of the Flowing Water. Diversion of the valley's water via aqueduct, completed in 1913, and ground water pumping, beginning in 1970, to supply water to the Los Angeles area, has drastically changed the valley's environment. (Snehitdesign/Dreamstime.com)

growing environment for food crops, some of which are not grown anywhere else in the nation. Mediterranean climates have warm, dry summers and rainy winters. Some vegetable, fruit, and nut crops thrive in these growing regions, given the long days of sunlight, low humidity, and mild winters.

Climate change has had an impact on both of these climate variables. According to the California Climate Adaption Strategy, the state has already experienced an increase in 1°F with some regions exceeding 2°F. Temperatures are expected to increase by 4.4–5.8°F by mid-century and 5.6–8.8°F by 2100. Precipitation has also changed over time with recent drought years. Precipitation has become more extreme, with record-breaking precipitation in October and December 2021, followed by the driest January, February, and March 2022 in more than 100 years. Climate change is memorialized as greater extreme weather patterns, which make agricultural food production more challenging given unpredictable weather conditions. Climate change also induces other weather impacts, making farming in California more challenging. Regardless of the challenges, California has adapted to be the leading agricultural state in the United States.

California's 69,000 farms with 9.5 million acres of irrigated land lead the nation in agricultural food crop production with $51.1 billion in cash receipts for output in 2022. About 400 different crops are grown in the state, according to the California Department of Food and Agriculture, with farmers focusing on producing high-value crops called specialty crops defined as fruits and vegetables, tree nuts, dried fruits, horticulture, and nursery crops (including floriculture). These crops, when compared to other crops such as cereal grains, generally are more costly to a consumer at the grocery store. These crops also offer unique nutritional content. Their production can also be unique, different, and sometimes labor-intensive, compared to grain crops produced in the Midwest and central parts of the United States. For example, the processing of tomatoes grown in California requires specialized harvesting technology, whereas other specialty crops are hand-picked (e.g., avocados) and labor-intensive. Several specialty crops, such as vegetables and fruits, have a shorter shelf life than grain crops, which can be dried and stored for extended periods without refrigeration, adding to their higher price point.

The production and focus on specialty crops in California can be attributed to several factors, including the higher cost of agricultural land, availability of water resources, climate, academic research centers that support the agricultural sector in California, technological innovations, and existing logistical distribution systems. For instance, according to the USDA National Agricultural

Statistics Service, agricultural land prices on average in California are $12,000 per acre, whereas in states such as Arizona, the average is $1,060 per acre, and in Colorado it is $1,770. A corresponding estimate on cropland value also shows similar patterns where the per acre value for California is $15,410, whereas it is $2,480 for Colorado. Although agricultural land prices are high in California, they are not the highest in the United States. New Jersey, Rhode Island, and Massachusetts all have higher land prices for agriculture than California, most probably because those states are much smaller. The demand is, therefore, much more significant for a limited amount of land, which subsequently increases the cost of the land when considered in the context of simple supply–demand economics.

Another focus on specialty crop production in California can be attributed to efficient irrigation. There are approximately five months of the year (May through September) when California's major agricultural production regions receive little or no precipitation in comparison with the rest of the nation. Most of the nation's agriculture is rain-fed and supplemented by irrigation during the summer months. In California, however, agriculture relies on winter snowpack, which melts and is captured and distributed through various water projects that move water from the northern part of the state to the south. Water is moved from the Sierra Nevada in the north to the south providing water for agricultural food production, allowing growers to access water on a need-and-demand basis, with groundwater pumped for irrigation during droughts. Captured water from winter rains and subsequent spring and summer snowmelt is used to irrigate agricultural food crops using several efficient irrigation methods, including drip irrigation, micro-sprinkler irrigation, and subsurface drip irrigation. These technologies allow growers to align their irrigation with evapotranspiration events during the day. Over the years these more efficient irrigation methods have outpaced historic irrigation methods such as furrow and flood irrigation.

Flood and furrow irrigation has declined by more than a third over the last thirty years, and at the same time, more efficient irrigation management practices have increased. In California, low-volume irrigation methods such as micro-sprinkler and drip irrigation have more than tripled from 15 percent in 1990 to 49 percent in 2016. Subsurface drip irrigation has increased from 1 percent to 7 percent. Many of California's specialty agricultural crops utilize efficient low-volume irrigation methods. Of the approximately 9 million irrigated acres of agricultural food crops grown in California, more than 60 percent of the acreage utilizes efficient irrigation management practices. California continues to grow field crops, which do not utilize efficient drip or micro-sprinkler irrigation techniques. Continued use and expansion of irrigation technologies and utilization of efficient irrigation techniques allow growers in California to efficiently operate water and engage in efficient fertilizer application using fertigation methods (movement of fertilizers through efficient irrigation systems).

Despite the gains in water efficiency, the state's agriculture sector continues to be blamed for high water use. Many references have been made to California agriculture using as much as 80 percent of the state's water. A simple internet search using "water use, California, agriculture" will provide information that California agriculture uses 80 percent of all water used by homes and businesses. This value conflicts with other references stating that agriculture, on average, uses 40 percent of the water in California. The California Department of Water Resources website (as of September 20, 2023) states, "Yet, considering that agriculture accounts for approximately 80 percent of all the water used in California, even small improvements in agricultural water use efficiency can be significant". The presentation of these values has confused the general public, who think agriculture utilizes the majority of the water that arrives in the state. This presentation of water uses and villainization of agriculture, which produces food for human sustenance and existence, is factually incorrect.

The 2022–23 water year in California was historic in that it broke several snowpack and precipitation records, given the unprecedented winter rains that brought water to the state. Total water in terms of million-acre-feet (maf) was unavailable for the 2022–2023 water year at the time of this writing. Therefore, a similar year (2006) was used when there was a total of 254 maf of water that the state received from winter rains and snowpack. Less than half of this water was captured and stored for beneficial use (103 maf). The percentage distribution of the captured water for 2006 was 29 percent for agriculture, 62 percent for the environment, and 8 percent for domestic use. Approximately 151 maf flowed without capture through the state's streams and rivers to the ocean in 2006. This water is not defined as "environmental" water even though it flows to the "environment." These data show that the environment and not agriculture receives the majority of captured water in the state in a year with high precipitation. If the calculations include uncaptured water as "environmental" water, the environmental allocations increase to 85 percent. Agriculture and the urban sector do not receive uncaptured water because it flows out to the ocean during winter rains. Therefore, agriculture uses only 12 percent or four times domestic/urban use of the total water that arrives in the state. The data show that the environment and not agriculture receives 80 percent or more of the water.

Agricultural food production is an essential sector of the nation's economy and human food security system. Agriculture is often seen as a polluter, environmental disrupter, and natural resource burden. However, agriculture only uses four times the water of the domestic sector. It is not the largest user of water in the state in years of high precipitation, like 2022–2023, given the sector's highly efficient irrigation systems. The environment receives significantly more water allocations, especially in a year with above-than-average precipitation. Agricultural food production in California should be appreciated more, farmers should be recognized and acknowledged for their innovation and contributions to food security, water allocations should be increased to balance the distribution between the environment and food production, and true and accurate information should be distributed to the public.

About the Author

Dr. Amrith Gunasekara is Director of Science and Research for the California Bountiful Foundation. The California Bountiful Foundation is the 501c(3) non-profit science, research, and education organization of the California Farm Bureau.

Further Reading

California Department of Food & Agriculture. 2022. *California Agricultural Statistics Review 2021–2022.* https: cdfa.ca.gov/Statistics/PDFs/2022_Ag_Stats_Review.pdf.

California Department of Water Resources. 2023. https://water/ca/gov/Programs/Water-Use-And-Efficiency-Agricultural-Water-Use-Efficiency/.

Guo, Jeff. 2015. "Agriculture Is 80 Percent of Water Use in California. Why Aren't Farmers Being Forced to Cut Back? *The Washington Post.* https://www.washingtonpost.com/blogs/govbeat/wp/2015/04/03/agriculture-is-80/percent-of-water-use-in-california-why-arent-farmers-being-forced-to-cut-back/.

State of California. 2022. Summary of Projected Climate Change Impacts on California. *California Climate Adaptation Strategy.* https://climateresilience.ca.gov/overview/impacts.html#:text=temperature,°F%C2%B0F%20by%20late%20century/.

The Colorado River Can be a Model of Resilience

Taylor Hawes

I have been working on Colorado River issues since the mid-1990s, before we began experiencing the drought of the last two decades. I was working in the headwaters of the Colorado River in 2002 when we got our first taste of an extremely dry year. In fact, 2002 is still the driest year on record in the Colorado River Basin. It was our wake-up call. Little did we know it was just the beginning of a multidecade trend.

During 2002, Colorado experienced some of its first big wildfires, including the Hayman fire, which ranked as Colorado's largest ever wildfire for eighteen years. During the spring runoff that year, the rivers and streams were a trickle when they would normally be rushing and full of snowmelt. Cities and agricultural irrigators drew down reservoirs quickly, leaving exposed lake beds, which then became a health concern as communities saw an increase in asthma cases due to localized dust storms. In 2003, the Colorado legislature introduced and passed many laws focused on conservation and drought. People who had never thought about water were now debating or discussing water with their neighbors and friends. A crisis will do that.

Unfortunately, the water crisis in the region continues today. The story of climate change is being written in water: too much or too little or at different times. Places that have historically had droughts are expected to experience longer and more intense periods of drought. In some areas, droughts may be punctuated by extreme weather and rain events that feel like "weather whiplash," such as what California experienced in the winter of 2022–23.

History is filled with examples of water mismanagement leading to societal, economic, and environmental crises (e.g., the Aral Sea, the Tigris–Euphrates, the Nile, etc.). These crises often stem from one sector or government trying to dominate the other stakeholders, putting their water needs above others' interests. In all cases, the environment was an afterthought. Today, about 4 billion people, representing nearly two-thirds of the global population, experience severe water scarcity during at least one month of the year. That number is expected to rise due to more extreme weather events, extended droughts, and growing demands, which will likely lead to more conflict and water crises as communities and sectors fight for a dwindling share.

In the Colorado River Basin, for every 1°F increase, we are experiencing a 3–9 percent reduction in river flows. Less precipitation, thirstier soils, and a drier atmosphere leads to more evaporation, which accounts for much of the reduction in flow. And although the Colorado River has often experienced drought, climate change is intensifying the impacts of those droughts. It is a slow-moving crisis and one that we can adapt to and learn to live with as our new reality, but it requires that we rethink how we manage our water supplies and our rivers and that we do so quickly.

Up until a few decades ago, we had enough water in the Colorado River Basin to go around. Since 2002, however, the overall drying trend has continued with only a few "good" years, while demands have steadily increased. The result is an imbalanced system, characterized by shrinking rivers and reservoirs.

I believe there is a path forward that includes three "no regrets" steps. (1) Reducing water use in the region (not easy but definitely possible); (2) investing in the health of the entire watershed to allow more precipitation to make it to our rivers; and (3) adopting a governance structure and policies that promote sustainable use of the Colorado River (e.g., the Post-2026 Operating Rules, the next Agreement with Mexico, and state laws).

I used to think we just had to reduce our water use to balance the supply-demand equation and "fix" our laws and policies that had not kept pace with the changing climate. The last three years have caused me to re-evaluate my thinking. In addition to reducing demands and adopting amended policies, which we still must do, I now realize we must improve the health of the watershed. In 2020 and 2021, we experienced near-normal snowpack, but a much smaller portion made it to the rivers. Due to very dry soils, a thirsty atmosphere, and unhealthy forests, much of the snowpack was absorbed by the soils, air, and forests before it reached the rivers. In addition to low stream flows, we also experienced an extreme wildfire season that lasted until October. To ignore the health and resilience of our environment will only make our water scarcity challenges more difficult to address.

Tackling the challenges in the Colorado River is like playing three-dimensional chess. Everything is interrelated, and there is no single solution. If we solve one aspect of the challenge, we might unknowingly create a new problem. We all have something to lose. People's livelihoods, health and safety, community welfare, and our quality of life are all at stake. We must develop solutions that meet the needs of people *and* nature.

Related to governance and policies, there have been many efforts in the Basin over the last twenty years to staunch the overuse. Unfortunately, after a few years of implementing a new policy to reduce the region's water use (the Drought Contingency Plan of 2017), the decision-makers end up back at the negotiating table. This recurring band-aid approach to water supply issues leaves the water user community scrambling to address crisis after crisis.

The next set of agreements and policies that govern Colorado River operations must balance water demands with available supply, including recovery of reservoir storage. The agreements must be flexible enough to adapt to what Mother Nature provides, not what we hope she will provide. Finding ways to reduce water use will be challenging for everyone in every state and every sector that depends on this river. The region, however, has the chance to be a model of sustainability and resilience—only if we can embrace the concept of balancing our supplies and demands and always remember that this is a shared river system.

To craft a successful path forward, every solution must have multiple co-benefits and every drop of water will need to meet multiple needs as it flows downstream. As a recent example of this approach, The Nature Conservancy entered into an agreement with the New Mexico Interstate Stream Commission (NMISC) and Jicarilla Apache Nation that allows the NMISC to lease up to 20,000-acre-feet (6 billion gallons) of water per year (for ten years) from the Nation. The lease benefits threatened and endangered fish, increases water security for New Mexico, and provides income to help build the Nation's economic self-sufficiency. It is truly a win–win–win solution at a scale that is meaningful.

The decisions that lie ahead for the Colorado Basin will be difficult. Every path forward includes trade-offs. As lawmakers, state, local, and federal officials, and community and business leaders take action and finalize their plans, they must include measures to protect and restore the environment—the very foundation of this iconic river system. We must all recognize that the Colorado River's increasingly depleted and degraded ecosystems are not just another category of "water user" whose interests must be balanced against other competing priorities in the Basin for the simple reason that the integrity of the Colorado River's remaining natural systems is foundational to ensuring the continued viability of the river system itself.

Environmental non-profits in the region have been working on the ground to test and implement solutions that work for nature, people, and business.

If we work across sectors, tapping the broad expertise of all the interests that depend on this river system, including environmental and Tribal Nations, we can develop a plan that recovers this river system before it's too late. We don't have to look far to see examples around the world of the negative consequences if we fail to develop an approach that brings the river back into balance.

What will our future look like? Will we be a model of sustainability and resilience for water-scarce regions of the world, or will the Colorado River be another example of the Tragedy of the Commons? My hope is that we will be a model, which requires that we focus on our common interests, find shared solutions, and take bold action while we still have the chance. The river we depend on depends on us and it is time for us to fulfill our side of the bargain.

About the Author

Taylor Hawes is the Colorado River Program Director for The Nature Conservancy.

Whiplash Again!—Learning from the Frequent Extremes of Western Water

Dr. Jay Lund, Deirdre Des Jardins, and Kathleen Schaefer

The western United States is famous for its frequent floods and droughts in a semi-arid climate. This is well illustrated by recent years in California, which have been among both the wettest and driest years in a century. The West's extreme-heavy climate is exacerbated by ongoing climate changes, particularly increasing temperatures.

Societies and economies in the American West have long had to adapt to this high variability and have mostly adapted quite successfully, at least in overall economic terms (Pinter et al. 2019). Regional and interbasin systems of dams, aqueducts, and groundwater shift water from the wet season to address the West's 6–8 months of seasonal drought that the West experiences every year. The region's flood management system of levees, dams, and bypasses has greatly reduced (but not eliminated) economic and life losses from floods and makes some flood water available for agricultural and urban water supplies. Damages to ecosystems are another matter, and remain the most difficult water challenge for the region as a whole. In addition, long-term reductions in average water use (especially from groundwater) are needed for a drying climate, greater extremes, and sustaining ecosystems.

This essay compares two wet water years in California, October 1982–September 1983 (the 1983 water year), the wettest year on record, and October 2022–September 2023 (water year 2023), the most recent wet year. This comparison gives a good sense of how water managers in California (and other regions) have long understood the challenges and limitations of water management in extreme climates and how water management in the western United States will likely adapt as its climate becomes more extreme.

In July 1984, the California Department of Water Resources issued Bulletin 69–83, *California High Water 1982–83*. It insightfully reviewed what is still California's wettest water year in more than a century. "Old superlatives have been dusted off and new ones count to better describe the tragedy, damage, and trauma associated with the State's latest 'unusual' weather experience," the report noted. "California's climate has often been described as variable, inconsistent, and unpredictable. The meteorological events of the last few years give additional credence to those observations. The two extremes of weather patterns—the record back-to-back dry years of 1976–77 and the all-time record of consecutive wet water years, 1981–82 and 1982–83—have now been recorded in less than a single decade!"

Here are a few long-term lessons from the 1983 and 2024 experiences:

1. California often has wet and very wet years, just as it often has dry and very dry years.
2. Flooding can occur in all parts of California, and many parts can flood in the same year. Few areas should feel entirely safe from floods. Flood hazard zones should be updated to consider subsidence and changes in land use and climate.
3. Floods have many causes, including regional flooding from major rivers, local tributaries, very local storm drainage, coastal storm driven waves, and infrastructure failures. All causes can cause sizable property damage and deaths.
4. Effective infrastructure helps. For major river flooding, California's systems of flood bypasses, levees, and reservoirs were highly effective, but will have vulnerabilities for extreme wet conditions, which are becoming more likely with greater climate variability. Flood-fighting by local and state agencies greatly improve levee reliability, but local levee breaks must be expected and prepared for in a system with thousands of miles of levees.

5. Warnings and evacuations greatly reduce deaths from flooding, but reducing property damage requires investments and regulations to reduce flooding and flood vulnerabilities. Most flood deaths in 2023 were from people attempting to travel through flood waters (often by car) and local levee failures.
6. California's Flood Operation Center was a beehive of activity in the winter of 2023, as it was in 1983. The co-located activities of the Department of Water Resources and the National Weather collaboration are a valuable service. Sharing resources, expertise, and technology across levels of government has been an excellent and effective investment.
7. 2023's emergency conditions in the Tulare Lake Basin also occurred in 1983 when they disrupted agricultural production in the region for two years due to partial re-emergence of naturally occurring Tulare Lake.
8. Agency postmortems for major events are vital to improving our understanding of present and future problems. However, public agency documents usually find it easier to recount the history of events, losses, and successes than to identify specific and broad causes of failures. Identifying systemic improvements, though, is vitally important. It is important to systematically reflect on, discuss, and learn from the experiences of each extreme event, wet or dry. Postmortem reports from major extreme events are opportunities to improve the understanding and functioning of California's water system and should be expected, available, and discussed to facilitate improvements.

The 2023 water year was lucky enough to have a cool spring to slow snowmelt. The same was true 40 years earlier, as the 1984 report noted, "Recall the termination of the rainfall and the unseasonably cool temperatures during the peak of the snowmelt period in the southern Sierra Nevada, which moderated the melt and possibly averted disastrous flooding in the San Joaquin Valley." Luck always helps, but cannot be relied upon.

Floods and droughts require serious long-term organization and preparation for past and still larger extremes. Prepare with diligence and humility, for preparation is never perfect. "There is no question that the various entities involved achieved some degree of success in managing the 1982–83 flood fight. We must realize that, although man's ability to manage the extremes of the elements is sometimes successful, Nature bats last!"

Let's hope that new and old agency postmortems and reflections can become available on the web to help us reflect on present and coming challenges. These are helpful for understanding and restoring faith and pride in government, and perhaps more important for fostering the kinds of conversations and trust needed professionally and publicly.

California has seen incredible floods and flooding in the past and must prepare for major floods and droughts in the future. California must accept the fact that absolute protection is not possible and plan for exceedance. Floods and droughts are inevitable in California, just as hurricanes are inevitable on the US eastern seaboard and tornadoes are inevitable in the Midwest. In all these cases, loss of life and economic damages are greatly reduced by preparation, infrastructure, warnings, and analytically informed discussions and decisions. Be prepared.

About the Authors

Jay Lund is Professor of Civil and Environmental Engineering and Vice-Director of the Center for Watershed Sciences at the University of California, Davis.

Deirdre Des Jardins is a tenacious researcher and policy advocate on climate adaptation in California water.

Kathleen Schaefer is a PhD Candidate at the University of California, Davis completing a dissertation on community-based flood insurance.

Further Reading

Bertino, Michael. 2023. "Tulare Lake Basin Flooding: An Update for Early May." *Bountiful* (blog) May 12, 2023. https://blog.beautiful.ag/Tulare-lake-basin-flooding-sat-imagery-update.

California Department of Water Resources. 2021. *California's Drought of 2012–2016: An Overview*. https://water.ca.gov/-/media/DWR-Website/Web-Pages/Water-Basics/Drought/Files/Publications-And-Reports/033021_2012-16-Drought-Report_v4_ay11.pdf.

Lund, Jay R. 2012. "Flood Management in California." *Water* 4: 157–169. https://doi.org/10.3390/w.4010157.

Pinter, Nicholas., Jay Lund, and Peter Moyle. 2019. "The California Water Model: Resilience Through Failure." *Hydrological Processes* 22 (12): 1775–1779. https://doi.org/10.1002/hyp.13447.

Tulare County Master Flood Control Plan. 1971. https://tularecunty.ca.gov/_api/render/file/?fileID=8045B502-5056-A959-DB0F3AB7DEC64B50.

Impacts of Groundwater Export in Owens Valley, Inyo County, California

Dr. Sara J. Manning

"In conclusion," I said, "results show that groundwater pumping by the Los Angeles Department of Water and Power in the Owens Valley leads to: loss of perennial native grasses; an increase in shrubs and nonnative weeds relative to grasses; die off of less tolerant 'rare' plant species; and an overall decline in live vegetation. These vegetation changes expose bare surfaces, leading to wind erosion and airborne dust. As healthy, diverse meadows convert to shrub monocultures, wildlife habitat is lost. There is less forage for domestic livestock, adversely affecting our local economy. The changes in vegetation we see are not supposed to happen according to management under the Inyo/Los Angeles Water Agreement. Thank you."

It was April 2004. The audience in the high school auditorium sat wide-eyed and applauded politely considering the depressing information I had just dropped into their laps. As the attendees dispersed, one man approached. I recognized Harry Williams, a member of the local Bishop Paiute Tribe. Harry was one of the most outspoken critics of Los Angeles Department of Water and Power (LADWP) and the Water Agreement, and I admired him for it! He never missed an opportunity to point out that Inyo County, which employed me as the Vegetation Scientist, was allowing LADWP to pump too much water.

Harry did not need to sit through my presentation with its tables, graphs, and statistics to arrive at the same conclusion: groundwater pumping sucks the life out of the valley. Harry had lived in Owens Valley all his life; his ties to the land are something that transplants like me find difficult to fathom. His body and blood came from the soil, air and water of the valley, and because his ancestors are buried here, his being contains them too. Harry had spent nearly all his forty-seven years venturing throughout his homeland, observing, studying, remembering, and, now, grieving as he witnessed its desiccation.

LADWP justified its taking of Owens Valley's water, which began early in the twentieth century, by claiming the water otherwise went to waste. Snow and rain falling east of California's Sierra Nevada crest flowed into Inyo County's hydrologically closed Owens River Basin, providing water for plants, animals, and a large lake. The Indigenous Paiute people dug ditches to spread the water, and the plants and habitat they tended provided for their needs. Eventually, western-trained engineers arrived, and they saw an arid climate, green plants, and a lake with no outlet to the sea. They reasoned they were entitled to take the water that was being "lost" to evapotranspiration. So they hatched a plan to build an aqueduct, divert Owens River and its tributaries, and export flows south over 233 miles of desert to Los Angeles. The first barrel of the LA Aqueduct was completed in 1913, depriving half of the Owens River of water and causing the vast and beautiful Owens Lake to go dry. The lakebed became the largest single source of particulate matter (PM 10) in the nation.

The next step was for LADWP to take ground water. In 1970, LADWP completed construction of the aqueduct's second barrel. LADWP now had the means to take all the surface runoff in heavy precipitation years and pump ground water to keep their conduits full in normal or dry years.

Pumping began in earnest in 1970. Immediately, springs and wetlands dried up, and gradually, trees and groundwater-dependent vegetation died. Soon dust and tumbleweeds blew everywhere. The County of Inyo responded by filing a suit under the new California Environmental Quality Act demanding LADWP prepare an environmental impact report on its plans to continuously pump and take more water from the valley. LADWP demurred. After two decades of arguing, the two parties settled by signing the Inyo/LA Water Agreement in 1991.

The Water Agreement allowed LADWP to pump the valley's ground water as long as the pumping caused no significant adverse environmental impacts. Inyo County and LADWP officials sold the agreement to a skeptical public by asserting: Inyo County would have a say in water management; management would be based on science; any further damage to native vegetation would be avoided; inadvertent impacts to the environment would be mitigated; and LADWP would continue to provide water for in-valley purposes.

I had arrived in Owens Valley in 1985 to work on my graduate research in plant ecology and was quite surprised to learn Inyo County actually *needed* a plant ecologist! The county put me to work measuring groundwater depth, plant water stress, evapotranspiration, root depth, and leaf area index. I soon realized the need to scale up and monitor plant communities to track vegetation changes at the landscape level. The signing of the Water Agreement in 1991 was my opportunity to step into the role of the county's full-time Vegetation Scientist and lead the program to collect data on vegetation response to pumping. If monitoring results indicated that problems were occurring, pumping could be curtailed before serious damage occurred, and thus the Water Agreement goal of avoiding adverse changes would be achieved.

By 1999, the data were clearly confirming the common sense verdict that groundwater-dependent ecosystems need groundwater to remain healthy. Year after year as I was adding the next data points to the graphs, a downward trend was obvious. In the late 1990s, I collaborated with university researchers, comparing the field-collected data with satellite-derived estimates of plant vigor. We could see the downward trend from outer space. Vegetation health was correlated with groundwater depth: they rose and fell together, and mostly fell. Grass was dying in meadows as shrubs and weeds moved in. Before-and-after photographs showed changes. Results were reported publicly in documents prepared by Inyo County and at meetings between Inyo County and LADWP. Pumping had lowered the water table deeper than plant roots could reach, and plants were stressed and dying as a result.

The data I delivered seemed more than sufficient for our decision-makers to act and minimize pumping. How naïve I was to think LADWP, a very wealthy and powerful municipal utility, would be swayed by data! One senior LADWP official announced that if those plant species grew in his yard in Hollywood, he would immediately send his gardener to eradicate them. Inyo County leadership crumbled when LADWP threatened retaliation, for example, by crippling county projects if pumping was reduced. Stopping the pumps seemed the only chance to protect vast living resources throughout the valley from blinking off into oblivion, but it became obvious that the hydrologists, engineers, lawyers, and politicians did not give a damn about a perennial native grass.

However, Harry did. My tedious scientific investigations had led me to the same conclusions that were instilled in him since time immemorial: the Owens Valley environment mattered. His people had lived within and cultivated these lands, which in turn provided their needs, for thousands of years prior to the arrival of Euro Americans. What principle allows "western" society to designate some lands as exploitable to the point where the water and life may be taken and the lands designated worthless? LADWP's practice of ecocide made the valley less livable and brought harm to human health and the economy. Harry would sum it up: "If you don't take care of Mother Nature, she will not take care of you."

Presently, we are at a crossroads: The climate noose is tightening, and LADWP controls the valley's water. Decades ago, LADWP used its deceptive strategies to prevent the valley's tribes from accessing rights to water, and later, the tribes were barred from having a seat at the Water Agreement table. Tribal representatives attend water meetings and speak to the injustices; however, years ago, LADWP made sure that the valley's tribes remain politically marginalized. Tribes have no legal tools strong enough to allow them to level the playing field.

Water in Los Angeles is a renewable, sustainable resource, and if steps were taken to update water infrastructure and management, LA could abandon its stranglehold on Owens Valley. Like a plastic bag, Owens Valley's water is "single use" in LA, flowing from the High Sierra through their toilets then into the ocean. Los Angeles' unsustainable water practices were recently analyzed by their resident UCLA scientists and policy makers. Results showed that by implementing water conservation, wastewater recycling, groundwater quality intervention, and stormwater capture—and without resorting to desalination—LA could dramatically increase its own water supply and become self-sufficient.

After that 2004 presentation, Harry Williams and I became good friends. I left my Inyo County job and career as a plant ecologist. I could not face a future of being ignored as my eyes and data recorded systematic, predictable plant death. Within months, in 2009, I was hired as Environmental Director for the Big Pine Paiute Tribe of the Owens Valley.

With the Tribe and others, I work toward a vision of water and environmental justice. My hope is the day will come when LADWP will leave Owens Valley, allowing for restoration of tribal jurisdiction. Using a national monument/working landscape approach, the valley could tell the story of what *not* to do to an incredibly beautiful and productive land and the original inhabitants of that land. Food could be raised sustainably and energy generated as people from all over the world visit to share the beauty of an integrated landscape and culture.

Years of breathing Owens Valley dust weakened Harry's lungs, and he died much too young in June 2021. He is, of course, still in the land, air, and water all around us.

About the Author

Sara J. Manning is Environmental Director, Big Pine Paiute Tribe.

Further Reading

Inyo County. California. 1990. *Agreement Between the County of Inyo and the City of Los Angeles and its Department of Water and Power on a Long Term Groundwater Management Plan for Owens Valley and Inyo County*. https://inyowater.org/documents/governing-documents/water-agreement.

Mika, Katie, Elizabeth Gallo, Erik Porse, Terri Hogue, Stephanie Pincetl, and Mark Gold. 2018. *LA Sustainable Water Project: Los Angeles City-Wide Overview*. This report is a product of the UCLA Grand Challenges, Sustainable LA; UCLA Institute of the Environment and Sustainability; and Colorado School of Mines https://cloudfront.escholarship.org/dist/prd/content/qt4tp3x8g4/qt4tp3x8g4.pdf?t=p4u0ld.

National Academies of Sciences, Engineering, and Medicine. 2020. *Effectiveness and Impacts of Dust Control Measures for Owens Lake*. Washington, DC: The National Academies Press. https://doi.org/10.17226/25658.

4

Profiles

Alan H. Bible (1909–1988)

Sometimes an individual who has started from humble beginnings can have a tremendous influence on something later in their life. That person may not end up being especially well known, or may be soft-spoken in demeanor, but has chosen a path that makes them instrumental in affecting the lives of many others. Such is the case of Alan H. Bible, the man who consumer advocate Ralph Nader once called one of the US Senate's most productive members.

Few members of the Senate have as humble a start as Alan Bible. Born on November 20, 1909, he grew up in the tiny northern Nevada community of Lovelock at a time when there were less than 1,000 residents. Lovelock was known originally as Big Meadows, a stop for settlers in wagon trains heading on the Humboldt Trail to California. The town was named for George Lovelock, a Welsh settler who bought 320 acres of land, and with it, water rights on the Humboldt River. Lovelock became the home of a depot for the Central Pacific Railroad, but the town was not incorporated until 1917.

Alan Bible was the son of Jacob Harvey Bible and his wife, Isabel Welsh, attending class in the town's two-room schoolhouse. The family lost all of their possessions when a fire burned down their house in 1919, so they moved to nearby Fallon where the younger Bible became known for his skill in public speaking and as a member of the debate team. After graduating from high school, he attended the University of Nevada, Reno, receiving a bachelor's degree in economics in 1930, and from there, despite the worsening economic depression, attended Georgetown Law School in Washington, DC. Finances forced him to look for work while he was in law school, and Nevada's Senator

---

John Wesley Powell overlooking the Rio Virgen with Paiute chief Tau-Gu circa 1873. Powell's reports to Congress and to the Department of the Interior explained the arid nature of much of the West and indicated that irrigation would be required for settlement. (U.S. National Park Service.)

Pat McCarran found him a job as an elevator operator in the Capitol building. Once he graduated in 1934, he joined McCarran's law firm.

Entering politics for the first time, Bible was appointed as District Attorney for Storey County in 1935, winning election to the position in 1936. His political connections in the state led to a position as Deputy Attorney General from 1938 to 1942, and then in 1942, he was elected as Attorney General for Nevada, becoming the youngest attorney general in the nation. He served for eight years. His friend and mentor McCarran died in 1954, and Bible was elected to fill the remaining two years of McCarran's term, then won the office on his own in 1956. He served in that capacity until his retirement in 1974.

Bible's Senate career focused on crafting water rights policy and legislation designed to expand the Nevada economy, but he was also an advocate for national parks and monuments. During his tenure as chair of the Interior Committee's Subcommittee on Parks and Recreation, he helped create more than eighty-five parks, historic sites, and national monuments. In 1986, Congress established Great Basin National Park in eastern Nevada, a project he had worked on for much of his final years in the Senate.

As a protégé of Senator McCarran, Bible recognized the importance of having a sufficient supply of water for the state, understanding that the resource was key to the future growth of Las Vegas. For years, there had been little concern about the issue, as many believed Las Vegas was so small there would never be a need for more water. Bible was troubled, though, about federal government encroachment and the decline of the mining industry in Nevada. He took on the cause of bringing reclamation projects to the state, as well as fighting to make sure that Nevada received an adequate share of water from the Colorado River.

From early in his career until he left the Senate, Bible watched over the implementation of the Colorado River Compact and his state's meager allotment of 300,000 acre-feet from the river. Realizing that Nevada's needs for water would balloon as Las Vegas (and especially its tourist industry) continued to grow, Bible sought to intervene in the 1952 US Supreme Court case of *Arizona v. California*, worried that it was essential for the state to protect its interests. As special Assistant Attorney General, he argued that Nevada needed both a stable and predictable source of water, and after twelve years of litigation, the court agreed. In the late 1950s and early 1960s, he took on a new role as state officials began to consider a project that would bring water through a pipeline from Lake Mead to Las Vegas. He pressed the Bureau of Reclamation to consider the water needs of the entire Las Vegas Valley, and used his relationships with presidents John F. Kennedy and Lyndon B. Johnson to seek federal funding.

Bible supported regional cooperation in water planning, but worried that the seven states involved in the Colorado River Compact too often fought for their own narrow interests. He then sought support for a separate Southern Nevada Water Project that would allow Nevada to use its own allotment of the Colorado through the construction of six pumping plants, a reservoir, a four-mile-long tunnel, and over 31 miles of pipeline at a cost of $72 million. The legislation cleared Congress and was signed by President Lyndon B. Johnson in October 1965. Despite several hiccups that were largely political, the money was eventually appropriated and by June 1971, the first phase of the project was dedicated in ceremonies in which Bible was honored as the "Father of the Project."

Further Reading

Elliott, Gary E. 1989. "Senator Alan Bible and the Southern Nevada Water Project." *Nevada Historical Society Quarterly*. Vol. 32, No. 3: 181–196. https://epubs.nsla.nv.gov/statepubs/epubs/210777-1989-3Fall.pdf.

Elliott, Gary E. 1994. *Senator Alan Bible and the Politics of the New West*. Reno: University of Nevada Press.

n.a. 1988. "Nevada Ex-Sen. Alan H. Bible; Political Force for 40 Years." *Los Angeles Times*, September 14, 1988. https://www.latimes.com/archives/la/xpm-1988-09-14-mn-1677-story.html.

Delph E. Carpenter (1877–1951)

Delphus Emory Carpenter, better known as Delph, was a key figure in the development of water law in the West, and his legacy as negotiator of the first interstate agreement for sharing water is as important today as it was in the early 1920s.

His parents, Leroy and Martha Carpenter, decided to leave their Iowa home in 1877 to relocate to Weld County, Colorado, where they became members of the Union Colony in the town of Greeley. The colony was a pioneer settlement that Horace Greeley, editor of the *New York Tribune*, had backed financially. The utopian community, whose religious foundation called those of "high moral standards" to join their farming homestead, was located at the confluence of two rivers, the Cache la Poudre and South Platte. Operating in a manner similar to what today might be called a commune, the Union Colony used ditch irrigation to manage the area's scarce water resources. The Carpenters arrived in Greeley, however, at a time when Colorado was facing disputes over the diverging priorities of mining and agricultural interests.

Delph was their second son, born May 13, 1877, joining Alfred Bennett, and a third son, Fred George, would later be added to the small family. He graduated from Greeley High School, and left the colony in 1896 to attend the University of Denver in the literature department, and receiving a law degree in 1899. He decided to return to Greeley to start his law practice, marrying Ann Michaela "Dot" Hogarty, who had been his classmate in high school, in 1901. They had four children—three girls and a boy—while Delph became involved in several types of agriculture-related disputes. He and his family operated a cattle ranch and were closely associated with the state's livestock industry. In order to support his family, he also defended an accused murderer in a 1907 case, and the publicity he gained by convincing the jury his client had acted in self-defense propelled Carpenter into a political career.

In 1908, he became the first native-born citizen of Colorado to be elected to the state senate, running as a Republican Party member. Although he only served one four-year term, as part of his tenure he served on a committee examining the state's surface water and interstate streams. In his final report, he advocated for states' rights and supported what was known as the Colorado Doctrine, the concept best known as prior appropriation. He and others endorsed the idea of "first in time, first in right" that was becoming the standard throughout the West.

As a lawyer, he understood that Colorado's water was a valuable resource that needed to be legally protected from other states and interests that wanted it for their own use in irrigating the arid land. But he also knew that Colorado's rivers ultimately flowed across state lines into other arid states. Rather than allowing the federal government make the decisions on western water, as had happened in 1907 when the US Supreme Court had affirmed its authority to settle interstate water disputes, he began looking at other models that could protect Colorado's rights to this valuable resource.

He wore a different hat as the attorney representing the Greeley-Poudre Irrigation District. In a case that would be argued twice before the US Supreme Court, *Wyoming v. Colorado*, Carpenter was the defense attorney for the state when the irrigation district built a tunnel to divert water from the Laramie River in Wyoming to the nearby Cache la Poudre River. The case began in 1911 but was not decided until 1922; Colorado lost. But it once again demonstrated the need for Colorado to defend its water rights as a headlands state, preferably without litigation.

While the case was still being heard by the Court, Carpenter advocated the idea that there was an alternative to having states battling over water rights in a courtroom. At a 1920 meeting of the League of the Southwest, he called for a multistate agreement—a compact—that would delineate how the Colorado River's waters would be shared among the states. This mechanism would be legal under the Compact Clause of the US Constitution, but would need congressional approval. The issue of the division of the river and where the water would go was already being debated, especially by Californians. In January 1922, Carpenter served as Colorado's representative to the newly formed Colorado River Commission, with the Secretary of Commerce, Herbert Hoover, serving as the federal government's representative. Carpenter's drafts of a pact that would be acceptable to the other six states, as well as Hoover, were considered the model for an interstate agreement, which was reached in November 1922. The compact took years to be completely ratified, but it became the foundation of the West's interstate water law. Later, Carpenter would negotiate other interstate water compacts, and although not all of them would end up as legal instruments, his work protecting Colorado's resources were evidence of his bargaining skills.

Carpenter's health limited his work in his later years, and due to Parkinson's Disease, he relied on his wife's help to assist him while he remained bedridden and unable to travel. He passed away on February 27, 1951, in Greeley, where he and his wife are buried together.

Further Reading

Hudson, Bill. 2019. "Editorial: The Murder and Resurrection of the Colorado River, Part One." *Pagosa Daily Post*, October 15. https://pagosadailypost.com/2019/10/15/editorial-the-murder-and-resurrection-of-the-colorado-river-part-one.

Rettig, Patricia J. 2023. "Delph E. Carpenter." *Colorado Encyclopedia*. https://coloradoencyclopedia.org/article/delph-e-carpenter.

Tyler, Daniel. 2003. *Silver Fox of the Rockies: Delphus E. Carpenter and the Western Water Compacts*. Norman: University of Oklahoma Press.

Floyd E. Dominy (1909–2010)

Among the most important figures in the history of water reclamation, Floyd Dominy has been praised, revered, and despised for his record as the longest-serving Commissioner of the US Bureau of Reclamation. Dominy's supporters described him as candid, smart, self-reliant, politically connected, and hard-driving, whereas critics called him an impulsive, reckless, and profane womanizer who wanted to harness all of the West's water resources for human use. Even the Bureau's official biography calls him "easily the most colorful Commissioner in Reclamation's history."

He was born December 24, 1909 on a 160-acre homestead in Hastings, Nebraska that did not have indoor plumbing. One of six children born to Charles and Emma May Dominy, he secretly married his teenage sweetheart, Alice Criswell, in Georgia. Dominy attended Hastings College for two years and studied civil engineering, then graduated from the University of Wyoming, Laramie in 1932 with a bachelor's degree in agricultural economics. One year later he added a master's degree from the school. Soon after graduation he became an agricultural agent in Campbell County, Wyoming. During the Depression he helped cattle ranchers who built small dams on local creeks fed by stormwater. In 1942, he served as coordinator for the Inter-American Affairs Bureau in Latin and Central America, where he worked to obtain raw materials for the war effort and to counter the Nazi influences in that part of the world. From there he moved on to assist several Pacific islands as they were recaptured from the Japanese, establishing small farms to feed American troops on Guam.

After the Second World War he landed work as a land settlement specialist with the Bureau of Reclamation. He steadily rose up through the ranks of the agency, serving as assistant commissioner in 1957 and associate commissioner in 1958 (a position that had never existed before). In May 1959, he was appointed to serve as commissioner of the agency.

Despite the fact that he was not an engineer, Dominy was the driving force behind the construction and completion of multiple dams, power plants, and the expansion of units within the Colorado River Storage Project, the Central Valley Project, the Central Arizona Project, and at Grand Coulee. He was a forceful, influential advocate in cultivating members of Congress throughout the administrations of presidents Eisenhower, Kennedy, Johnson, and Nixon. In *Cadillac Desert*, author Marc Reisner writes that Dominy kept a professional diary and lists of those who had supported and opposed him, frequently threatening to resign, going after a sitting governor, impugning the engineering profession, and defying his superiors. He vilified the Bureau's headquarters in Denver, and was audacious enough to have his plans for a new building included in a bill authorizing dams, later to be called the Dominy Building.

In the late 1960s and early 1970s, Dominy decided to take on the environmental movement and its titular leader, David Brower, who was the Sierra Club's first paid executive director. Brower and other conservationists had successfully blocked the appropriation for Utah's Echo Park dam in exchange for not opposing the construction of the Glen Canyon Dam, which created Lake Powell on the Utah/Arizona border. Glen Canyon, which began construction in 1956, has been called the most contested dam in America; others refer to it as one of the worst environmental sins in the West. Dominy, who called it his crowning jewel, made no apologies for building a dam that was 700 feet above the canyon floor, referring to Lake Powell as a drag strip for power boats. Despite six years' worth of archaeological salvage at a cost of about $1 million, the dam drowned Native American cultural and historical sites and destroyed important natural wildlife habitats. When dedicated on September 22, 1966, it was the world's highest steel-arch bridge, and its construction site/town was home to 4,500 residents, many of whom lived in trailers in what has been described as a boomtown on the frontier, Page, Arizona.

Dominy's exploits and lack of discretion were his undoing. Richard Nixon's Secretary of the Interior James Watt was assigned the task of telling Dominy that an FBI investigation had come back with a thick file of improprieties, and that although he was being fired, he was allowed to stay on at the Bureau long enough that his government pension would be vested. Upon leaving the Bureau, Dominy and his wife moved to Virginia, where they raised Angus cattle. She died in 1982, and he passed on April 20, 2010 at the age of 100. They were survived by two daughters, a son, and multiple grandchildren and great-grandchildren.

Dominy's legacy might be the completion of the Glen Canyon, Flaming Gorge, and Navajo dams as elements in the Colorado River Storage Project, and the Central Arizona Project. He was, for most of his years as commissioner, the public face of the Bureau of Reclamation, especially to members of Congress. But archaeologists also criticize Dominy for the destruction of over 2,250 important historical and Native American sites, including petroglyphs at Glen Canyon, at water projects across the American West.

Further Reading

Boxall, Bettina. 2010. "Floyd E. Dominy Dies at 100; Federal Water Official Oversaw Major Dam Projects." April 28. https://www.latimes.com/local/obituaries/la/floyd/dominy-20100428-story.html.

Martin, Douglas. 2010. "F.E. Dominy, Who Harnessed Water in the American West, is Dead at 100." *The New York Times*, April 28. https://www.nytimes.com/2010/04/29/us.29dominy.html.

McPhee, John. 1971. *Encounters with the Archdruid*. New York: Farrar, Straus, and Giroux.

U.S. Bureau of Reclamation. "Floyd E. Dominy, Commissioner, Bureau of Reclamation, 1959–1969." https://www.usbr.gov/history/CommissBiods/dominy.html.

John Samuel Eastwood (1857–1924)

Although a lot has been written about political figures who made impact on decisions about allocating water in the West, much less is known about the men (and the small number of women) who played pioneering roles in developing facilities and structures to divert and store water. Among those individuals, the designation "dam design specialist" applies to only a few, one of whom, John S. Eastwood, played a key role in western water engineering. His designs were called "avant garde," and "high tech," but he struggled to breach the interpersonal barriers of professional engineers, dam regulators, and businesses seeking traditional solutions to dam building within western hydraulic culture. Many of his most advanced designs were created after he had reached age sixty.

Eastwood was born into an immigrant Dutch family on a farmstead near Minneapolis in Scott County, Minnesota. He attended the University of Minnesota between 1877 and 1880, taking classes in what was then called the "Scientific Course," and then traveled to the Pacific Northwest in 1880 to work on the building of the Northern Pacific Railroad. He left that project around 1883 to move to Fresno, California, intending to work as an engineer and surveyor. Fresno had been founded in 1872 as a stop on the newly established Southern Pacific Railroad, but the small community had not yet been incorporated as a city.

Soon after his arrival, Eastwood became active in the effort to formally incorporate Fresno. He thought it would mean better municipal services for residents and help to promote growth of the city, the population of which was just over 1,000 in 1880. The need for municipal services had already become apparent in the area before Eastwood arrived. An entire block of Fresno was destroyed in 1882, with another large blaze a year later because firefighting resources were scarce and firefighters were mostly untrained. A ballot measure to incorporate was approved by the city's voters in 1885; the population had already tripled to more than 3,000 in that short time.

For his efforts during the incorporation efforts, Eastwood was appointed as Fresno's first city engineer and as secretary of the health board. He stayed in public service only a year before he decided to work on his own to learn more about the fields of engineering and hydroelectric power technology. He became familiar with California's San Joaquin Valley and its watershed, working for the San Joaquin Electric Company. When severe drought hit the region in the late 1890s, the utility suffered financially because it did not have the capital to build a dam and a reservoir on the San Joaquin River.

Eastwood moved on to the Pacific Light & Power Corporation, working on the upper San Joaquin's Big Creek system and developing the design for what would become the reinforced concrete multiple-arch dam. This model of dam building would be less expensive than conventional rock-filled gravity dams by using less concrete, as he demonstrated in 1908 when the Hume Lake Dam was built in the Sierra Nevadas. Two years later, he designed a larger dam in Southern California, the Big Bear Valley Dam, that would provide water for irrigation in the San Bernardino area, home to numerous citrus producers and field agriculture.

In an effort to develop a reputation for cost-effective dam building, he began designing smaller structures before receiving two commissions for larger ones in Salt Lake City and San Diego, followed by one for flood control for the city of Phoenix, and others for various irrigation districts in the West. He gained acclaim for his innovative structures that minimized the amount of concrete needed, reducing costs for the owners, using efficiency as their underlying principle. Disagreements with other dam designers led to what historian/biographer Donald C. Jackson has called "professional conflict." The multiple-arch dam designs Eastwood created were not nearly as massive in appearance as more conventional designs, and for some, did not give the public confidence in the structures' ability to withstand earthquakes or floods. The concept of structural art and visual interest proposed by historian David Billington resonates today but not during Eastwood's time, when engineers were considered technicians and scientists were considered the innovators.

Despite the industry's preference for massive concrete gravity dams, Eastwood continued to work on his unique dam designs as he expanded his clientele to Canada and Mexico. He had purchased a small ranch along the Kings River near Fresno in the 1890s, and spent time there with his wife Ella. While at the ranch in 1924, he suffered a heart attack while swimming in the river. In an ironic twist, Eastwood's ranch land is now covered with water from the lake of the Pine Flat Dam (not one of his own designs) built by the US Army Corps of Engineers and completed thirty years after his death. No multiple-arch dams were built after the Second World War. John S. Eastwood Elementary School in Big Creek, California is named in his honor.

Further Reading

Jackson, Donald C. 1995. *Building the Ultimate Dam: John S. Eastwood and the Control of Water in the West*. Lawrence: University of Kansas Press.

Whitney, Charles Allen. 1969. "John Eastwood: Unsung Genius of the Drawing Board." *Montana*, Vol. 19, No. 3: 38–49. https://www.jstor.org/stable/4517382.

Benjamin Harrison Eaton (1833–1904)

Although a substantial amount of history has been written about the impact of bringing irrigation to California and other arid regions in the West, less is published about the historical struggle to bring water to Colorado. Benjamin H. Eaton played an important role in Colorado's development of its water resources and irrigation policies before, during and after his tenure as the state's governor from 1885 to 1887.

Born in Coshocton, Ohio, he worked for the Ohio Line Railroad as a surveyor, helping in the building of road beds as westward expansion accelerated. He became familiar with the canals being built across the state as the population began to grow. In 1856, he married Delilah Wolfe and had a dual life of farming and teaching school. Delilah died during childbirth in 1857, and Eaton left his new son with his wife's family in West Bedford, Ohio. He relocated to the Iowa River valley to farm, but left in 1859 to join the Columbus City, Iowa-Pikes Peak Expedition as one of many men attracted to what began as the 1858 Gold Rush in Colorado.

The words "Gold Rush" usually are used in connection with California and the discovery of gold, but the second largest mining attraction of the mid nineteenth century was the Pikes Peak Gold Rush. The "Fifty-Niners" as they were called, referring to the peak of prospecting in 1859, brought an estimated 100,000 people to the region, which was, at that time, part of Kansas and Nebraska territory. The new arrivals displaced many of the native population in their hurry to get to the gold.

Colorado became a territory in 1861, and a state in 1876. Much of the prospecting fury focused near Denver, which served as a supply station for those heading to the gold mines. Others moved on along the South Platte River and an economic center called "The Richest Square Mile on Earth." However, gold prospecting in Colorado was not easy, complicated by the harsh winters, difficult terrain, and the fact that unlike California, most of the gold ore had to be hard rock mined—difficult and expensive to process. As a result, within a few years, Colorado mining was in a depression and most of the miners left the state.

Ben Eaton was not one of them. Although the other members of the Iowa expedition returned home, Eaton moved on to what was considered unchartered wilderness in San Juan County in northern Colorado, becoming one of the most extensive farmers in the state. From there, Eaton moved south to work along Mexican farmers on the Maxwell Land Grant in New Mexico, where he began learning about irrigation ditches. He joined Kit Carson and the New Mexico

Volunteers in 1862, and as the Civil War wound down, he returned to Ohio to visit his family, remarry, and in 1866, moved to Weld County, Colorado to homestead. With his familiarity with irrigation, he bought up thousands of acres of barren land from the Union Pacific Railroad, claimed water rights to the waters of the Cache le Poudre River, and created a share leasing irrigation system that made him a wealthy man. He developed the Millpower Canal in 1871, the Plumb, Larimer, and Weld Canal in 1877, the Highline Canal in 1880, and Windsor Reservoir in 1882, bringing water to northeastern Colorado's sugar beet industry and turning the South Platte River valley into a valuable agricultural region.

His political career began in 1866 when he was elected justice of the peace and served as a commissioner in Weld County. He became a Republican member of the Colorado territorial legislature in 1872, and in 1884, became the fourth governor of the state. He is considered a pioneer champion of water diversion, the creation of reservoirs and irrigation ditches, and proposals to reduce the waste of water. The town of Eaton, where he built a mill, is named in his honor. He died in Greeley, Colorado on October 29, 1904, leaving behind him a vision of what Colorado might look like if its leaders could obtain a sufficient amount of water to power the growing agriculture industry, build storage reservoirs, and followed the irrigation practices of the Spanish. He has been called a conservationist before his time.

Eaton is also known for being one of the founding officers of the Greeley Colony, also known as the Union Colony or the Union Temperance Colony. Named for New York newspaperman Horace Greeley, the colony was settled around 1870 by immigrants who sought to become part of an experimental utopian agricultural community. Their success at setting up irrigation systems, thanks to Eaton, and proximity to the railroad, attracted even more settlers, and the colony changed its name and was incorporated as Greeley in 1886. By the 1920s, Greeley manufactured one-fourth of all the sugar sold and consumed in the United States.

Further Reading

Abbot, Carl, et al. 2013. *Colorado: A History of the Centennial State*. 5th ed. Denver: University Press of Colorado.

Norris, Jane E., and Lee G. 1990. *Written in Water: The Life of Benjamin Harrison Eaton*. Athens: Ohio University Press.

Carl Hayden (1877–1972)

"Every federal program which has contributed to the development of the West—irrigation, power, reclamation—bears his mark." Those words, spoken by President John F. Kennedy at a dinner in Phoenix honoring Arizona Senator Carl Hayden, are just one expression of the regard the Arizona native is still held by so many. His work on securing approval, and more importantly, appropriations, for water projects in his home state are only part of a politically powerful career that changed much of the way the West approached water scarcity.

When Carl Hayden was born, Arizona was still a territory, not yet a state. His Connecticut-born father, Charles Hayden, had moved west for health reasons and homesteaded along the Salt River at Hayden's Ferry, now known as Tempe. His mother, Sallie Davis, was a schoolteacher who later became part of several family businesses, including a mercantile, flour mill, and the river ferry service that bore the Hayden name. His mother, who called him "the senator" as a boy because of his love of reading history and reciting great political speeches, was said to have told friends that someday Carl would be the greatest man in the US Senate. He attended local area schools, including the Arizona Territorial Normal School that is now Arizona State University. In 1896, Hayden enrolled at Stanford University, where he met his wife Nan Downing. Although Hayden had planned to attend law school after he graduated from Stanford, when his father died in 1900, Hayden dropped out of school to settle the estate and manage the family's businesses. He was successful as a manager, and moved his two sisters and his mother to Palo Alto, California, where the girls could attend college. He enlisted in the Arizona National Guard in 1903.

His political career began when Hayden was in his twenties, working his way up from local Democratic Party positions to a term as county treasurer, and then was elected as Maricopa County Sheriff. He made his first run for Congress in 1911 (just as Arizona was approaching statehood in 1912). Recognizing the importance of water to his largely agricultural district, he worked tirelessly over fifteen years in the House of Representatives to secure funding for reclamation projects and irrigation projects, especially the Salt River Project. He opposed the Colorado River Compact that apportioned the river's water, and initially opposed the Boulder Canyon Project. In 1926, he decided to run for the US Senate, using his platform as a candidate to oppose the Boulder Dam project, which was unpopular in his home state. But the appeal of the dam was growing, and he eventually dropped his opposition in favor of supporting dams and irrigation projects through the West. Notably, his first speech as a senator was a nine-hour-long filibuster on the floor of the Senate in 1928 opposing the Boulder Canyon Project. Although Congress enacted the project a few months later, Hayden did gain some concessions for his home state while continuing to oppose appropriations for the dam itself.

One of his achievements involving a local water project involved the transfer of the Salt River Project from the Bureau of Reclamation to a local government body, a model that would later be repeated throughout the West. He was unsuccessful, however, in his efforts to have a flood control dam built on the Gila River in 1914 when critics argued that Arizona had received more than its fair share of reclamation dollars. Instead, Hayden switched tactics and began including his reclamation appropriation requests in legislation that would benefit the local Pima Indians.

One of his most impressive accomplishments was the Central Arizona Project (CAP) to bring Colorado River water to the growing megalopolis that would become the corridor between Phoenix and Tucson. Proposed in 1947, the project did not gain congressional approval until 1968. He said that he considered his success in winning passage of the CAP legislation the most significant accomplishment of his lengthy career. Hayden also co-sponsored the legislation leading to the construction of the Glen Canyon Dam and other projects that were approved, in part, due to his position as chair of the powerful Senate Appropriations Committee for fourteen years.

Hayden also played a key role in the passage of the legislation establishing Grand Canyon National Park, and was a sponsor of the 19th Amendment that would give women the right to vote. But in addition to being called "the Dean of the Senate" he was also known as "the silent senator" because he rarely spoke at all on the Senate floor. After fifty-six years in Congress, Carl Hayden retired in 1969, and his Senate seat was won by Barry Goldwater. Hayden died in Mesa, Arizona in 1972. A Phoenix high school was named in his honor, as was the visitor center that overlooks Glen Canyon Dam.

Further Reading

August, Jack L., Jr. 1999. *Vision in the Desert: Carl Hayden and Hydropolitics in the American Southwest.* Fort Worth: Texas Christian University Press.

Kennedy, John F. 1961. "Remarks in Phoenix at the 50th Anniversary Dinner Honoring Senator Hayden." *The American Presidency Project.* https://www.presidency.ucsb.edu/documents/remarks-phoenix-the-50th-anniversary-dinner-honoring-senator-hayden.

Rice, Ross R. 1994. *Carl Hayden: Builder of the American West.* Lanham, MD: University Press of America.

Elwood Mead (1858–1936)

Lake Mead, located on the Nevada–Arizona border, is often in the headlines, either as a well-known area for boating and recreation, as one of the reservoirs that stores the water that irrigates much of the West, or because it holds back the water behind Hoover Dam. But the lake's namesake, Elwood Mead, is hardly a household name despite his close association with this body of water.

Elwood was born to Daniel and Lucinda Davis Mead on a farm along the Ohio River about an hour southeast of Cincinnati in Patriot, Indiana. He attended Purdue University, where he received a Bachelor of Science degree in agriculture in 1882 while working for the county as a surveyor. He received his doctoral degree in civil engineering from Iowa State College (now Iowa State University) in 1883, a Master of Science degree from Purdue in 1884, and an honorary Doctorate of Engineering degree from Purdue in 1904. Later in life he would receive several other honorary degrees.

After completing his master's degree, he worked for a year as an assistant engineer with the Army Corps of Engineers on improvements to the Wabash River before accepting a first-of-its-kind position in 1883 as a professor in irrigation engineering at Colorado State Agricultural College in Fort Collins and also became an assistant to the State Engineer. In 1884, he returned to Indiana to join a law firm in Lafayette, going back to Colorado in 1886. He moved to the territory of Wyoming in 1888 when he was appointed to the new position as territorial engineer, where he served until 1899. Mead also made an unlikely business partnership with William (Buffalo Bill) Cody in 1894. Both men supported the settlement of the West and hoped to attract New York investors to an irrigation project along the Shoshone River, a plan that failed to generate financial success.

Mead then moved again, this time to the University of California where he had been recruited to become a professor in the institutions and practice of irrigation. He was also asked to organize a new Department of Irrigation, which he headed. Once again, he also held a dual job working with the United States Department of Agriculture as a drainage expert, but resigned in 1907, traveling to Australia where he was chair of the State Rivers and Water Supply Commission from 1907 to 1915. That career change involved helping government officials create thirty-two irrigated settlements. Mead felt a similar irrigation strategy would work in the United States, and in 1917, convinced the state legislature in California to appropriate $260,000 for a 10,000-acre settlement project, the

Dunham Colony in Butte County. In 1915, Mead was also serving as professor of rural institutions at the University of California and served as chair of the state land settlement board, but the settlement project failed.

Despite those challenges, Mead was in demand internationally, and in 1923, he took a leave of absence from the university and the state board so he could travel to Palestine to advise officials on how they might irrigate the Jordan Valley for agricultural use. His visit only convinced him that the area was economically unstable and that there should be limited settlement there. He also traveled to Haiti and Cuba and advised officials in Mexico, Java, Canada, and South Africa who sought out his expertise. His interest in sustainable farming never gained him the accolades of his other accomplishments, but was of great personal interest to him throughout his life.

President Calvin Coolidge also became aware of Mead's talents, and in April 1924, offered to name him as head of the United States Bureau of Reclamation. The appointment was somewhat ironic, since Mead had opposed the Federal Reclamation Act of 1902 that would fund western irrigation projects. In his position as commissioner, he led the construction of the $48.8 million Boulder (later Hoover) Dam between 1931 and 1935, which at the time was the largest federal appropriation in the country. The dam was completed two years ahead of schedule. He also wrote extensively for engineering publications and was named to several professional organizations. Mead also aided in the development of Washington state's Grand Coulee Dam and the Owyhee Dam in Oregon, among others. In another nod to irony, Mead died in January 1936, just four months after Hoover Dam was dedicated. He and his wife, Florence Chase had three children and seven grandchildren.

The country's largest reservoir in terms of capacity, Lake Mead, was named in his honor a month after his death. At full capacity, the surface area is 157,418 acres. Lake Mead holds 9.3 trillion gallons of water with 759 miles of shoreline. The National Park Service entered into an agreement with the Bureau of Reclamation to manage the newly established Boulder Dam National Recreation Area in 1936. In 1947, the name was officially changed to Lake Mead National Recreation Area, and in 1964, Congress designated the recreation area as an official unit of the National Park Service.

Further Reading

"Elwood Mead." *Iowa State University Biographical Dictionary*. https://isubios.pubpub.org.pub/ppq0duz3v/release/1.

U.S. Bureau of Reclamation. Elwood Mead, Commissioner, Bureau of Reclamation, 1924–1936. https://www.usbr.gov/history/CommissBios/mead.html.
Water Education Foundation. "Elwood Mead." https://www.watereducation.org/aquapedia/elwood-mead.

William Mulholland (1855–1935)

It is doubtful that William Mulholland's parents had any idea that their son, born in Belfast, County Antrim, Ireland just after The Great Famine ended in 1852, would transform from a life as a Dublin jackeen—a young, irresponsible, ne'er do well—to become one of the most influential men in the history of the American West. He has been vilified for stealing precious water from the residents of California's Owens Valley to feed the explosive growth of Los Angeles, both in population and in economic importance to the wider American West. Self-taught as a civil engineer, he was even once considered a potential candidate for mayor of Los Angeles (he said he'd rather give birth to a porcupine backward).

He was one of four children—two brothers, Thomas and Hugh, and a sister, Sarah—born to Hugh Mulholland and Ellen Deakers Mulholland on September 11, 1855. His father worked as a guard for the Royal Mail. His mother died in 1862 when he was 7 years old, and his father remarried. While living in Dublin, he attended the O'Connell School run by the Christian Brothers, and as a young boy, he ran away from home. As a 15-year-old, Mulholland joined the British Merchant Marine, sailing to North America and the Caribbean until in 1874, he decided to leave a sailor's life behind to make his fortune and travel the United States. He eventually found his way to his uncle Hugh's home in Pittsburgh, where he read Charles Nordhoff's book *California: For Health, Pleasure, and Residence.* Local promoters had already begun to sell the frontier's virtues of sunshine, as a place where all kinds of ailments could be cured, and as a land of endless opportunity. It was enough to convince Willie and his brother Hugh to find their way to the land he envisioned, and in 1877, he arrived in Los Angeles.

Mulholland began working for the Los Angeles City Water Company in 1878 in the unglamorous position as a ditch tender. He worked his way up the career ladder with the company, first with construction projects, and then as superintendent. The city took control of the water company in 1902 at a time when the area was in the midst of a decade-long drought. Mulholland inherited a Los Angeles River that was nearly dry, mountain lakes that looked more like mudflats, a growing city population, and an undercapitalized municipal utility, the Los Angeles Department of Water and Power.

Mulholland married Lillian (Lillie) Ferguson in 1890 in Los Angeles. They had six children: Rose Ellen, William Perry, Thomas Ferguson, Lucile, Ruth, and Richard James Mulholland. Lillian died in 1915 at the age of forty-seven.

As a self-taught engineer who never went to college, he was given an honorary doctorate degree from the University of California in 1914. During his career, he was a member of the American Society of Civil Engineers, the Pacific Association of Consulting Engineers, the Engineers and Architects Association of Southern California, among others. He described himself as non-partisan when it came to politics, although he was a member of several political and progressive organizations. In some circles, he might have been called a utilitarian—the greater good for the greatest number—whereas others believe he exploited the few for personal gain. Biographer Les Standiford writes that Mulholland has not received sufficient credit for many of his other achievements that involved the growing city of Los Angeles. For example, the residents of the city used about 300 gallons of water per day in 1900. Concerned about sustainability long before the word had entered our environmental consciousness, Mulholland decided to introduce water meters that charged households for the water they used. The meters cut water use in half.

With the Department of Water and Power, he took on the challenge of finding new sources of water for the city's growing population. He and a colleague began investigating the Owens Valley east of the Sierra Nevada, where the expected snowmelt was seen as being reliable and clean. They secretly began purchasing land in Inyo County for a planned aqueduct that would run more than 250 miles west to Los Angeles. The project was kept a secret because it competed with a similar federal project that would have benefitted the Owens Valley's ranchers and farmers. Some biographers believe the land purchases were unethical, made for monetary gain in what might be considered insider trading by the two men. Then with the city's approval, Mulholland went forward with a massive public works project, and was able to win overwhelming voter support for funding it. The aqueduct planning began in 1906 and was completed on November 5, 1913.

Opposition to the Owens Valley project continued for several more years, mostly from local residents who felt that Mulholland had "stolen" their water to ship it south to Los Angeles. Bombings and protests characterized the California Water War, so Mulholland decided to build closer to the city itself to insure a reliable water supply. One of the projects, the St. Francis Dam, was built about 50 miles northwest of Los Angeles in San Francisquito Canyon, and completed in 1926. Two years later, just after midnight, the dam collapsed, killing more than 400 people and causing millions of dollars in damage as a result of the flooding. Although investigations and a coroner's inquest cleared Mulholland of criminal negligence, his decisions on where to build the dam were blamed for the disaster. He stayed on as a consultant to the Los Angeles Department of Water and Power, but formally resigned his position as Chief Engineer. After he died on July 22, 1935, his body lay in state in the rotunda of City Hall, and waters from the Los Angeles Aqueduct and the Colorado River aqueduct were stopped for 60 seconds as he was interred at Forest Lawn cemetery, where Lillian was also buried.

Further Reading

Mulholland, Catherine. 2002. *William Mulholland and the Rise of Los Angeles*. Berkeley: University of California Press.

Water Education Foundation. "William Mulholland." https://www.watereducation.org/aquapedia/william-mulholland.

"William Mulholland of Aqueduct Fame Dies." *Los Angeles Times*, July 23, 1935. https://www.latimes.com/local/obituaries/archives/la-me-william-mulholland-19350723-story.html.

Patricia Mulroy (1953–)

Patricia "Pat" Mulroy served from 1989 to 2014 as general manager of both the Las Vegas Valley Water District and the Southern Nevada Water Authority (SNWA), the regional agency responsible for acquiring, treating, and delivering water to 2 million residents of southern Nevada (including Las Vegas) and 40 million annual visitors. During her quarter-century in those positions, Mulroy became one of the most visible and influential shapers of water policy in the American West.

Mulroy was born Elizabeth Patricia Gallagher in 1953 in Frankfurt, Germany to an American father who was a civilian working with the Air Force, and a German mother who had grown up in India and spoke five languages. In 1974, she came to Las Vegas on a college scholarship to the University of Nevada where she received her bachelor's degree, followed by a master's degree in German Literature. From there, she attended Stanford University to pursue her doctoral studies, but she returned to Las Vegas doing intergovernmental affairs for Clark County as a junior management analyst. She became the county's first-ever justice court administrator, and in 1985, joined the Las Vegas Valley Water

District as its deputy general manager. Four years later she became the agency's first female general manager.

During Mulroy's tenure with the water district, and then with the SNWA she became a formidable and controversial figure in water policymaking. Part of the controversy stemmed from her 1991 decision to place a moratorium on any new building projects, both commercial ones like casinos, and residential subdivisions, because southern Nevada was running out of water. In her role as lead negotiator for the state's interests in Colorado River issues, especially during the droughts of the early 2000s, she helped usher in one of the most aggressive water conservation efforts in the country, combining both incentives and penalties with strong enforcement mechanisms. She also took part in the negotiations with Mexico that led to an agreement on agricultural water storage. They were part of what she calls "soft conservation" while at the same time, she advertised in Colorado newspapers that Nevada wanted to buy water from its neighbor state. She cites as her main accomplishment the creation of the SNWA and the 2007 agreements that basically threw out the concept of priority water rights among the Colorado River Basin states' water in favor of a shared allocation agreement.

Critics contend that Mulroy used her expertise and connections to push for whatever water was needed to keep Las Vegas expanding in both commercial and residential growth, with insufficient consideration for sustainable water use. In 1998, she was part of the team that pushed for the Southern Nevada Land Management Act that allowed the Department of the Interior to sell tens of thousands of federal acres to private developers, and then insisted that the SNWA get 10 percent of the sale of each lot that was sold to pay for the staff and infrastructure needed to supply water to the land. That generated almost $300 million, allowing SNWA to buy up valuable land and the aquifers underneath. The rapid growth created extensive suburbs and pushed the city's boundaries further and further out. To supply sufficient water for the growth and reduce dependence on the Colorado River, officials launched a controversial proposal for a $3.2 billion, 300-mile pipeline across much of the state, drawing water from eastern Nevada and sending it west to Las Vegas. The proposal died after a judge's decision in March 2020. The SNWA also built a $1.4 billion tunnel and pumping station below Lake Mead as part of its overall plan to make sure Las Vegas had sufficient water resources.

After retiring from the SNWD Mulroy started her own consulting firm, Sustainable Strategies, and became a fellow at the Brookings Institution. From there, she became a Senior Fellow for Climate Adaptation and Environmental

Policy and as a Practitioner in Residence for the Saltman Center for Conflict Resolution at the Boyd School of Law at the University of Nevada, Las Vegas. As a proponent of desalination, she suggested officials begin looking more at the Salton Sea in California. She has been active in the creation of the Springs Preserve in Las Vegas, a 180-acre cultural attraction that was once the site of the waters that were home to the native people of the area, as well as a stopping place for Mormon settlers and those traveling along the Old Spanish Trail. On a personal note, she and her husband Robert have two children.

Further Reading

Lustgarten, Abraham. 2015. "The 'Water Witch': Pat Mulroy Preached Conservation while Backing Growth in Las Vegas." *ProPublica*, June 2. https://www.propublica.org/article/killing-colorado-pat-mulroy0las-vegas-water-witch.

"Pat Mulroy: Secrets to Success on the Colorado River." *Municipal Water Leader*. Vol. 8, Issue 1, January 2021. https://municipalwaterleader.com/pat-mulroy-secrets-to-success-on-the-colorado-river.

University of Nevada, Las Vegas. "Business Hall of Fame Inductee: Pat Mulroy." https://www.unlv.edu/content/business-hall-fame-inductee-pat-mulroy.

Francis G. Newlands (1846–1917)

Francis G. Newlands was an attorney, banker, millionaire, land developer, and progressive, member of both the US House of Representatives and the Senate, who made a huge and enduring impact on water development policies in the American West. In that regard he is best known as one of the men responsible for promoting federal efforts to irrigate the West through laws such as the National Reclamation Act of 1902. But that accomplishment (and others) is tainted by his support for white supremacy and what he called "race complications."

Francis Griffith Newlands' southern roots were in Natchez, Mississippi, where he was born to Scottish immigrants James and Jessie Newlands. Newlands attended Yale University for one year before moving to Washington, DC, where he earned a law degree from Colombian College. He moved to San Francisco after being admitted to the bar and married Clara Adelaid Sharon, whose father William Sharon was one of the richest men in the West and also a US Senator from Nevada. The Newlands moved to San Francisco, where he partnered with his father-in-law to reopen the Bank of California. His wife was an active socialite but also raised four children, and when she died in childbirth in 1882, he was appointed trustee of the Sharon estate, making him a millionaire. He married a second time a few years later, but his sons both died in infancy.

He later moved back to Washington and established the Chevy Chase Land Company, buying up land in the area, operating a streetcar line to connect the suburb to the capitol. The community had numerous amenities, including an amusement park as well as schools and churches, but it also prohibited people of color and immigrants, as well as Jews, from moving in or using those amenities. In 1893, he decided to use the same development strategies to create the city of Burlingame, south of San Francisco, on property that had been part of the Sharon estate.

In 1893, he began a ten-year career representing Nevada in the US House of Representatives, and in 1902 lobbied for the creation of the Federal Reclamation Fund under the Newlands Reclamation Act. Passage of the legislation was due to the growing political influence of those lobbying for the federal government to undertake, as well as pay for through subsidies, infrastructure improvements in the West, including roads, railroads, and harbors. Their efforts were one of the hallmarks of the Progressive Movement. Pro-irrigation planks were inserted into both the Republican and Democratic Party platforms in 1900. A western congressional filibuster against a rivers and harbors bill favored by eastern interests who opposed western irrigation opened the door for the Act's passage. The legislation required that water users repay construction costs of projects from which they received benefits.

Shortly thereafter, the Secretary of the Interior established the United States Reclamation Service within the US Geological Survey (USGS). The new agency began assessing proposed water development projects in each western state that included federal land, and not coincidentally, Nevada benefitted from Newlands' support. In 1903, the Newlands Reclamation Project provided funding for irrigation projects in Washoe, Ormsby, Churchill, and Lyon counties in Nevada, including the building of dams and canals. The projects were funded initially from the sale of public lands. From the Act's passage in 1902 through 1907, when the Reclamation Service became an independent bureau separate from the USGS, the agency started about thirty projects in the West.

Newlands believed in an enhanced role of federal government in many sectors as part of a demonstration of the efficiency of controlling public utilities. For him, the federal government was to be the great engine of American life. He had a vision of the country as a harmonious, homogeneous society in which whites would continue to enjoy sweeping social, legal, political, and economic advantages over people of color. Newlands' white supremacist views were apparent in his efforts to repeal the Fifteenth Amendment, his support for training Negro children to be servants, anti-Japanese initiatives, and support for new immigration and citizenship restrictions.

Nevada historian William Rowley, who has studied Newlands' career, has written that the man's racial views were a mirror of his views about progress, including support for reclamation: "If the reclamation engineers could successfully bring water to the Nevada desert, proper Progressive legislation at the national level on matters of race could also engineer the viable and homogeneous society for the future and avoid the complications of racial and cultural diversity."

Newlands died in 1917 of heart failure in Washington, DC. His widow, Edith McCallister Newlands, provided the funds for a memorial fountain in Chevy Chase Circle on the border between Washington and Maryland in her husband's honor. The fountain was authorized by an Act of Congress and erected in 1933, and is a part of Rock Creek Park, a unit of the National Park Service. Although officials and residents have attempted to have the fountain renamed and rededicated, and a memorial plaque removed because of Newlands' racial views, the decision on what to do, if anything, lies with the National Park Service.

Further Reading

Newlands, Francis G. 2018. *Development of the West: Articles on Western Topics Entitled Watering the Desert, National Irrigation as a Social Problem, and Dry Farming.* London: Forgotten Books.

Rowley, William D. 1996. *Reclaiming the Arid West: The Career of Francis G. Newlands.* Bloomington: Indiana University Press.

U.S. National Park Service. "Senator Francis G. Newlands." https://www.nps.gov/people/senator-francis-g-newlands.htm.

John Wesley Powell (1834–1902)

There are numerous approaches for looking at the life of John Wesley Powell: his experiences during the Civil War; as the leader of the Colorado River Exploring Expedition; as a student of Native Americans and their culture; as an educator despite only a year's formal schooling; as a naturalist, scientist, and museum curator. All are important understanding the man most closely associated with the Colorado River.

"Wes" Powell was born on March 24, 1834 in Mount Morris, New York to English immigrants who named him after the co-founder of the Methodist faith. He was one of eight children, and the family moved often as he was growing up, settling in southern Ohio. The family did not fit well there, and in 1846, they moved to the Wisconsin territory. Powell decided he needed a more formal education, and after only a year, he decided to seek a job as a teacher, securing a position in a one-room school at $14 per month. From there he moved to Illinois and by 1859 he was employed as a school principal in Hennepin, Illinois.

When President Abraham Lincoln called for volunteers to support the Union cause, and at age twenty-seven Powell mustered into the Twentieth Illinois Infantry Regiment, becoming its "consulting engineer." He took leave from his duties to marry his half-cousin, Emma Dean, in November 1861. Just a few months later, Powell was injured by a Confederate musket ball at the Battle of Shiloh and had to have his arm amputated two inches below his elbow. He applied for a federal disability pension, but in 1865, decided he would accept a teaching position at Illinois Wesleyan University, leaving in his second year to become the curator of a small museum at Illinois State Normal University. He left that position in 1867 to lead a party of naturalists, including his wife Emma, who was an ornithologist and the only woman in the group, to Colorado.

The trip inspired Powell to look for financing for a second trip to the region the maps listed as "unexplored," and with support from Congress, the expedition left Chicago in June 1868. The small group spent the summer in Colorado, doing "altitude science," staying with members of the Ute tribe, and preparing for a trip down the Colorado River the following year.

The 1869 trip was planned as a government (and Smithsonian Institution) sanctioned scientific expedition that would map the two major rivers that had been explored, rather than studied, the Green and the Colorado. Powell and his party left on May 24 in four boats made in Chicago to Powell's specifications. The party traveled downriver, losing provisions, a boat, facing a fire in their camp that caused members of the crew to leave unexpectedly, and meanwhile collected fossil specimens, facing what some could argue was almost a mutiny, heavy rains, and finally, after sixty-nine days, made their way to the confluence of the Colorado River and the Virgin River. Powell retraced part of the 1869 route on a second expedition in the winter 1871–72. In 1875, at the urging of members of Congress, he published an account of the first expedition (interspersed with elements from the second) called *Exploration of the Colorado River of the West and Its Tributaries.*

Powell is perhaps best known, however, for his commentary on the reports that were being made to Congress and to Department of the Interior officials who sought more practical analyses of the areas of grass, timber, and mineral lands. In one 1874 letter to the House Committee on Public Lands, Powell wrote that "two-fifths of the country has a climate so arid that agriculture cannot be pursued without irrigation." In 1878 he published *Report on the Lands of the Arid Region of the United States*, in which he delineated his version of how the public lands might be managed, explained how climate divided the country into wet and dry, emphasized the need for irrigation districts so that settlers could build and manage their own water system, and warned that the region he explored was only capable of supporting limited numbers of people and economic activities. The report stirred up tremendous antagonism and outright hostility toward Powell, whose portrayal of a land with extremely limited water resources was a stark contrast to the inexhaustible Eden that many hoped to exploit.

Much of his later life was spent in Washington, DC. Powell was appointed by President Rutherford B. Hayes as a civilian member of the Public Lands Commission in 1879, but the commission's recommendations had no impact on Congress. In 1881, he became director of the U.S Geological Survey (USGS) while also heading the Bureau of Ethnology he had established at the Smithsonian in 1879. In the 1890s, Powell was a central figure in the debate whether the West could be amply irrigated. Boosters in Southern California pointed to the growing metropolis of Los Angeles, the agricultural riches of Riverside, and the potential of irrigation as the secret to prosperity. Powell gave a sober appraisal of the future, warning that no matter what efforts were made, "there is still not sufficient water to irrigate all this arid region."

In 1894, Powell announced his resignation from the USGS, telling President Grover Cleveland that the wounds he had suffered during the Civil War needed surgery. He had, at that point, lost much of his motivation and physical capacity. In mid-September 1902, he suffered a cerebral hemorrhage, and died in his bed in his bungalow in Maine. His body is buried in Arlington National Cemetery in Washington, DC, where the inscription reads, "Soldier. Explorer. Scientist."

Further Reading

Dolnick, Edward. 2001. *Down the Great Unknown: John Wesley Powell's 1869 Journey of Discovery and Tragedy through the Grand Canyon*. New York: HarperCollins.

Powell, J. W. 1879. *Report on the Lands of the Arid Region of the United States.* Washington, DC: Government Printing Office.
Stegner, Wallace Earle. 1954. *Beyond the Hundredth Meridian: John Wesley Powell and the Second Opening of the West.* Boston: Houghton Mifflin.

Marc Reisner (1948–2000)

Marc Reisner was an environmental journalist and author of *Cadillac Desert: The American West and Its Disappearing Water* (1986), listed as No. 61 on Modern Library's 100 Best Non-Fiction Books of the 20th Century. *Cadillac Desert* continues to be regarded today as a provocative and seminal work in explaining the West's relationship with water. The executive director of the Natural Heritage Institute called the book Reisner's "permanent monument," and others have ranked *Cadillac Desert* with Rachel Carson's *Silent Spring* in terms of importance and impact.

Reisner was born in St. Paul, Minnesota, the son of a lawyer and a scriptwriter, Konrad and Else, and had one sister, Jacqui. Reisner graduated with a bachelor's degree from Earlham College, a private liberal arts school in Richmond, Indiana, in 1970. The college was established in 1847 by the Religious Society of Friends and has a strong focus on Quaker values. He worked for a time in Washington, DC for two non-profit groups, Environmental Action and The Population Institute, before taking a position in New York as staff writer and communications director for the Natural Resources Defense Council (NRDC). After working with the NRDC at the apex of the growing environmental movement from 1972 to 1979, he was awarded an Alicia Patterson Journalism Fellowship that allowed him to focus on water policy. His research into the Bureau of Reclamation and the role of dams, excessive use of fertilizers, and water waste would form the basis of his best-selling work of non-fiction, *Cadillac Desert.* In 1997, the book was the basis for a Public Broadcasting System documentary that won a Columbia University Peabody Award. He wrote or co-authored two other books, including *Overtapped Oasis: Reform or Revolution for Western Water* (with Sarah Bates in 1989), and *Game Wars: The Undercover Pursuit of Wildlife Poachers* (1991). As a freelance writer, he also wrote for Colorado-based *High Country News*, as well as *The New York Times*, *The Los Angeles Times*, the *Washington Post*, and several magazines. His expertise and knowledge were sought after as a consultant and public speaker.

Toward the end of his career, Reisner turned to serving as a consultant to groups on other environmental issues, including the Pacific Coast Fishermen's Association, where he worked on efforts to remove antiquated dams that were interfering with salmon runs. That project led to a 2000 Pew fellowship which would have funded the restoration of native salmon habitats in California. He was one of two non-PhD's that received one of the prestigious awards in 2000.

He also taught as a distinguished visiting professor at the University of California's Davis campus, where he lectured on the interaction of human civilization and the environment. In addition to the honors that *Cadillac Desert* received, Reisner was a member of the board of the Natural Heritage Institute for six years, and he received a special commendation from the non-profit organization American Whitewater for his efforts to promote river conservation. He also was named an honorary trustee of the Tuolumne River Preservation Trust, a Rene Dubois Fellow, and the winner of the San Francisco Bay Institute's Bay Education Award.

At one point joking that he was "not too old to be making money," Reisner became involved with two private for-profit companies, joining the Vidler Water Company, which focuses on the development of reliable water supplies by identifying, acquiring, and developing water rights. Then in 1997, Reisner became interested in the development of migratory bird habitat in California's rice fields, co-founding the Ricelands Habitat Partnership, described as an eco-collaboration between the rice industry and environmental advocates in California's Sacramento Valley. The group promotes environmentally friendly agriculture, and helps develop waterfowl habitat. That led to a partnership to make fiberboard and other products from discarded and then compressed rice straw. The latter project seemed in some ways to contradict his opinions about growing rice in an arid climate, but it was countered by his conviction that the farmers he was working with were also creating habitat for migratory birds. Writing was never far from his interests, though. He was working on a third book dealing with California and natural disasters when he died.

A second edition of *Cadillac Desert* was printed in 1993, with a new postscript by Lawrie Mott, Reisner's wife, who he married in 1985. They had two daughters together, Ruthie and Margot. Until his death, she was a senior staff scientist at the Natural Resources Defense Council. Mott provides updates of water issues, and warns about the long-term impact of climate change. The book that Reisner was working on at the time of his death from colon cancer in 2000, *A Dangerous Place: California's Unsettling Fate*, was published posthumously in 2003.

In an article published three years after Reisner's death, the environmentalist/writer side of the author is contrasted with a much more human, and personal description of the man and the life he led. In interviews, his wife recalls that he was an incredible cook, preparing almost all the family's meals. He was a clotheshorse, even when hiking, wearing the very latest apparel. He liked BMW motorcycles. And the Three Stooges. And Volvos. His wife referred to him as Marco. He wanted to write about the impact of wildfires. But Reisner's name remains synonymous with *Cadillac Desert*, and it probably always will.

Further Reading

Marston, Ed. 2000. "Farewell, Marc Reisner." *High Country News*, August 14. https://www.hcn.org/issues/183/5929.

Oliver, Myrna. 2000. "Marc Reisner, Environment Writer, Dies." *Los Angeles Times*, July 25. https://www.latimes.com/archives/laxpm-2000-jul-25-mn-58530-story.html.

Reed, Christopher. 2000. "Marc Reisner: The Man Who Blew the Whistle on America's Western Water Scandal." *The Guardian*, July 27. https://www.theguardian.com/news/2000/jul/28/guardianobituaries.

Reisner, Marc. 1986. *Cadillac Desert: The American West and Its Disappearing Water*. New York: Viking Press.

Philip David Swing (1884–1963)

Anyone who has visited San Diego, California may recall the beautiful fountain near the San Diego Civic Center and Community Concourse. There is a plaque there, dedicated by city officials and benefactors in 1967, with an image of a man that honors one of California's own heroes, Phil Swing, as the Father of Boulder Dam, the All-American Canal, the San Diego Aqueduct, and the Metropolitan Water District. But the fountain is now gone, replaced by a desert garden and signage explaining that in 1933, Swing introduced legislation that would transfer federal lands to the state of California to create the Anza-Borrego Desert State Park. Now California's largest state park, and the nation's first desert park, it took eight years for the park to gain sufficient funding and political and public support before it was dedicated. Whether the cacti and succulents honor Swing for that achievement, or the space was repurposed because of drought conditions in San Diego, Swing has failed to achieve the prominence of many other western water pioneers.

Born in San Bernardino, California, the son of James Wesley Swing and Mary Frances Garner, he was one of six children—five boys and one girl. He attended public schools before enrolling at Stanford University in 1905. In an early career that would mirror that of his colleague, Carl Hayden of Arizona, Phil Swing joined the California National Guard, serving from 1906 to 1908, and returned to his hometown. In 1907, after being admitted to the state bar, he joined the law office of his older brother, Ralph Swing, who also served as a member of the California state senate. The younger Swing subsequently moved to a new political jurisdiction, Imperial County, southeast of San Bernardino, when it was formed by the state legislature in 1907. There he served as acting district attorney in 1908 and then district attorney from 1911 to 1915. It was in this position with the county that Swing began providing guidance on a new model for an irrigation district that would be owned by the public, rather than a private company, becoming the Imperial Irrigation District's legal counsel while also working in private practice in El Centro at his firm Eshleman & Swing from 1907 to 1912. He married Nell Cremeens in 1912, and they had two daughters, Margaret and Phyllis. During World War I he was a private in the Army Officers Training Camp in Kentucky. After serving as district attorney, Swing was appointed as a judge on the county's superior court from 1919 to 1921, running successfully for Congress and serving six terms from 1921 to 1933. The district included both Imperial and San Diego counties, allowing him to represent constituents deeply interested in water resources, agriculture, and the growth in the region.

Congressman Swing's otherwise obscure career in the US House of Representatives included serving as chair of the Committee on Expenditures in the Post Office Department, and the Committee on Public Lands, where he sponsored legislation in 1927 to direct the Secretary of the Interior to allow public lands to be used to build highways in Imperial County. But his most notable achievement had nothing to do with post offices. He became an advocate in support of the Boulder Canyon Project, resulting in legislation authorizing the dam in 1928. Recognizing southern California's increasing need for water as the population in the region expanded, Swing helped establish the Boulder Dam Association and the Colorado River Aqueduct Association, partnering with California Senator Hiram Johnson on legislation that bears their names. As Beverly Moeller notes in her biography of Swing, the congressman had to overcome opposition to the Boulder Dam from developers, power companies, and the state of Arizona, as well as what she calls bureaucratic inertia and easterners uninterested in the project. In that role, she writes, Swing really became the father of Boulder Dam. In 1947, a partisan Congress renamed the structure as Hoover Dam in honor of the president, who had initially opposed the project. But it was Swing who is credited with writing the legislation and stipulating the design of the dam and lobbying for its funding. Swing also became an important congressional player in virtually every major project involving water and power production in the Southwest, including interstate and international agreements and compacts and water litigation.

Swing chose not to run for re-election in 1932, and after leaving Washington, DC he moved to San Diego and became a partner in the law firm of Stearns, Luce, Forward, and Swing. As a lawyer and advocate, he represented the state of California, both the City and County of San Diego, and the Imperial Irrigation District in matters related to the Colorado River. His expertise in water issues led to an appointment to the California State Water Resources Board in 1945, where he served until 1958. Buried in San Diego, his quiet legacy includes an elementary school named after him in Brawley, California.

Further Reading

Moeller, Beverly Bowen. 1971. *Phil Swing and Boulder Dam*. Berkeley: University of California Press.

San Diego History Center. "Hon. Philip David Swing (1884–1963)." https://www.sandiegohistory.org/archives/biographysubject/philswing.

Mark Wilmer (1903–1994)

Mark Wilmer's father, John Bernard Wilmer, was a farmer when Mark Bernard Wilmer was born to Elizabeth Johnston Wilmer in East Troy, Wisconsin on July 18, 1903. Mark was the sixth of seven children, growing up in the small community of about 300 people, Honey Creek, where his parents had purchased a dairy and farm in 1904, and where he went to public school. Although Honey Creek was primarily made up of Baptist farmers, the Wilmers were Catholic, so Mark took the milk train (the train that carried dairy milk all the way to Chicago) the seven miles to parochial school in Burlington, Wisconsin for a fare of 10 cents. An average student in school, but a voracious reader, Wilmer's parents encouraged him to consider college when he graduated from high school in 1922. His work experience at that time, in addition to working on his parents' farm, was driving an ice cream truck in Burlington. Wilmer would rise from this humble setting to become one of the least known but most important figures in securing water for Arizona.

He left home to work in Milwaukee, and spent two years studying pre-law at Marquette University. He would later recall that he had an older brother who had gone to law school, but he never was quite sure why he was attracted to the field. A dean at the university discouraged Mark from going to Marquette's law school, so he applied and was accepted to Georgetown University, which he attended from 1926 to 1929. During the summer, he returned to Honey Creek to work on the farm to pay for his tuition. After graduation from Georgetown, he and an acquaintance headed to Texas with their diplomas and in October 1929, after driving through the state trying to decide where to live, decided to open a law practice in San Angelo. When the stock market imploded, the two men opened a satellite office in the oil field area of Iraan, Texas. The mother of a Georgetown classmate operated a boarding house in Iraan, and her son had opened a practice in Phoenix, Arizona, she told him, so Wilmer headed there to visit. With the promise of a job through another connection, he passed the Arizona Bar Examination in May 1931, and began working on bonds for water resource development infrastructure. He later served as a deputy county attorney, and was then appointed as Assistant Attorney General. In 1938, Wilmer joined the law firm of Snell, Strouss & Salmon. He had been on Frank Snell's radar with a reputation as an outstanding trial attorney—a label he was about to enhance. Over the years, he and the firm did work related to water rights in the state.

As the US Bureau of Reclamation notes, "You won't see his name on any libraries or government buildings. There aren't any freeways or airports named after him. You would even be hard pressed to find any mention of him in Arizona history books. However, Mark Wilmer is probably one of the most important people in Arizona's history. He is largely responsible for securing Arizona's future."

Those accolades from the Bureau are because of a US Supreme Court case filed in 1952 in which Wilmer played the key role arguing on behalf of the state of Arizona. Wilmer, representing the State of Arizona, filed a complaint before the US Supreme Court arguing that the justices should apportion the waters of the Colorado River, and his job was to ensure that the state's water rights were protected. Since 1922 there had been disputes between the Upper Basin states and the Lower Basin states, and California refused to settle matters with Arizona despite petitions to the Supreme Court that had been filed four times.

The state of Arizona's lawyers changed lawyers early on after disagreements about how the case was being handled. Arizona's governor, Ernest McFarland, called Wilmer and Snell, who had been recommended to him by the state's Bar Association, for a meeting about the case. In an oral history session with the Arizona Historical League in 1994, just before he died, Wilmer said the governor did not ask them if he could win the case, just whether or not he would take it. Wilmer said that he felt that at least part of what the state had tried to prove wasn't provable. "I had a good feeling I could win it. But I wasn't betting any money on it," he said.

Wilmer completely changed the approach that the previous legal team had been taking, and filed a Change of Position document with the court. The actual trial in the case, *Arizona v. California*, lasted more than two years with over 340 witnesses and thousands of exhibits. One judge had passed away, and a second judge was appointed to continue the hearings. The case was not decided until 1963—eleven years after it had been filed, becoming the longest case in the court's history. In the end, Wilmer and Arizona both won what was considered to be an equitable share of the Colorado River. That share then led to the construction of the Central Arizona Project (CAP), which would allow both Phoenix and Tucson to continue to grow with a sufficient amount of water resources (discussed in Chapter 2).

In addition to his career as an attorney, Wilmer served as president of the Chamber of Commerce in Phoenix in 1958, and he received numerous professional awards. He was considered by many to be the Dean of Arizona's trial lawyers long before his death on December 8, 1994. Wilmer was posthumously honored by officials of the CAP by having the pumping plant in Parker, Arizona that takes Arizona's share out of the Colorado named in his honor.

Further Reading

August, Jack L., Jr. 2007. *Dividing Western Waters: Mark Wilmer and Arizona v. California*. Fort Worth: Texas Christian University Press.

n.a. 1994. "Mark B. Wilmer." *Arizona Republic*, December 11. https://www.newspapers.com/article/arizona-republic-mark-b-wilmer-obituary/14645169.

Lorig, Zona Davis. 2004. "Mark Wilmer Oral History." Arizona Historical Society. https://www.historicalleague.org/wilmer/%20m-ohOf6o6d1-cd1f-45dc-bc9a-de51Coc33867.pdf.

5

Data and Documents

Figure 5.1 Colorado River Allocation by State, Upper Basin

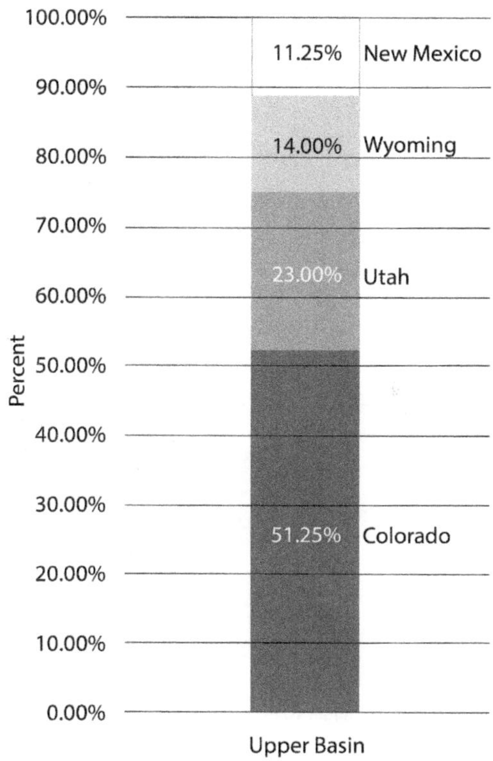

Source: U.S. Bureau of Reclamation. Upper Colorado River Basin Compact, 1948. https://www.usbr.gov/lc/region/g1000/lawofrvr.html

---

President Theodore Roosevelt and John Muir on Glacier Point in Yosemite Valley, CA, in 1903. Both men were dedicated conservationists. Roosevelt understood the need to protect forests in order to protect water supplies. Muir fought, but failed, to prevent the flooding of the Hetchy Hetchy Valley in the creation of a reservoir for the city of San Francisco. (Library of Congress.)

Figure 5.2 Colorado River Allocation by State, Lower Basin

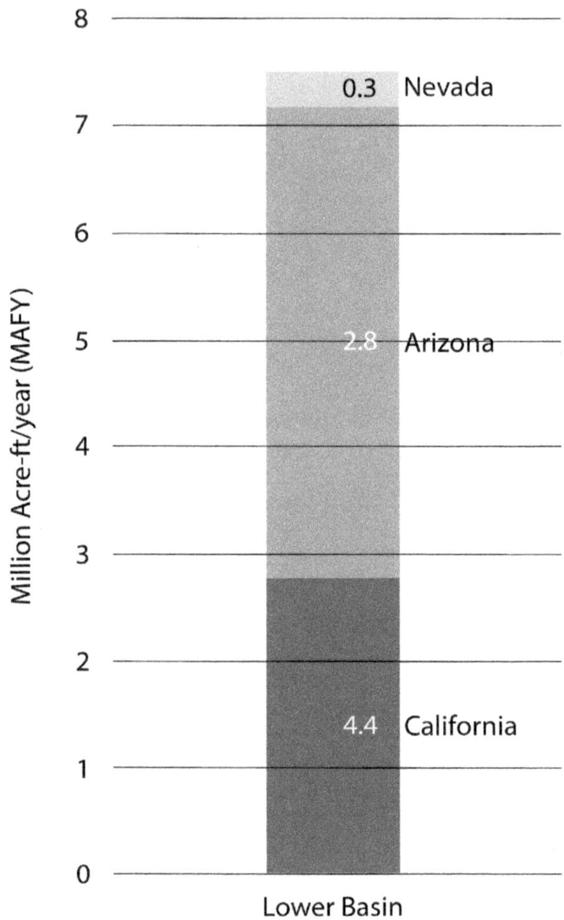

Source: U.S. Bureau of Reclamation. Boulder Canyon Project Act, 1928. https://www.usbr.gov/lc/region/g1000/pdfiles/bcpact.pdf.

Table 5.1 Interstate Water Allocation Agreements of the West

Arkansas River Compact of 1949 (Kansas and Colorado)
Bear River Compact of 1978 (Idaho, Wyoming, and Utah)
Belle Fourche River Compact of 1943 (South Dakota and Utah)
Colorado River Compact of 1922 (Arizona, California, Colorado, Nevada, New Mexico, Utah, and Wyoming)
Costilla Creek Compact of 1944 (Colorado and New Mexico)
Klamath River Basin Compact of 1957 (California and Oregon)
La Plata River Compact of 1922 (Colorado and New Mexico)
Pecos River Compact of 1948 (New Mexico and Texas)
Republican River Compact of 1942 (Colorado, Kansas, and Nebraska)
Rio Grande Interstate Compact of 1938 (Colorado, New Mexico, and Texas)
Sabine River Compact of 1953 (Louisiana and Texas)
Snake River Compact of 1949 (Idaho and Wyoming)
South Platte River Compact of 1923 (Colorado and Nebraska)
Upper Colorado River Compact of 1948 (Arizona, Colorado, New Mexico, Utah, and Wyoming)
Upper Niobrara River Compact of 1962 (Nebraska and Wyoming)
Yellowstone River Compact of 1950 (Montana, North Dakota, and Wyoming)

Table 5.2 WaterSense Statistics and Facts

- According to a 2014 Government Accountability Report, 40 out of 50 state water managers expect water shortages under average conditions in some portion of their states over the next decade.
- Each American uses an average of 82 gallons of water a day at home (USGS, Estimated Use of Water in the United States in 2015).
- We can all use at least 20 percent less water by installing water-efficient fixtures and appliances.
- The average family spends more than $1,000 per year in water costs, but can save more than $380 annually from retrofitting with WaterSense-labeled fixtures and ENERGY STAR certified appliances.

WaterSense and Water Savings

- WaterSense labels products that are 20 percent more water-efficient and perform as well as or better than standard models.
- The average family can save 13,000 gallons of water and $130 in water costs per year by replacing all old, inefficient toilets in their home with WaterSense -labeled models.
- Replacing old, inefficient bathroom faucets and aerators with WaterSense-labeled models can save the average family $250 in water and electricity costs over the faucets' lifetime.
- Replacing showerheads with WaterSense-labeled models can reduce the average family's water and electricity costs by $70 and can save the average family more than 2,700 gallons of water per year, equal to the amount of water needed to wash 88 loads of laundry.
- Giving a home's main bathroom a high-efficiency makeover by installing a WaterSense-labeled toilet, showerhead, and faucet aerator can pay for itself in as little as 1 year.
- Replacing a clock-based controller with a WaterSense-labeled irrigation controller can reduce an average home's irrigation water use by up to 30 percent and can save an average home up to 15,000 gallons of water annually.

Water Stats

- The average family can waste 180 gallons per week, or 9,400 gallons of water annually, from household leaks. That's equivalent to the amount of water needed to wash more than 300 loads of laundry.
- Household leaks can waste approximately nearly 900 billion gallons of water annually nationwide. That's equal to the annual household water use of nearly 11 million homes.
- Running the dishwasher only when it's full can eliminate one load of dishes per week and save the average family nearly 320 gallons of water annually.
- Turning off the tap while brushing your teeth can save 8 gallons of water per day and, while shaving, can save 10 gallons of water per shave. Assuming you brush your teeth twice daily and shave 5 times per week, you could save nearly 5,700 gallons per year.

- Letting your faucet run for five minutes while washing dishes can waste 10 gallons of water and uses enough energy to power a 60-watt light bulb for 18 hours.
- Outdoor water use accounts for more than 30 percent of total household water use, on average, but can be as much as 60 percent of total household water use in arid regions.
- If the average-sized lawn in the United States is watered for 20 minutes every day for 7 days, it's like running the shower constantly for 4 days or taking more than 800 showers. That's equivalent to the amount of water needed for the average family to take 1 year's worth of showers.
- As much as 50 percent of the water we use outdoors is lost due to wind, evaporation, and runoff caused by inefficient irrigation methods and systems. A household with an automatic landscape irrigation system that isn't properly maintained and operated can waste up to 25,000 gallons of water annually.
- When hiring a professional to install or audit your landscape irrigation system, be sure he or she is certified by a WaterSense-labeled irrigation program. If the system is well managed, a household's irrigation water use can be reduced by 15 percent, or nearly 7,600 gallons of water, annually. That's the amount of water needed to take 480 showers.

Source: U.S. Environmental Protection Agency. *WaterSense: Statistics and Facts.* https://www.epa.gov/watersense/statistics-and-facts. Updated April 2, 2024.

President Theodore Roosevelt, First Annual Message to the Congress (1901): Excerpt

On December 3, 1902, in his first opportunity to address Congress after the assassination of President McKinley, newly sworn in President Theodore Roosevelt outlined an expansive list of policies and projects that reflected not only his personal views about conservation but also his perspective on presidential power. In this excerpt from that speech, he focuses on the role of the national government in reclaiming the arid deserts of the West. Not only does the president outline his view that the government be responsible for building dams and reservoirs, but also irrigation systems as part of the national interest, rather than for the personal gain of settlers. Most importantly, he shows his support for water laws that would tie rights to use, rather than perpetual rights.

The forests alone cannot, however, fully regulate and conserve the waters of the arid region. Great storage works are necessary to equalize the flow of streams and to save the flood waters. Their construction has been conclusively shown to be an undertaking too vast for private effort. Nor can it be best accomplished by the individual States acting alone. Far-reaching interstate problems are involved; and the resources of single States would often be inadequate. It is properly a national function, at least in some of its features. It is as right for the National Government to make the streams and rivers of the arid region useful by engineering works for water storage as to make useful the rivers and harbors of the humid region by engineering works of another kind. The storing of the floods in reservoirs at the headwaters of our rivers is but an enlargement of our present policy of river control, under which levees are built on the lower reaches of the same streams.

The Government should construct and maintain these reservoirs as it does other public works. Where their purpose is to regulate the flow of streams, the water should be turned freely into the channels in the dry season to take the same course under the same laws as the natural flow.

The reclamation of the unsettled arid public lands presents a different problem. Here it is not enough to regulate the flow of streams. The object of the Government is to dispose of the land to settlers who will build homes upon it. To accomplish this object water must be brought within their reach.

The pioneer settlers on the arid public domain chose their homes along streams from which they could themselves divert the water to reclaim their holdings. Such opportunities are practically gone. There remain, however, vast areas of public land which can be made available for homestead settlement, but only by reservoirs and main-line canals impracticable for private enterprise. These irrigation works should be built by the National Government. The lands reclaimed by them should be reserved by the Government for actual settlers, and the cost of construction should so far as possible be repaid by the land reclaimed. The distribution of the water, the division of the streams among irrigators, should be left to the settlers themselves in conformity with State laws and without interference with those laws or with vested fights. The policy of the National Government should be to aid irrigation in the several States and

Territories in such manner as will enable the people in the local communities to help themselves, and as will stimulate needed reforms in the State laws and regulations governing irrigation.

The reclamation and settlement of the arid lands will enrich every portion of our country, just as the settlement of the Ohio and Mississippi valleys brought prosperity to the Atlantic States. The increased demand for manufactured articles will stimulate industrial production, while wider home markets and the trade of Asia will consume the larger food supplies and effectually prevent Western competition with Eastern agriculture. Indeed, the products of irrigation will be consumed chiefly in upbuilding local centers of mining and other industries, which would otherwise not come into existence at all. Our people as a whole will profit, for successful home-making is but another name for the upbuilding of the nation.

The necessary foundation has already been laid for the inauguration of the policy just described. It would be unwise to begin by doing too much, for a great deal will doubtless be learned, both as to what can and what cannot be safely attempted, by the early efforts, which must of necessity be partly experimental in character. At the very beginning the Government should make clear, beyond shadow of doubt, its intention to pursue this policy on lines of the broadest public interest. No reservoir or canal should ever be built to satisfy selfish personal or local interests; but only in accordance with the advice of trained experts, after long investigation has shown the locality where all the conditions combine to make the work most needed and fraught with the greatest usefulness to the community as a whole. There should be no extravagance, and the believers in the need of irrigation will most benefit their cause by seeing to it that it is free from the least taint of excessive or reckless expenditure of the public moneys.

Whatever the nation does for the extension of irrigation should harmonize with, and tend to improve, the condition of those now living on irrigated land. We are not at the starting point of this development. Over two hundred millions of private capital has already been expended in the construction of irrigation works, and many million acres of arid land reclaimed. A high degree of enterprise and ability has been shown in the work itself; but as much cannot be said in reference to the laws relating thereto. The security and value of the homes created depend largely on the stability of titles to water; but the majority of these rest on the uncertain foundation of court decisions rendered in ordinary suits at law. With a few creditable exceptions, the arid States have failed to provide for the certain and just division of streams in times of scarcity. Lax and uncertain laws have made it possible to establish rights to water in excess of actual uses or necessities, and many streams have already passed into private ownership, or a control equivalent to ownership.

Whoever controls a stream practically controls the land it renders productive, and the doctrine of private ownership of water apart from land cannot prevail without causing enduring wrong. The recognition of such ownership, which has been permitted to grow up in the arid regions, should give way to a more enlightened and larger recognition of the rights of the public in the control and disposal of the public water supplies. Laws founded upon conditions obtaining in humid regions, where water is too abundant to justify hoarding it, have no proper application in a dry country.

In the arid States the only right to water which should be recognized is that of use. In irrigation this right should attach to the land reclaimed and be inseparable therefrom. Granting perpetual water rights to others than users, without compensation to the public, is open to all the objections which apply to giving away perpetual franchises to the public utilities of cities. A few of the Western States have already recognized this, and have incorporated in their constitutions the doctrine of perpetual State ownership of water.

The benefits which have followed the unaided development of the past justify the nation's aid and co-operation in the more difficult and important work yet to be accomplished. Laws so vitally affecting homes as those which control the water supply will only be effective when they have the sanction of the irrigators; reforms can only be final and satisfactory when they come through the enlightenment of the people most concerned. The larger development which national aid insures should, however, awaken in every arid State the determination to make its irrigation system equal in justice and effectiveness that of any country in the civilized world. Nothing could be more unwise than for isolated communities to continue to learn everything experimentally, instead of profiting by what is already known elsewhere. We are dealing with a new and momentous question, in the pregnant years while institutions are forming, and what we do will affect not only the present but future generations.

Source: Roosevelt, Theodore. First Message to Congress, December 3, 1901. Available online at https://www.presidency.ucsb.edu/documents/first-annual-message-16

Newlands Reclamation Act (1902): Excerpt

Named after its primary sponsor in Congress, Representative Francis Newlands of Nevada, the Newlands Reclamation Act (also known as the National Reclamation Act) was the federal government's response to the demands of western settlers for a system that would store the runoff water from precipitation to irrigate their fields. The term "reclamation" became widely used as a method for reclaiming the arid lands of the West, driven by the irrigation movement that had gained strength at the turn of the century. Although there was strong support for some type of government assistance in developing irrigation and water storage projects, debates simmered over whether responsibility should rest with the state or federal government. The measure was strongly supported by President Theodore Roosevelt, who traveled widely in the region and was convinced that the West could be settled if water was made available. This legislation was somewhat unique because it not only called for the creation of a United States Reclamation Service within the US Geological Survey, but the act also called for money from the sale of federal public lands to be set aside in a Reclamation Fund to construct and maintain irrigation projects, rather than paid for by the US Treasury. The act is credited with giving the federal government the means for beginning a wave of dam building that brought both economic and cultural changes to the West.

An Act Appropriating the Receipts from the sale and disposal of public lands in certain States and Territories to the construction of irrigation works for the reclamation of arid lands.

Be it enacted by the Senate and House of Representatives of the United States of America in Congress assembled, That all moneys received from the sale and disposal of public lands in Arizona, California, Colorado, Idaho, Kansas, Montana, Nebraska, Nevada, New Mexico, North Dakota, Oklahoma, Oregon, South Dakota, Utah, Washington, and Wyoming, beginning with the fiscal year ending June thirtieth, nineteen hundred and one, including the surplus of fees and commissions in excess of allowances to registers and receivers, and excepting the five per centum of the proceeds of the sales of public lands in the above States set aside by law for educational and other purposes, shall be, and the same are hereby, reserved set aside, and appropriated as a special fund in the Treasury to be known as the "reclamation fund," to be used in the examination and survey for and the construction and maintenance of irrigation works for the storage, diversion, and development of waters for the reclamation or arid and semiarid lands in the said States and Territories, and for the payment of all other expenditures provided for in this Act: Provided, That in case the receipts from the sale and disposal of public lands other than those realized from the sale and disposal of lands referred to in this section are insufficient to meet the requirements for the support of agricultural colleges in the several States and Territories, under the Act of August thirtieth, eighteen hundred and ninety, entitled "An Act to apply a portion of the proceeds of the public lands to the more complete endowment and support of the colleges for the benefit of agriculture and the mechanic arts, established under the provisions of an Act of Congress approved July second, eighteen hundred and sixty-two," the deficiency, if any, in the sum necessary for the support of the said colleges shall be provided for from any moneys in the Treasury not otherwise appropriated.

SEC. 2. That the Secretary of the Interior is hereby authorized and directed to make examinations and surveys for, and to locate and construct, as herein provided, irrigation works for the storage, diversion, and development of waters, including artesian wells, and to report to Congress at the beginning of each regular session as to the results of such examinations and surveys, giving estimates of cost of all contemplated works, the quantity and location of the lands which can be irrigated therefrom, and all facts relative to the practicability of each irrigation project; also the cost of works in process of construction as well as of those which have been completed.

SEC. 3. That the Secretary of the Interior shall, before giving the public notice provided for in section four of this Act, withdraw from public entry the lands required for any irrigation works contemplated under the provisions of this Act, and shall restore to public entry any of the lands so withdrawn when, in his judgment, such lands are not required for the purposes of this Act; and the Secretary of the Interior is hereby authorized, at or immediately prior to the time of beginning the surveys for any contemplated irrigation works, to withdraw from entry, except under the homestead laws, any public lands believed to be susceptible of irrigation from said works: Provided, That all lands entered and entries made under the homestead laws within areas so withdrawn during such withdrawal shall be subject to all the provisions, limitations, charges, terms, and conditions of this Act; that said surveys shall be prosecuted diligently to completion, and upon the completion thereof, and of the necessary maps, plans, and estimates of cost, the Secretary of interior shall determine whether or not said project is practicable and advisable, and if determined to be impracticable or unadvisable he shall thereupon restore said lands to entry; that public lands which it is proposed to irrigate by means of any contemplated works shall be subject to entry only under the provisions of the homestead laws in tracts of not less than forty nor more than one hundred and sixty acres, and shall be subject to the limitations, charges, terms, and conditions herein provided: Provided, That the commutation provisions of the homestead laws shall not apply to entries made under this Act.

SEC. 4. That upon the determination by the Secretary of the Interior that any irrigation project is practicable, he may cause to be let contracts for the construction of the same, in such portions or sections are available in the reclamation fund, and irrigable under such project, and limit of area per entry which limit shall represent the acreage which, in the opinion of the Secretary, may be reasonably required for the support of a family upon the lands in question; also of the charges which shall be made per acre upon the said entries, and upon lands in private ownership which may be irrigated by the waters of the said irrigation project, and the number of annual installments, not exceeding ten, in which such charges shall be paid and the time when such payments shall commence. The said charges shall be determined with a view of returning to the reclamation fund the estimated cost of construction of the project, and shall be apportioned equitably: Provided, That in all construction work eight hours shall constitute a day's work, and no Mongolian labor shall be employed thereon.

SEC. 5. That the entryman upon lands to be irrigated by such works shall, in addition to compliance with the homestead laws, reclaim at least one-half of the total irrigable area of his entry for agricultural purposes, and before receiving patent for the lands covered by his entry shall pay to the Government the charges apportioned against such tract, as provided in section four. No right to the use of water for land in private ownership shall be sold for a tract exceeding one hundred and sixty acres to any one landowner, and no such sale shall be made to any landowner unless he be an actual bona fide resident on such land, or occupant thereof residing in the neighborhood of said land, and no such right shall permanently attach until all payments therefor are made. The annual installments shall be paid to the receiver of the local land office of the district in which the land is situated, and a failure to make any two payments when due shall render the entry subject to cancellation, with the forfeiture of all rights under this Act, as well as of any moneys already paid thereon. All moneys received from the above sources shall be paid into the reclamation fund. Registers and receivers shall be allowed the usual commissions on all moneys paid for lands entered under this Act.

SEC. 6. That the Secretary of the Interior is hereby authorized and directed to use the reclamation fund for the operation and maintenance of all reservoirs and irrigation works constructed under the provisions of this Act: Provided, That when the payments required by this Act are made for the major portion of the lands irrigated from the waters of any of the works herein provided for, then the management and operation of such irrigation works shall pass to the owners of the lands irrigated thereby, to be maintained at their expense under such form of organization and under such rules and regulations as may be acceptable to the Secretary of the Interior: Provided, That the title to and the management and operation of the reservoirs and the works necessary for their protection and operation shall remain in the Government until otherwise provided by Congress.

Source: Newlands Reclamation Act. https://www.usbr.gov/lc/region/programs/contracts/Legislation.pdf.

Convention between the United States and Mexico for the Equitable Distribution of the Waters of the Rio Grande (1906): Excerpt

When this convention was signed, it represented the United States' intention to develop more amicable relations with Mexico, especially over disputes related to the waters of the Rio Grande. In what might seem to be an unusual balance of responsibility, the United States agreed to ensure that Mexico would receive a secure amount of water from a storage facility being built near Engle, New Mexico at no cost to Mexico. Known in the United States as the Rio Grande and in Mexico as the Rio Bravo, the 1906 treaty dealt with a small portion of river basin in the northwest, considered the international reach of the river between the El Paso–Juarez Valley and Fort Quitman, Texas. The agreement was originally quite narrow in scope, but its importance is that it became the framework for an even more important document, the treaty between Mexico and the United States for the Utilization of Waters of the Colorado and Tijuana Rivers and of the Rio Grande.

Whereas a Convention between the United States of America and the United States of Mexico, providing for the equitable distribution of the waters of the Rio Grande for irrigation purposes, and to remove all causes of controversy between them in respect thereto, was concluded and signed by their respective

Plenipotentiaries at Washington on the twenty-first day of May, one thousand nine hundred and six, the original of which Convention being in the English and Spanish languages, is word for word as follows:

The United States of America and the United States of Mexico being desirous to provide for the equitable distribution of the waters of the Rio Grande for irrigation purposes, and to remove all causes of controversy between them in respect thereto, and being moved by considerations of international comity, have resolved to conclude a Convention for these purposes.

Article I. After the completion of the proposed storage dam near Engle, New Mexico, and the distributing system auxiliary thereto, and as soon as water shall be available in said system for the purpose, the United States shall deliver to Mexico a total of 60,000 acre-feet of water annually in the bed of the Rio Grande at the point where the head works of the Acequia Madre, known as the Old Mexican Canal, now exist above the city of Juarez, Mexico.

Article II. The delivery of the said amount of water shall be assured by the United States and shall be distributed through the year in the same proportions as the water supply proposed to be furnished from the said irrigation system to lands in the United States in the vicinity of El Paso, Texas. In case, however, of extraordinary drought or serious accident to the irrigation system in the United States, the amount delivered to the Mexican Canal shall be diminished in the same proportion as the water delivered to lands under said irrigation system in the United States.

Article III. The said delivery shall be made without cost to Mexico, and the United States agrees to pay the whole cost of storing the said quantity of water to be delivered to Mexico, of conveying the same to the international line, of measuring the said water, and of delivering it in the river bed above the head of the Mexican Canal. It is understood that the United States assumes no obligation beyond the delivering of the water in the bed of the river above the head of the Mexican Canal.

Article IV. The delivery of water as herein provided is not to be construed as a recognition by the United States of any claim on the part of Mexico to the said waters; and it is agreed that in consideration of such delivery of water, Mexico waives any and all claims to the waters of the Rio Grande for any purpose whatever between the head of the present Mexican Canal and Fort Quitman, Texas, and also declares fully settled and disposed of, and hereby waives, all claims heretofore asserted or existing, or that may hereafter arise, or be asserted, against the United States on account of any damages alleged to have been sustained by the owners of land in Mexico, by reason of the diversion by citizens of the United States of waters of the Rio Grande.

Article V. The United States, in entering into this treaty, does not thereby concede, expressly or by implication, any legal basis for any claims heretofore asserted or which may be hereafter asserted by reason of any losses incurred by the owners of land in Mexico due or alleged to be due to the diversion of the waters of the Rio Grande within the United States; nor does the United States in anyway concede the establishment of any general principle or precedent by the concluding of this treaty. The understanding of both parties is that the arrangement contemplated by this treaty extends only to the portion of the Rio Grande which forms the international boundary, from the head of the Mexican Canal down to Fort Quitman, Texas, and in no other case.

Source: Convention between the United States and Mexico Providing for the Equitable Distribution of the Waters of the Rio Grande for Irrigation Purposes. Office of the Historian, U.S. State Department. Available online at https://history.state.gov/historicaldocuments/frus1906p2/ch70.

Winters v. United States (1908): Excerpt

Disputes over the water rights of Native American tribes in the West date back to the time when their people lived on the land before European conquest. As settlers began to move onto their lands, they often diverted water for their use without any consultation with the indigenous people who believed the water was theirs. With the establishment of reservations, and sometimes the forced relocation of the tribe itself, treaties between the tribe and the federal government were the mechanism for determining water rights on tribal lands. After spending five years in exile and internment in New Mexico, an 1868 treaty allowed the Navajo (Dine) people to return to their ancestral homeland as a permanent home. This case is critical to the Navajo's understanding that the government's designation of a reservation implied the land included water rights, tying the need for water to the development of an agricultural economy.

This suit was brought by the United States to restrain appellants and others from constructing or maintaining dams or reservoirs on the Milk River in the State of Montana, or in any manner preventing the water of the river or its tributaries from flowing to the Fort Belknap Indian Reservation.

An interlocutory order was granted enjoining the defendants in the suit from interfering in any manner with the use by the reservation of 5,000 inches of the water of the river. The order was affirmed by the circuit court of appeals (143 F. 740). Upon the return of the case to the circuit court, an order was taken *pro confesso* against five of the defendants. The appellants filed a joint and several answer, upon which and the bill a decree was entered making the preliminary injunction permanent. The decree was affirmed by the circuit court of appeals (148 F. 684).

The allegations of the bill, so far as necessary to state them, are as follows: on the first day of May 1888, a tract of land, the property of the United States, was reserved and set apart "as an Indian reservation as and for a permanent home and abiding place of the Gros Ventre and Assiniboine bands or tribes of Indians in the State (then Territory) of Montana, designated and known as the Fort Belknap Indian Reservation."

The tract has ever since been used as an Indian reservation and as the home and abiding place of the Indians. Its boundaries were fixed and defined as follows:

> Beginning at a point in the middle of the main channel of Milk River, opposite the mouth of Snake Creek; thence due south to a point due west of the western extremity of the Little Rocky Mountains; thence due east to the crest of said mountains at their western extremity, and thence following the southern crest of said mountains to the eastern extremity thereof; thence in a northerly direction in a direct line to a point in the middle of the main channel of Milk River opposite the mouth of People's Creek; thence up Milk River, in the middle of the main channel thereof, to the place of beginning.

Milk River, designated as the northern boundary of the reservation, is a non-navigable stream. Large portions of the lands embraced within the reservation are well fitted and adapted for pasturage and the feeding and grazing of stock, and since the establishment of the reservation, the United States and the Indians have had and have large herds of cattle and large numbers of horses grazing upon the land within the reservation, "being and situate along and bordering upon said Milk River." Other portions of the reservation are "adapted for and susceptible of farming and cultivation and the pursuit of agriculture, and productive in the raising thereon of grass, grain, and vegetables," but such portions are of dry and arid character, and, in order to make them productive, require large quantities of water for the purpose of irrigating them. In 1889, the United States constructed houses and buildings upon the reservation for the occupancy and residence of the officers in charge of it, and such officers depend entirely for their domestic, culinary, and irrigation purposes upon the water of the river. In the year 1889, and long prior to the acts of the defendants complained of, the United States, through its officers and agents at the reservation, appropriated and took from the river a flow of 1,000 miners' inches, and conducted it to the buildings and premises, used the same for domestic purposes and also for the irrigation of land adjacent to the buildings and premises, and by the use thereof raised crops of grain, grass, and vegetables. Afterwards, but long prior to the acts of the defendants complained of, to-wit, on the fifth of July, 1898, the Indians residing on the reservation diverted from the river for the purpose of irrigation a flow of 10,000 miners' inches of water to and upon divers and extensive tracts of land, aggregating in amount about 30,000 acres, and raised upon said lands crops of grain, grass, and vegetables. And ever since 1889 and July, 1898, the United States and the Indians have diverted and used the waters of the river in the manner and for the purposes mentioned, and the United States "has been enabled by means thereof to train, encourage, and accustom large numbers of Indians residing upon the said reservation to habits of industry and to promote their civilization and improvement."

It is alleged with detail that all of the waters of the river are necessary for all those purposes and the purposes for which the reservation was created, and that, in furthering and advancing the civilization and improvement of the Indians, and to encourage habits of industry and thrift among them, it is essential and necessary that all of the waters of the river flow down the channel uninterruptedly and undiminished in quantity and undeteriorated in quality.

It is alleged that, "notwithstanding the riparian and other rights" of the United States and the Indians to the uninterrupted flow of the waters of the river, the defendants, in the year 1900, wrongfully entered upon the river and its tributaries above the points of the diversion of the waters of the river by the United States and the Indians, built large and substantial dams and reservoirs, and, by means of canals and ditches and waterways, have diverted the waters of the river from its channel, and have deprived the United States and the Indians of the use thereof. And this diversion of the water, it is alleged, has continued until the present time, to the irreparable injury of the United States, for which there is no adequate remedy at law.

The allegations of the answer, so far as material to the present controversy, are as follows: that the lands of the Fort Belknap Reservation were a part of a much larger area in the State of Montana which, by an Act of Congress approved April 15, 1874, 18 Stat. 28, c. 96, was set apart and reserved for the occupation of the Gros Ventre, Piegan, Blood, Blackfeet, and River Crow Indians, but that the right of the Indians therein "was the bare right of the use and occupation thereof at the will and sufferance of the government of the United States." That the United States, for the purpose of opening for settlement a large portion of such area, entered into an agreement with the Indians composing said tribes by which the Indians "ceded, sold, transferred, and conveyed" to the United States all of the lands embraced in said area, except Fort Belknap Indian Reservation, described in the bill. This agreement was ratified by an Act of Congress of May 1, 1888, 25 Stat. 113, c. 213, and thereby the lands to which the Indians' title was thus extinguished became a part of the public domain of the United States and subject to disposal under the various land laws, "and it was the purpose and intention of the government that the said land should be thus thrown open to settlement, to the end that the same might be settled upon, inhabited, reclaimed, and cultivated, and communities of civilized persons be established thereon."

That the individual defendants and the stockholders of the Matheson Ditch Company and Cook's Irrigation Company were qualified to become settlers upon the public land and to acquire title thereto under the homestead and desert land laws of the United States. And that said corporations were organized and exist under the laws of Montana for the purpose of supplying to their said stockholders the water of Milk River and its tributaries, to be used by them in the irrigation of their lands.

That the defendant the Empire Cattle Company is a corporation under the laws of Montana, was legally entitled to purchase, and did purchase, from those who were qualified to acquire them under the desert and homestead land laws of the United States, lands on the Milk River and its tributaries, and is now the owner and holder thereof.

That the defendants, prior to the fifth day of July, 1898, and before any appropriation, diversion, or use of the waters of the river or its tributaries was made by the United States or the Indians on the Fort Belknap Reservation, except a pumping plant of the capacity of about 250 miners' inches, without having notice of any claim made by the United States or the Indians that there was any reservation made of the waters of the river or its tributaries for use on said reservation, and believing that all the waters on the lands open for settlement as aforesaid were subject to appropriation under the laws of the United States and the laws, decisions, rulings, and customs of the State of Montana, in like manner as water on other portions of the public domain, entered upon the public lands in the vicinity of the river, made entry thereof at the United States land office, and thereafter settled upon, improved, reclaimed, and cultivated the same and performed all things required to acquire a title under the homestead and desert land laws, made due proof thereof, and received patents conveying to them, respectively, the lands in fee simple.

That all of said lands are situated within the watershed of the river, are riparian upon the river and its tributaries, but are arid and must be irrigated by artificial means to make them inhabitable and capable of growing crops.

That, for the purpose of reclaiming the lands, and acting under the laws of the United States and the laws of Montana, the defendants, respectively, posted upon the river and its tributaries at the points of intended diversion, notices of appropriation, stating the means of diversion and place of use, and thereafter filed in the office of the clerk and recorder of the county wherein the lands were situated a copy of the notices, duly verified, and within forty days thereafter commenced the construction of ditches and other instrumentalities, and completed them with diligence, and diverted, appropriated, and applied to a beneficial use more than 5,000 miners' inches of the waters of the river and its tributaries, of 120 cubic feet per second, irrigating their lands and producing hay, grain, and other crops thereon. The defendants and the stockholders of the defendant corporations have expended many thousands of dollars in constructing dams, ditches, and reservoirs and in improving said lands, building fences and other structures, establishing schools, and constructing highways and other improvements usually had and enjoyed in a civilized community, and that the only supply of water to irrigate the lands is from Milk River. If defendants are deprived of the waters, their lands cannot be successfully cultivated, and they will become useless and homes cannot be maintained thereon.

That there are other lands within the watershed of the Milk River and its tributaries and dependent upon its waters for irrigation, upon which large numbers of persons have settled under the land laws of the United States, and are irrigating and cultivating the same by means of said waters, and have assisted the defendants in establishing a civilized community in said country and in building and maintaining churches, schools, villages, and other elements and accompaniments of civilization; that said communities consist of thousands of people, and, if the claim of the United States and the Indians be maintained, the lands of the defendants and the other settlers will be rendered valueless, the said communities will be broken up, and the purpose and object of the government in opening said lands for settlement will be wholly defeated.

It is alleged that there are a large number of springs on the reservation and several streams from which water can be obtained for stock and irrigation purposes, and particularly these: People Creek, flowing about 1,000 inches of water; Big Horn Creek, flowing about 1,000 inches; Lodge Pole Creek, flowing about 600 inches of water; Clear Creek flowing about 300 inches. That all of the waters of these streams can be made available for use upon the reservation, and that it was not the intention of the government to reserve any of the waters of Milk River or its tributaries. That the respective claims of the defendants to the waters of the river and its tributaries are prior and paramount to the claims of the United States and the Indians, except as to 250 inches used in and around the agency buildings, and at all times there has been sufficient water flowing down the river to more than supply these 250 inches.

And it is again alleged that the waters of the river are indispensable to defendants, are of the value of more than $100,000 to them, and that, if they are deprived of the waters, "their lands will be ruined, it will be necessary to abandon their homes, and they will be greatly and irreparably damaged, the extent and amount of which damage cannot now be estimated, but will greatly exceed $100,000," and that they will be wholly without remedy if the claim of the United States and the Indians be sustained.

148 F. 684, affirmed.

MCKENNA, J., delivered the opinion of the Court, in which FULLER, C.J., HARLAN, WHITE, PECKHAM, HOLMES, DAY, AND MOODY, JJ. Joined. BREWER. J., dissents.

Source: *Winters v. United States*, 207 U.S. 564, 1908. Available at https://tile.loc.gov/storage-services/service/ll/usrep/usrep207/usrep207564/usrep207564.pdf.

John Muir, *The Yosemite* (1912): Excerpt

John Muir, America's premier naturalist, had a special place in his heart for the California wilderness, especially for the part that became Yosemite National Park in 1890. In this book, Muir writes in great detail about the park's treasures, from when the visitor enters Yosemite, to its trees, flowers, storms, floods, and peaks. It is in the very last chapter that he brings up the controversial project under consideration by Congress to build a dam in Yosemite's Hetch Hetchy Valley to provide the growing city of San Francisco with a stable water supply. Muir led the opposition to the dam proposal as leader of the preservationists who argued that the valley should be protected from human intrusion and development. On the other side were the people of San Francisco and those within the conservation movement who believed that natural resources should be used to benefit society. Congress eventually agreed, and President Woodrow Wilson signed a measure that enabled the O'Shaughnessy Dam to be built between 1914 and 1923. Muir lost the campaign to save his beloved valley before he died in 1914, but this early example of raising public awareness about the natural environment would serve as a touchstone for activism throughout the rest of the century and beyond.

Hetch Hetchy Valley, far from being a plain, common, rock-bound meadow, as many who have not seen it seem to suppose, is a grand landscape garden, one of Nature's rarest and most precious mountain temples. As in Yosemite, the sublime rocks of its walls seem to glow with life, whether leaning back in repose or standing erect in thoughtful attitudes, giving welcome to storms and calms alike, their brows in the sky, their feet set in the groves and gay flowery meadows, while birds, bees, and butterflies help the river and waterfalls to stir all the air into music–things frail and fleeting and types of permanence meeting here and blending, just as they do in Yosemite, to draw her lovers into close and confiding communion with her.

Sad to say, this most precious and sublime feature of the Yosemite National Park, one of the greatest of all our natural resources for the uplifting joy and peace and health of the people, is in danger of being dammed and made into a reservoir to help supply San Francisco with water and light, thus flooding it from wall to wall and burying its gardens and groves one or two hundred feet deep. This grossly destructive commercial scheme has long been planned and urged (though water as pure and abundant can be got from outside of the people's park, in a dozen different places), because of the comparative cheapness of the dam and of the territory which it is sought to divert from the great uses to which it was dedicated in the Act of 1890 establishing the Yosemite National Park.

The making of gardens and parks goes on with civilization all over the world, and they increase both in size and number as their value is recognized. Everybody needs beauty as well as bread, places to play in and pray in, where Nature may heal and cheer and give strength to body and soul alike. This natural beauty-hunger is made manifest in the little window-sill gardens of the poor, though perhaps only a geranium slip in a broken cup, as well as in the carefully tended rose and lily gardens of the rich, the thousands of spacious city parks and botanical gardens, and in our magnificent National parks—the Yellowstone, Yosemite, Sequoia, etc.—Nature's sublime wonderlands, the admiration and joy of the world. Nevertheless, like anything else worth while, from the very beginning, however well guarded, they have always been subject to attack by despoiling gainseekers and mischief-makers of every degree from Satan to Senators, eagerly trying to make everything immediately and selfishly commercial, with schemes disguised in smug-smiling philanthropy, industriously, shampiously crying, "Conservation, conservation, panutilization," that man and beast may be fed and the dear Nation made great. Thus long ago a few enterprising merchants utilized the Jerusalem temple as a place of business instead of a place of prayer, changing money, buying and selling cattle and sheep and doves; and earlier still, the first forest reservation, including only one tree, was likewise despoiled. Ever since the establishment of the Yosemite National Park, strife has been going on around its borders and I suppose this will go on as part of the universal battle between right and wrong, however much its boundaries may be shorn, or its wild beauty destroyed.

The first application to the Government by the San Francisco Supervisors for the commercial use of Lake Eleanor and the Hetch Hetchy Valley was made in 1903, and on December 22nd of that year it was denied by the Secretary of the Interior, Mr. Hitchcock, who truthfully said:

Presumably the Yosemite National Park was created such by law because within its boundaries, inclusive alike of its beautiful small lakes, like Eleanor, and its majestic wonders, like Hetch Hetchy and Yosemite Valley. It is the aggregation of such natural scenic features that makes the Yosemite Park a wonderland which the Congress of the United States sought by law to reserve for all coming time as nearly as practicable in the condition fashioned by the hand of the Creator–a worthy object of national pride and a source of healthful pleasure and rest for the thousands of people who may annually sojourn there during the heated months.

In 1907 when Mr. Garfield became Secretary of the Interior the application was renewed and granted; but under his successor, Mr. Fisher, the matter has been referred to a Commission, which as this volume goes to press still has it under consideration.

The most delightful and wonderful camp grounds in the Park are its three great valleys—Yosemite, Hetch Hetchy, and Upper Tuolumne; and they are also the most important places with reference to their positions relative to the other great features—the Merced and Tuolumne Cañons, and the High Sierra peaks and glaciers, etc., at the head of the rivers. The main part of the Tuolumne Valley is a spacious flowery lawn four or five miles long, surrounded by magnificent snowy mountains, slightly separated from other beautiful meadows, which together make a series about twelve miles in length, the highest reaching to the feet of Mount Dana, Mount Gibbs, Mount Lyell and Mount McClure. It is about 8500 feet above the sea, and forms the grand central High Sierra camp ground from which excursions are made to the noble mountains, domes, glaciers, etc.; across the Range to the Mono Lake and volcanoes and down the Tuolumne Cañon to Hetch Hetchy. Should Hetch Hetchy be submerged for a reservoir, as proposed, not only would it be utterly destroyed, but the sublime cañon way to the heart of the High Sierra would be hopelessly blocked and the great camping ground, as the watershed of a city drinking system, virtually would be closed to the public. So far as I have learned, few of all the thousands who have seen the park and seek rest and peace in it are in favor of this outrageous scheme.

One of my later visits to the Valley was made in the autumn of 1907 with the late William Keith, the artist. The leaf-colors were then ripe, and the great godlike rocks in repose seemed to glow with life. The artist, under their spell, wandered day after day along the river and through the groves and gardens, studying the wonderful scenery; and, after making about forty sketches, declared with enthusiasm that although its walls were less sublime in height, in picturesque beauty and charm Hetch Hetchy surpassed even Yosemite.

That any one would try to destroy such a place seems incredible; but sad experience shows that there are people good enough and bad enough for anything. The proponents of the dam scheme bring forward a lot of bad arguments to prove that the only righteous thing to do with the people's parks is to destroy them bit by bit as they are able. Their arguments are curiously like those of the devil, devised for the destruction of the first garden—so much of the very best Eden fruit going to waste; so much of the best Tuolumne water and Tuolumne scenery going to waste. Few of their statements are even partly true, and all are misleading.

Thus, Hetch Hetchy, they say, is a "low-lying meadow." On the contrary, it is a high-lying natural landscape garden, as the photographic illustrations show.

"It is a common minor feature, like thousands of others." On the contrary it is a very uncommon feature; after Yosemite, the rarest and in many ways the most important in the National Park.

"Damming and submerging it 175 feet deep would enhance its beauty by forming a crystal-clear lake." Landscape gardens, places of recreation and worship, are never made beautiful by destroying and burying them. The beautiful sham lake, forsooth, should be only an eyesore, a dismal blot on the landscape, like many others to be seen in the Sierra. For, instead of keeping it at the same level all the year, allowing Nature centuries of time to make new shores, it would, of course, be full only a month or two in the spring, when the snow is melting fast; then it would be gradually drained, exposing the slimy sides of the basin and shallower parts of the bottom, with the gathered drift and waste, death and decay of the Upper Basins, caught here instead of being swept on to decent natural burial along the banks of the river or in the sea. Thus the Hetch Hetchy dam-lake would be only a rough imitation of a natural lake for a few of the spring months, an open sepulcher for the others.

"Hetch Hetchy water is the purest of all to be found in the Sierra, unpolluted, and forever unpollutable." On the contrary, excepting that of the Merced below Yosemite, it is less pure than that of most of the other Sierra streams, because of the sewerage of camp grounds draining into it, especially of the Big Tuolumne Meadows camp ground, occupied by hundreds of tourists and mountaineers, with their animals, for months every summer, soon to be followed by thousands from all the world.

These temple destroyers, devotees of ravaging commercialism, seem to have a perfect contempt for Nature, and, instead of lifting their eyes to the God of the mountains, lift them to the Almighty Dollar.

Dam Hetch Hetchy! As well dam for water-tanks the people's cathedrals and churches, for no holier temple has ever been consecrated by the heart of man.

Source: Muir, John. "The Hetch Hetchy Valley." In *The Yosemite* (New York: The Century Co., 1912, pp. 249–262).

Colorado River Compact (1922): Excerpt

From a political perspective, this agreement is critical to understanding the deliberations now underway that revisit the 1922 division of the waters of the Colorado River. For the first time, the federal government designated how the seven states located within the drainage system of the Colorado will be apportioned their share of the river's water. By dividing the system into Upper and Lower

Division states, the parties to the agreement recognized the need to assure both divisions a stable supply of water, and their relationship to Mexico. In addition, the compact notes that the use of the Colorado for navigation becomes secondary to its importance for domestic, agricultural, and power purposes. This section of the agreement recognizes the changes taking place in the West as industrialization spreads and agricultural production increases.

ARTICLE I. The major purposes of this compact are to provide for the equitable division and apportionment of the use of the waters of the Colorado River System; to establish the relative importance of different beneficial uses of water, to promote interstate comity; to remove causes of present and future controversies; and to secure the expeditious agricultural and industrial development of the Colorado River Basin, the storage of its waters, and the protection of life and property from floods. To these ends the Colorado River Basin is divided into two Basins, and an apportionment of the use of part of the water of the Colorado River System is made to each of them with the provision that further equitable apportionments may be made.

ARTICLE II. As used in this compact—(a) The term "Colorado River System" means that portion of the Colorado River and its tributaries within the United States of America. (b) the term "Colorado River Basin" means all of the drainage area of the Colorado River System and all other territory within the United States of America to which the waters of the Colorado River System shall be beneficially applied. (c) The term "States of the Upper Division" means the States of Colorado, New Mexico, Utah, and Wyoming. (d) The term "States of the Lower Division" means the States of Arizona, California, and Nevada. (e) The term "Lee Ferry" means a point in the main stream of the Colorado River one mile below the mouth of the Paria River. (f) The term "Upper Basin" means those parts of the States of Arizona, Colorado, New Mexico, Utah, and Wyoming within and from which waters naturally drain into the Colorado River System above Lee Ferry, and also all parts of said States located without the drainage area of the Colorado River System which are now or shall hereafter be beneficially served by waters diverted from the System above Lee Ferry. (g) The term "Lower Basin" means those parts of the States of Arizona, California, Nevada, New Mexico, and Utah within and from which waters naturally drain into the Colorado River System below Lee Ferry, and also all parts of said States located without the drainage area of the Colorado River System which are now or shall hereafter be beneficially served by waters diverted from the System below Lee Ferry. (h)

The term "domestic use" shall include the use of water for household, stock, municipal, mining, milling, industrial, and other like purposes, but shall exclude the generation of electrical power.

ARTICLE III (a). There is hereby apportioned from the Colorado River System in perpetuity to the Upper Basin and to the Lower Basin, respectively, the exclusive beneficial consumptive use of 7,500,000 acre-feet of water per annum, which shall include all water necessary for the supply of any rights which may now exist. (b) In addition to the apportionment in paragraph (a), the Lower Basin is hereby given the right to increase its beneficial consumptive use of such waters by one million acre-feet per annum. (c) If, as a matter of international comity, the United States of America shall hereafter recognize in the United States of Mexico any right to the use of any waters of the Colorado River System, such waters shall be supplied first from the waters which are surplus over and above the aggregate of the quantities specified in paragraphs (a) and (b); and if such surplus shall prove insufficient for this purpose, then, the burden of such deficiency shall be equally borne by the Upper Basin and the Lower Basin, and whenever necessary the States of the Upper Division shall deliver at Lee Ferry water to supply one-half of the deficiency so recognized in addition to that provided in paragraph (d). (d) The States of the Upper Division will not cause the flow of the river at Lee Ferry to be depleted below an aggregate of 75,000,000 acre-feet for any period of ten consecutive years reckoned in continuing progressive series beginning with the first day of October next succeeding the ratification of this compact. (e) The States of the Upper Division shall not withhold water, and the States of the Lower Division shall not require the delivery of water, which cannot reasonably be applied to domestic and agricultural uses. (f) Further equitable apportionment of the beneficial uses of the waters of the Colorado River System unapportioned by paragraphs (a), (b), and (c) may be made in the manner provided in paragraph (g) at any time after October first, 1963, if and when either Basin shall have reached its total beneficial consumptive use as set out in paragraphs (a) and (b). (g) In the event of a desire for a further apportionment as provided in paragraph (f) any two signatory States, acting through their Governors, may give joint notice of such desire to the Governors of the other signatory States and to The President of the United States of America, and it shall be the duty of the Governors of the signatory States and of The President of the United States of America forthwith to appoint representatives, whose duty it shall be to divide and apportion equitably between the Upper Basin and Lower Basin the beneficial use of the unapportioned water of the Colorado River System as mentioned in paragraph (f), subject to the legislative ratification of the signatory States and the Congress of the United States of America.

ARTICLE IV (a). Inasmuch as the Colorado River has ceased to be navigable for commerce and the reservation of its waters for navigation would seriously limit the development of its Basin, the use of its waters for purposes of navigation shall be subservient to the uses of such waters for domestic, agricultural, and power purposes. If the Congress shall not consent to this paragraph, the other provisions of this compact shall nevertheless remain binding. (b) Subject to the provisions of this compact, water of the Colorado River System may be impounded and used for the generation of electrical power, but such impounding and use shall be subservient to the use and consumption of such water for agricultural and domestic purposes and shall not interfere with or prevent use for such dominant purposes. (c) The provisions of this article shall not apply to or interfere with the regulation and control by any State within its boundaries of the appropriation, use, and distribution of water.

ARTICLE V. The chief official of each signatory State charged with the administration of water rights, together with the Director of the United States Reclamation Service and the Director of the United States Geological Survey shall cooperate, ex-officio: (a) To promote the systematic determination and coordination of the facts as to flow, appropriation, consumption, and use of water in the Colorado River Basin, and the interchange of available information in such matters. (b) To secure the ascertainment and publication of the annual flow of the Colorado River at Lee Ferry. (c) To perform such other duties as may be assigned by mutual consent of the signatories from time to time.

ARTICLE VI. Should any claim or controversy arise between any two or more of the signatory States: (a) with respect to the waters of the Colorado River System not covered by the terms of this compact; (b) over the meaning or performance of any of the terms of this compact; (c) as to the allocation of the burdens incident to the performance of any article of this compact or the delivery of waters as herein provided; (d) as to the construction or operation of works within the Colorado River Basin to be situated in two or more States, or to be constructed in one State for the benefit of another State; or (e) as to the diversion of water in one State for the benefit of another State; the Governors of the States affected, upon the request of one of them, shall forthwith appoint Commissioners with power to consider and adjust such claim or controversy, subject to ratification by the Legislatures of the States so affected. Nothing herein contained shall prevent the adjustment of any such claim or controversy by any present method or by direct future legislative action of the interested States.

ARTICLE VII. Nothing in this compact shall be construed as affecting the obligations of the United States of America to Indian tribes.

ARTICLE VIII. Present perfected rights to the beneficial use of waters of the Colorado River System are unimpaired by this compact. Whenever storage capacity of 5,000,000 acre-feet shall have been provided on the main Colorado River within or for the benefit of the Lower Basin, then claims of such rights, if any, by appropriators or users of water in the Lower Basin against appropriators or users of water in the Upper Basin shall attach to and be satisfied from water that may be stored not in conflict with Article III. All other rights to beneficial use of waters of the Colorado River System shall be satisfied solely from the water apportioned to that Basin in which they are situate.

ARTICLE IX. Nothing in this compact shall be construed to limit or prevent any State from instituting or maintaining any action or proceeding, legal or equitable, for the protection of any right under this compact or the enforcement of any of its provisions.

ARTICLE X. This compact may be terminated at any time by the unanimous agreement of the signatory States. In the event of such termination all rights established under it shall continue unimpaired.

ARTICLE XI. This compact shall become binding and obligatory when it shall have been approved by the Legislatures of each of the signatory States and by the Congress of the United States.

Source: Colorado River Compact, 1922. Available online at https://www.usbr.gov/lc/region/pao/pdfiles/crcompct.pdf.

Boulder Canyon Project Act (1928): Excerpt

At the turn of the twentieth century, control of the 1,450 miles of the Colorado River was one of the most contentious issues facing the West. The river was unpredictable but also essential to the communities along its course, and the damage floods caused every year was devastating to local economies. The political pressures that led to the passage of this bill also were a result of the nation's increasing reliance on electricity as the region developed, and the need to build a large dam on the Colorado. The measure drew the support of Secretary of Commerce

Herbert Hoover, who called the dam that would later bear his name, "the greatest engineering work of its character ever attempted by the hand of man." The act is important not only because it authorized the construction of an important dam on the Colorado but also because it called for construction of the All-American Canal providing irrigation water for California's fertile Coachella and Imperial Counties, and a system for dividing up the Colorado's waters among the Lower Basin states. All three of these provisions in the law are as controversial today as they were in the late 1920s as the seven states of the Colorado River Basin continue to debate the river's management.

AN ACT To provide for the construction of works for the protection and development of the Colorado River Basin, for the approval of the Colorado River compact, and for other purposes.

Be it enacted by the Senate and House of Representatives of the United States of America in Congress assembled, That for the purpose of controlling the floods, improving navigation and regulating the flow of the Colorado River, providing for storage and for the delivery of the stored waters thereof for reclamation of public lands and other beneficial uses exclusively within the United States, and for the generation of electrical energy as a means of making the project herein authorized a self-supporting and financially solvent undertaking, the Secretary of the Interior, subject to the terms of the Colorado River compact hereinafter mentioned, is hereby authorized to construct, operate, and maintain a dam and incidental works in the main stream of the Colorado River at Black Canyon or Boulder Canyon adequate to create a storage reservoir of a capacity of not less than twenty million acre-feet of water and a main canal and appurtenant structures located entirely within the United States connecting the Laguna Dam, or other suitable diversion dam, which the Secretary of the Interior is hereby authorized to construct if deemed necessary or advisable by him upon engineering or economic considerations, with the Imperial and Coachella Valleys in California, the expenditures for said main canal and appurtenant structures to be reimbursable, as provided in the reclamation law, and shall not be paid out of revenues derived from the sale or disposal of water power or electric energy at the dam authorized to be constructed at said Black Canyon or Boulder Canyon, or for water for potable purposes outside of the Imperial and Coachella Valleys: Provided, however, That no charge shall be made for water or for the use, storage, or delivery of water for irrigation or water for potable purposes in the Imperial or Coachella Valleys; also to construct and equip, operate, and maintain at or near said dam, or cause to be constructed, a complete plant and incidental structures suitable for the fullest economic development of electrical energy from the water discharged from said reservoir; and to acquire by proceedings in eminent ...

... SEC. 18. Nothing herein shall be construed as interfering with such rights as the States now have either to the waters within their borders or to adopt such policies and enact such laws as they may deem necessary with respect to the appropriation, control, and use of waters within their borders, except as modified by the Colorado River compact or other interstate agreement.

SEC. 19. That the consent of Congress is hereby given to the States of Arizona, California, Colorado, Nevada, New Mexico, Utah, and Wyoming to negotiate and enter into compacts or agreements, supplemental to and in conformity with the Colorado River compact and consistent with this Act for a comprehensive plan for the development of the Colorado River and providing for the storage, diversion, and use of the waters of said river. Any such compact or agreement may provide for the construction of dams, headworks, and other diversion works or structures for flood control, reclamation, improvement of navigation, division of water, or other purposes and/or the construction of power houses or other structures for the purpose of the development of water power and the financing of the same; and for such purposes may authorize the creation of interstate commissions and/or the creation of corporations, authorities, or other instrumentalities.

(a) Such consent is given upon condition that a representative of the United States, to be appointed by the President, shall participate in the negotiations and shall make report to Congress of the proceedings and of any compact or agreement entered into.

(b) No such compact or agreement shall be binding or obligatory upon any of such States unless and until it has been approved by the legislature of each of such States and by the Congress of the United States.

SEC. 20. Nothing in this Act shall be construed as a denial or recognition of any rights, if any, in Mexico to the use of the waters of the Colorado River system.

Source: Boulder Canyon Project Act, Pub.L. 70-642; 45 Stat. 1057. https://www.archives.gov/milestone-documents/boulder-canyon-project-act#transcript.

Interior Secretary Bruce Babbitt, Speech on the Sledgehammer Tour (1998): Excerpt

As Secretary of the Interior for eight years during the administration of President Bill Clinton, Bruce Babbitt brought new perspectives to the job, using his political skills and relying upon scientific data to address issues that had formerly been off limits to debate. Among the most challenging of those issues was whether many of the dams that had been built during the previous century, up until environmental groups questioned their utility, should be dismantled. New evidence had been gathered by environmental researchers indicating that dams had negative ecological impacts, ranging from the destruction of fish spawning grounds and wetlands to the flooding of ancient archaeological sites to the near extinction of key species. In 1998, Babbitt embarked on what he called his Sledgehammer Tour, speaking to groups across the country about what he refers to in this speech as America's "dam building frenzy" for which the public has "paid a steadily accumulating price."

Usually my trips to rivers involve a canoe and paddle, or flyfishing rod and reel. More recently I arrive with sledgehammer in hand, to celebrate the destruction of dams.

I suspect this breaks with tradition. Six decades ago, President Franklin Delano Roosevelt and his Interior Secretary Harold Ickes toured the country to dedicate dams, new dams, powerful dams, including four of the largest dams in the history of civilization. They built dams for barge traffic, for electricity, for irrigation, for drinking water, for flood control. For most of this century, politicians have eagerly rushed in, amidst cheering crowds, to claim credit for the construction of 75,000 dams all across America. Think about that number. That means we have been building, on average, one large dam a day, every single day, since the Declaration of Independence. Many of these dams have became monuments, expected to last forever.

You could say forever just got a lot shorter.

Starting last June 17, I hoisted a sledgehammer to mark the removal of four dams, opening 160 miles of the Menominee River flowing between Wisconsin and Michigan. In September, I visited the two Elwha River dams which the Administration plans to remove to restore one of the fabled chinook salmon runs of the river. Then on December 17, I took my sledgehammer to punch open the 55-year-old, 260-foot Quaker Neck Dam on the Neuse River, opening 925 miles of fish spawning habitat. And in July I took the first crack at breaking up

McPherrin Dam to restore chinook salmon to Butte Creek and, a day later, used the sledgehammer to breach Oregon's Bear Creek Dam.

Every stop on this dam-busting tour attracts enormous local, regional and national attention. I believe that huge public interest reflects a deep, widespread understanding that America overshot the mark in our dam building frenzy. In this century, dams that were clearly justified for their economic value gradually gave way to projects built with excessive taxpayer subsidies, then justified by dubious cost/benefit projections.

The public is now learning that we have paid a steadily accumulating price for these projects, in the form of fish spawning runs destroyed, downstream rivers altered by changes in temperature, unnatural nutrient load and seasonal flows, wedges of sediment piling up behind structures, and delta wetlands degraded by lack of fresh water and saltwater intrusion. Rivers are always on the move and their inhabitants know no boundaries; salmon and shad do not read maps, only streams.

The clang of the sledge hammer is one of the oldest sounds known to man. Yet now, at the end of the 20th century, we are using it to ring in an entirely new era of conservation history, moving beyond preservation or protection towards a deeper, more complex movement the affirmative act of restoration.

Beyond Preservation

Restoration grows out of the same stewardship impulse as preservation, but pushes beyond, as one might renovate an old, neglected farm to inhabit once again. The coming age of restoration requires the active involvement of the citizens who live on the entire watershed. Most of all it requires a creative act; we must see not only what is, but envision what can be. It requires us to reach back into our history in order to grasp the future in which we might live.

Restoration invites us to understand how the natural world with its complex storms, fires, forests, watersheds and wildlife functions as a whole. And the best unit to measure that whole how it is more than the sum of its parts is the river that runs through us. For that river reflects the condition of every single acre of the whole, integrated watershed. Thirty six centuries ago, Emperor Yu of China advised "To protect your rivers, protect your mountains."

That same rule applies today. To restore our aquatic ecosystems, look beyond the water's edge out onto the land that borders it. What happens on that land inevitably is reflected in our rivers.

But even protecting mountains, we discover, goes only so far. I doubt that Emperor Yu, for all his wisdom, could foresee the construction of Three Gorges Dam or what it would do to the life of that river. And lest we condemn China too quickly, I should point out that we in America have been slow to recognize the ecological costs of dams. And slower still to envision watershed restoration through dam removal.

I began to reflect on these issues over the course of many days and nights spent in the Grand Canyon over the last half century. I hiked and boated and camped beside the Colorado River before Glen Canyon was built in the 1960s. In those years it was a wild, unpredictable, brown, sediment-laden stream flooding into the early summer, then settling down in the winter. The gates of Glen Canyon were closed in 1963. Today, you see an ice cold, Jell-O-green river, manipulated up and down, rising and falling on a daily cycle, flushed with the regularity, and predictability, of a giant toilet.

Over time, as I floated down the river, I saw trees on talus slopes wither and die for lack of water. I saw sandbars once covered with yarrow, willow and cottonwood disappear. I saw once plentiful native fish driven back to the brink of survival in only a few isolated tributaries.

It may seem hard to comprehend now that, at the time, no one even considered the possibility of these dramatic changes. At the time Glen Canyon was built, we were still thinking of dams as stand alone projects that, lamentably, flooded out nice scenery upstream but without consequences for the entire river system. And the Grand Canyon is only one of thousands of examples.

Nowhere has the impact of dams been more visible than on aquatic life. We once believed that freshwater flowing to the sea was "wasted." By trying to hold it back as long as possible, we blocked out anadromous fisheries from their ancient spawning grounds. In the 19th century, from Maine to the Chesapeake on down to Florida, in the course of damming rivers, we virtually destroyed the rich Atlantic salmon, shad, striped bass, herring and sturgeon as they made their way inland from the Atlantic.

And in this century, with our massive projects up and down the Pacific-bound rivers, we have repeated this process of destruction, virtually decimating the great salmon and steelhead runs of the northwest, by continuing to build dams clear up into the 1970s. This year, we learn that roughly one third of all fish, two thirds of all crayfish, and three quarters of the bivalve freshwater mussels in America are rare or threatened with extinction.

Let's give the economists their due: We seem to value something only when it becomes rare. The loss of fisheries that we once took for granted has led to a new urgency demanding ways we can replenish them. Every single dam to which I brought my sledgehammer was removed for the benefit of one or more endangered aquatic species. Yet despite this progress there are still—if we use established figures—74,993 dams in America, blocking 600,000 miles of what had once been free flowing rivers.

But as we contemplate future ceremonies involving dams, here are some considerations:

- Dams are not America's answer to the pyramids of Egypt. We did not build them for religious purposes and they do not consecrate our values (even if some are named after Presidents). Dams do, in fact, outlive their function. When they do, some should go.
- There also comes a point in the life of a dam where we can get the same benefits in other ways. On Butte Creek, irrigation farmers could replace McPherrin Dam and three others with an irrigation pump and siphon. Quaker Neck Dam, which stored water for power generators, could be replaced with a different cooling system.
- Moreover, in some cases the price for the benefits is simply too high; the dam has grown too expensive relative to the loss of fish. Owners of dams coming out on the Menominee found that taking a holistic approach to the entire watershed would save them time, money and energy. Some could be phased out, while others reoperated with screens, fish passage and drawdowns.

But all these conditions rest on the values and the scientific understanding of the larger community. Who, besides nature, decides whether a dam stands or falls?

One recent column made a reference to "Babbitt, the nation's dam-remover-in-chief" as if I were some Roman emperor giving thumbs up or down. The truth is I have not brought my sledgehammer to a single dam that was not approved for removal by consensus of the inhabitants of the watershed. Each community made a thoughtful, deliberative choice in how they could restore their river. Many of these consensus-based decisions are brought about by democratic, voluntary watershed councils that are cropping up all over the country.

Larger dams pose more complex issues, for there are more, and bigger, economic stakeholders. Entire industries, the price of electricity for millions of people, water storage for cities. We are rapidly reaching a consensus with Congress to remove the dams at Elwha and Glines Canyon. The debate over four dams on the Snake River will surely continue for years. Yet even when a community decides that a dam should remain, it may discover progressive new ways to operate it that restore some of the ecological damage.

So what can you do as citizens and scientists to shape this restoration movement? What you can do as ecologists is research and examine and document the benefits that might be accrued by restoration of the aquatic ecosystem by removal or reoperation of a given dam in the watershed you may be involved in. We have plenty of powerful stakeholders willing to reassert the known, traditional benefits of dams irrigation, hydropower, urban water authorities, engineers. But the process of putting a value on the native life intrinsic to watersheds and ecosystems is something new, and the degree to which you can do so goes a long way.

There is another way of expressing this: My parents' generation gloried in the construction of dams across America's rivers. My generation saw how those rivers were changed, deformed, killed by dams. Your generation must help decide if, how and where those dams stand or fall.

I am reminded of Ecclesiastes: One generation passeth away, and another generation cometh: but the earth abideth always All the rivers runneth to the sea, yet the sea is not full; to the place where the rivers flow, there they flow again.

A beautiful passage, but now haunting, for it is no longer true. I think back to my beloved Colorado River: once one of the mightiest rivers in America, it no longer makes it to the sea. That is a shame. As our generation passes, the toughest decisions rest firmly in your hands.

Source: Babbitt, Bruce. "Dams Are Not Forever." Remarks of the Secretary of the United States Department of Interior to the Ecological Society of America Annual Meeting, August 4, 1998.

Arizona v. Navajo Nation (2023): Excerpt

An 1868 peace treaty between the United States and the Navajo Tribe established the Navajo Reservation that today spans some 17 million acres, almost entirely in the Colorado River Basin of the western United States. The federal government's reservation of land for an Indian tribe implicitly reserves the right to use needed water from various sources—such as groundwater, rivers, streams, lakes, and springs—that arise on, border, cross, underlie, or are encompassed within the reservation. Although the Tribe has the right to use needed water from the reservation's numerous water sources, the Navajos face the same water scarcity problem that many in the western United States face. In the Navajos' view, the federal government's efforts to assist the Navajos with their water needs did not fully satisfy the trust obligations of the United States under the 1868 treaty. The Navajos filed suit seeking to compel the United States to take affirmative steps to secure needed water for the Tribe—including by assessing the Tribe's water needs, developing a plan to secure the needed water, and potentially building pipelines, pumps, wells, or other water infrastructure. The States of Arizona, Nevada, and Colorado intervened against the Tribe to protect those States' interests in water from the Colorado River. The US District Court for the District of Arizona dismissed the Navajo Tribe's complaint, but the Ninth Circuit reversed, holding in relevant part that the United States has a duty under the 1868 treaty to take affirmative steps to secure water for the Navajos.

Held: The 1868 treaty establishing the Navajo Reservation reserved necessary water to accomplish the purpose of the Navajo Reservation but did not require the United States to take affirmative steps to secure water for the Tribe. (a) The Tribe asserts a breach-of-trust claim based on its view that the 1868 treaty imposed a duty on the United States to take affirmative steps to secure water for the Navajos. To maintain such a claim here, the Tribe must establish, among other things, that the text of a treaty, statute, or regulation imposed certain duties on the United States. See *United States v. Jicarilla Apache Nation*, 564 U. S. 162, 173–174, 177–178. The Federal Government owes judicially enforceable duties to a tribe "only to the extent it expressly accepts those responsibilities." Id., at 177. Whether the Government has expressly accepted such obligations "must train on specific rights-creating or duty-imposing" language in a treaty, statute, or regulation. See *United States v. Navajo Nation*, 537 U. S. 488, 506. Here, while the 1868 treaty "set apart" a reservation for the "use and occupation of the Navajo tribe," 15 Stat. 668, it contains no language imposing a duty on the United States to take affirmative steps to secure water for the Tribe. See *United States v. Navajo Nation*, 537 U. S., at 506. Notably, the 1868 treaty did impose a number of specific duties on the United States, but the treaty said nothing about any affirmative duty for the United States to secure water. As this Court has stated, "Indian treaties cannot be rewritten or expanded beyond their clear terms." See *Choctaw Nation v. United States*, 318 U. S. 423, 432. To be sure, this Court's precedents have stated that the

United States maintains a general trust relationship with Indian tribes, including the Navajos. See *United States v. Jicarilla Apache Nation*, 564 U. S., at 176. But unless Congress has created a conventional trust relationship with a tribe as to a particular trust asset, this Court will not "apply common-law trust principles" to infer duties not found in the text of a treaty, statute, or regulation. Id., at 178. Here, nothing in the 1868 treaty establishes a conventional trust relationship with respect to water. And it is unsurprising that a treaty enacted in 1868 did not provide for all of the Navajos' current water needs 155 years later. Under the Constitution, Congress and the President have the responsibility to update federal law as they see fit in light of the competing contemporary needs for water. (b) Other arguments offered by the Navajo Tribe to support its claims under the 1868 treaty are unpersuasive. First, that the 1868 treaty established the Navajo Reservation as a "permanent home" does not mean that the United States agreed to take affirmative steps to secure water for the Tribe. Second, the treaty's express requirement that the United States supply seeds and agricultural implements for a 3-year period to the Tribe does not, as the Tribe contends, mean that the United States has an additional duty to take affirmative steps to secure water, but rather demonstrates that the United States and the Navajos knew how to impose specific affirmative duties on the United States under the treaty. Third, the Tribe asserts that the United States's purported control over the reserved water rights supports the view that the United States owes trust duties to the Navajos. But the "Federal Government's liability" on a breach-of-trust claim "cannot be premised on control alone." See *United States v. Navajo Nation*, 556 U. S. 287, 301. Finally, the text of the treaty and records of treaty negotiations do not support the claim that in 1868 the Navajos would have understood the treaty to mean that the United States must take affirmative steps to secure water for the Tribe.

26 F. 4th 794, reversed. KAVANAUGH, J., delivered the opinion of the Court, in which ROBERTS, C. J., and THOMAS, ALITO, and BARRETT, JJ., joined. THOMAS, J., filed a concurring opinion. GORSUCH, J., filed a dissenting opinion, in which SOTOMAYOR, KAGAN, and JACKSON, JJ., joined.

Source: *Arizona v. Navajo Nation* (2023). https://www.supremecourt.gov/opinions/22pdf/21-1484_aplc.pdf.

6

Resources

Books

Abbott, Carol. 2008. *How Cities Won the West: Four Centuries of Urban Change in Western North America*. Albuquerque: University of New Mexico Press.

The author, a professor of urban studies, argues that western migration was fueled by a desire to build cities. He recounts the development of urban centers like Los Angeles, San Diego, San Francisco, Denver, and Las Vegas, noting that agriculture and homesteading were not at the forefront of western development.

Adams, John A. 1990. *Damming the Colorado: The Rise of the Lower Colorado River Authority, 1933–1939*. College Station: Texas A&M University Press.

This scholarly book is useful for anyone seeking to know more about the early history of attempts to control the Colorado. It covers just six years—1933 to 1939—of the Lower Colorado River Authority. This is a segment of the river that has had less attention than other parts, but it is a good example of how the federal–state relationship worked to build a reclamation movement.

Arax, Max. 2020. *The Dreamt Land: Chasing Water and Dust across California*. New York: Vintage.

Farmers are at the very heart of this 528-page book, ranging from the "the nut king, grape king, and the citrus queen." The author is himself a farmer/journalist, and he uses that lens to tell the stories of farming throughout California, and the thirst agriculture has for the state's waters. The book is highly readable.

An irrigation canal carries water to pipes used to flood a field in the Arizona desert. Large-scale irrigation projects made agriculture possible in the West but also had unintended environmental consequences. (Matthew Rogers/Dreamstime.com)

August, Jack L., Jr. 2005. *Vision in the Desert: Carl Hayden and Hydropolitics in the American Southwest*. Fort Worth: Texas Christian University Press.

Carl Hayden is one of the most intriguing figures in American politics, and this biography explains why. The author uses both Arizona and Washington, DC as the setting for a readable story about Hayden's fifty-seven-year career in Congress, his support for the Central Arizona Project, and how he engineered a major water supply for the state.

Benson, Jackson J. 1996. *Wallace Stegner: His Life and Work*. New York: Viking.

Benson, a friend of the subject of this biography, focuses primarily on Stegner's life as a Pulitzer Prize-winning author and calls him "possibly the most accomplished man of American letters in our time." Less attention is paid to Stegner's role in the environmental movement, his affection for the American West, or his personal life. One review refers to Benson as an admirer of Stegner—an observation that will ring true for most readers.

Burch, John R., Jr. 2015. *Water Rights and the Environment in the U.S.: A Documentary and Reference Guide*. Santa Barbara, CA: Greenwood Press.

This extensive, six-part collection of documents covers water law, management, and key issues by providing excerpts or complete materials that are both historic and contemporary. This includes US Supreme Court cases, legislation, reports, rulemakings, and treaties that are often difficult to find for novices. The author provides an analysis of each one, along with the source and selections for further reading.

Carle, David. 2003. *Water and the California Dream: Choices for a New Millennium*. Berkeley: University of California Press.

The author looks to the future rather than the past in determining where the state will get the amount of water it needs. He argues that unlimited growth in times of limited supply are problematic. The book is less useful than others because so much has changed in the last twenty years.

Clark, Ira G. 1987. *Water in New Mexico: A History of Its Management and Use*. Albuquerque: University of New Mexico Press.

Although the book's extensive coverage ends with its publication date, this could easily become the only volume needed if you wanted to know about the development of water policy and law in New Mexico. Most of the contents are divided into three historical sections: territorial New Mexico; the years surrounding early statehood; and the post-Second World War period. The author covers the conflicts over the use of early land grant water rights, how mining has affected water use, the processes by which groundwater is allocated, and how water will potentially involve new types of disputes. This is a lengthy book, but it covers everything.

Clemings, Russell. 1996. *Mirage: The False Promise of Desert Agriculture*. San Francisco: Sierra Club Books.

It seemed like a good idea at the time—irrigate the desert and the desert will bloom. But global experience says otherwise, as ecosystems are damaged and the consequences of farming practices in both India and the American West no longer are the hope they once were. Because this is a comparative study of two nations, the information on the West is limited in parts.

Cumbler, John T. 2001. *Reasonable Use: The People, the Environment, and the State, New England 1790–1930*. New York: Oxford University Press.

The author outlines the developments that changed the riparian rights doctrine in place in English law when it was brought by colonists to New England. Of particular interest is the concept of reasonable use and how it affected the shift from an agrarian society to one that was beginning to become an industrial one.

Davis, Margaret Leslie. 1993. *Rivers in the Desert: William Mulholland and the Inventing of Los Angeles*. New York: HarperCollins.

The author's award-winning biography of Mulholland reveres him as a legendary engineer and his life is portrayed as a classic tragedy. Davis gives him more credit than blame for the collapse of the St. Francis Dam, calling the event a "tragic downfall" as she attempts to rehabilitate his memory for a new generation of readers.

deBuys, William. 2011. *A Great Aridness: Climate Change and the Future of the American Southwest*. New York: Oxford University Press.

Arguing that the Southwest is already in the throes of rapid change, the author examines the impacts, present and future, of global climate change. He reviews the history of wildfires, biopolitics, precipitation, and other factors to explain why change is coming to the region faster than expected.

D'Eastree, Tamara Pearson, and Bonnie B. G. Colby. 2004. *Braving the Currents: Evaluating Environmental Conflict Resolution in the River Basins of the American West*. New York: Springer.

This book is a series of case studies of conflict resolution, with the goal of determining what elements are needed for success. Because the book is now twenty years old, it has a limited set of case studies for current research.

Deloria, Vine, Jr. ed. 1985. *American Indian Policy in the Twentieth Century*. Norman: University of Oklahoma Press.

There is a multitude of authors who have written about the history of Native people, but this author's work is useful because it covers a limited time period and focuses on policy rather than just historical coverage.

DeVilliers, Marq. 2001. *Water: The Fate of Our Most Precious Resource*. Boston: Mariner.

This assessment of both water quality and water quantity provides a global perspective, with the usual explanation of problems and solutions, written in an optimistic tone. The book is more useful for comparative analysis rather than for information about the West.

Elliott, Gary E. 1994. *Senator Alan Bible and the Politics of the New West*. Reno: University of Nevada Press.

Nevada Senator Bible was of the belief that his role in Congress was to do everything possible to provide for the needs of his constituents, and from 1954 to 1974, he did exactly that. His relationship with President Lyndon B. Johnson, along with his quiet style of lobbying his colleagues, is extensively outlined in this biography.

Fleck, John. 2016. *Water is for Fighting Over: And Other Myths About Water in the West*. Washington, DC: Island Press.

Although the author does not discount the challenges the West is facing in dealing with water resources, his tone is more optimistic than others. He provides examples of the types of collaborative efforts that make doomsday seem less likely, although the book was published before the most recent years of drought.

Fradkin, Philip L. 1996. *A River No More: The Colorado River and the West*. Berkeley: University of California Press.

Reviewers have described this acclaimed perspective on the Colorado as "definitive" and "comprehensive," but others refer to it as "depressing," perhaps in part because the author clearly is on the side of protecting and regulating, rather than using, the river's water. He argues that the Colorado's ecosystem has been mismanaged, that the water runs dry (hence the title), and that development and politics have ruined it forever.

Fradkin, Philip L. 2009. *Wallace Stegner and the American West*. Berkeley: University of California Press.

Pulitzer Prize-winning journalist Fradkin is recognized as one of the preeminent writers on the West, and this biography of Stegner traces the literary icon's life from his childhood into three relatively distinct life phases: teacher, conservationist, and writer. The book is very heavily researched and, for the most part, provides a factual portrait of the man.

Fraser, Mary Ann. 1995. *In Search of the Grand Canyon: Down the Colorado with John Wesley Powell*. New York: Henry Holt & Company.

This book covers just three months of Powell's life, focusing on the river trip but little more. There is detailed coverage of the trip itself, using Powell's coverage along with other members of the journey to give the reader a taste of what the trip must have been like.

Gahan, Andrew H., and William D. Rowley. 2012. *The Bureau of Reclamation: From Developing to Managing Water, 1945–2000, Volume* 2. Denver, CO: U.S. Department of the Interior, Bureau of Reclamation.

Published during the Bureau's 110th anniversary of its founding, this book covers the post-Second World War history of the agency as the world's foremost dam builder and hydroelectric development. The authors explore the shift from a utilitarian ethos from the Progressive Era to a more environmentally conscious period characterized by diverse demands for water. Extensively illustrated, with a timeline and comprehensive bibliography.

Gleick, Peter. 2023. *The Three Ages of Water: Prehistoric Past, Imperiled Present, and a Hope for the Future*. New York: PublicAffairs.

The author's three "ages" cover the ways in which water has shaped both the planet and humanity. He calls for a more sustainable future based on rethinking our water supply, utilizing non-traditional supply options, and rethinking demand—what he calls the "soft path."

Glennon, Robert J. 2004. *Water Follies: Groundwater Pumping and the Fate of America's Fresh Waters*. Washington, DC: Island Press.

Using case studies of Arizona's Santa Cruz and San Pedro Rivers, along with examples from Maine to Georgia to Texas, the author illustrates what happens when values collide. He calls groundwater pumping from aquifers a widespread but underappreciated phenomenon that causes numerous environmental problems.

Glennon, Robert J. 2009. *Unquenchable: America's Water Crisis and What to Do about It*. Washington, DC: Island Press.

Calling water extravagance and inefficiency a looming catastrophe, Glennon seeks market-based solutions rather than engineered ones or bizarre schemes. Perhaps in an attempt to bring this problem's importance to a broader audience, the author shows us the absurdity of how water scarcity is ignored in some places, but how it is at crisis proportions in others.

Gumprecht, Blake. 1999. *The Los Angeles River: Its Life, Death, and Possible Rebirth*. Baltimore, MD: Johns Hopkins University Press.

If you only know the Los Angeles River as something that snakes through the city's concrete flood control system, this book provides you with much more information that is worth knowing. The author is a geographer, not a historian, but he tells great stories about the river and its earliest inhabitants, from Native Americans to Spanish settlers. He also explains the river's importance in the building of the city, how degradation has changed its role, and the potential for returning it to a more natural state.

Hansman, Heather. 2019. *Downriver: Into the Future of Water in the West*. Chicago: University of Chicago Press.

A 730-mile raft trip down the Green River through Wyoming, Colorado, and Utah provides the setting for the author's journalistic account of the public policy issues facing the Colorado Basin and the people who live there, including those with differing perspectives and complex opinions. She includes valuable information about climate change, water conservation, and provides little-known background on the Green River itself.

Harden, Blaine. 2012. *A River Lost: The Life and Death of the Columbia*, rev. ed. New York: W. W. Norton & Company.

The author took a freight barge to rediscover the Columbia River, with his hometown on the river the basis for his story. Much of the book is about how the river's history is full of negative images, the cultural changes that have taken place, including the exploitation of Native Americans. It is less useful in dealing with the challenges the river faces, including the salmon fisheries and hydroelectric power.

Harrison, Christian S. 2023. *All the Water the Law Allows*. Norman: University of Oklahoma Press.

Despite all its efforts to conserve water, Las Vegas has faced a unique challenge—the Law of the River and the allocation of water to the states along its course. The author notes that concerns about growth in the region are tempered by the fact that no matter how hard it tries, the city is limited in what it can do by legal restrictions. He contends that reallocation of the Colorado's water may at some point force other cities to look more closely at the city's accomplishments.

Hart, John. 1996. *Storm Over Mono: The Mono Lake Battle and the California Water Future*. Berkeley: University of California Press.

In this book accompanied by beautiful nature photographs, the author explores how a small group of poorly financed but well-organized environmental activists sought to protect the lake as an important ecological resource. Taking on the California Water Resources Control Board and local and state officials, their grassroots efforts led to a key 1994 court decision restricting the use of the lake's waters. Valuable for its use of primary historical materials.

Hawley, Steven. 2012. *Recovering a Lost River: Removing Dams, Rewilding Salmon, Revitalizing Communities*. Boston: Beacon Press.

For those interested in salmon politics, the author, an environmental journalist, provides an overview of the Columbia Basin and its wild rivers like the Salmon, in this critique of dams. Citizen action plays a key role in this story of the efforts by the US, state, and Canadian governments to eliminate salmon from one of our most important watersheds.

Hawley, Steven. 2023. *Cracked: The Future of Dams in a Hot, Chaotic World*. Ventura, CA: Patagonia Publishing.

Grassroots organizing, says the author, is a key strategy in ridding the nation of dams that simply need to be removed in order to protect our rivers and the habitats within them. Like other environmental conflicts, the need to build consensus is a complex and difficult task, but he illustrates his ideas with multiple case studies of dedicated citizens organizing to build a better future.

Hoffman, Abraham. 1981. *Vision or Villainy: Origins of the Owens Valley–Los Angeles Water Controversy*. College Station: Texas A&M University Press.

Two factors set this book apart from others dealing with the Owens Valley controversy. First, it is written for scholars rather than casual readers, and those willing to sift through not only primary sources but also unpublished ones. Second, it is one of the only treatments that covers the conspiracy theories over how William Mulholland and the city of Los Angeles were said to have stolen the waters said to belong to those who lived in the valley.

Hoffman, Abraham. 2014. *Mono Lake: From Dead Sea to Environmental Treasure*. Albuquerque: University of New Mexico Press.

There are a number of lenses through which one can look at Mono Lake, and Hoffman provides a historical perspective, rather than a largely ecological one. From the early Paiute fly people who lived in the region, to the role of Mono Lake in the disputes between the Los Angeles Department of Water and Power, to the continuing fight by environmental groups, he provides the additional resources of maps and illustrations.

Holyoke, Thomas T. 2023. *Water Politics: The Fragmentation of West Water Policy*. London: Routledge.

This book provides a different perspective on water politics, using case studies to illustrate how politics influences the way water policy is developed. This is a textbook on the subject, one of the few that is highly readable for non-students as well.

Hundley, Norris, Jr. 2009. *The Colorado River Compact and the Politics of Water in the West*, 2nd ed. Berkeley: University of California Press.

The updated version of the book covers the late 1880s, through the development of the 1922 Colorado River Compact, to somewhat contemporary times. The coverage of the Compact makes you think the author was in the room, with more details about the infighting that took place until the agreement was reached and ratified. It provides excellent context for the current efforts to revise the guidelines for managing the Colorado.

Hundley, Norris, Jr. and Donald C. Jackson. 2015. *Heavy Ground: William Mulholland and the St. Francis Dam Disaster*. Berkeley: University of California Press.

Sadly, the tragedy of the failure of the St. Francis Dam is not well known by generations who have always been able to turn on the water faucet in their home. But the story of the dam built in 1926 about 50 miles north of Los Angeles is told in the 1974 movie *Chinatown*, and in this book. When the dam collapsed in 1928, more than 400 people were killed, and the authors provide a detailed analysis of the reasons why and the man behind the Los Angeles Department of Water and Power that built the facility.

Hunt, Constance E. 2004. *Thirsty Planet: Strategies for Sustainable Water Management*. New York: Palgrave Macmillan.

The author is one of the few who argue that conservation is the only strategy that must become an absolute priority if we are to have sufficient water for human use. Although noting that this is an extremely complex problem, she uses case studies to plead her case.

Igler, David. 2001. *Industrial Cowboys: Miller & Lux and the Transformation of the Far West, 1850–1920*. Berkeley: University of California Press.

This comprehensive analysis of the California Supreme Court case explores how common law and the riparian doctrine were rejected in 1886 as the court juggled the competing rights of different water users, eventually adopting the doctrine of prior appropriation for the state. The author identifies the factors that make these court cases exemplary of changes throughout the West and its land use.

Ingram, B. Lynn, and Frances Malamud-Roam. 2015. *The West without Water: What Past Floods, Droughts, and Other Climatic Clues Tell Us about Tomorrow*. Berkeley: University of California Press.

Combining history with research on climate change, the authors cover the West's weather and disasters from a unique perspective. They note that what has happened in the past will not only happen again, but that the looming changes in temperature may exacerbate what we already face.

Jackson, Donald C. 1995. *Building the Ultimate Dam: John S. Eastwood and the Control of Water in the West*. Lawrence: University Press of Kansas.

"Bigger is better" was the mantra of western water policy illustrated not only in the book itself but also in the career of John S. Eastwood, a hydraulic engineer who battled his colleagues, corporate interests, and the government to build seventeen dams across the West using his innovative multiple-arch design. The book also explores how corporate interests viewed big dams as profitable investments in the emerging West, and how the more cost-effective dam designed by Eastwood was considered not as reliable as the traditional gravity-fill structures designed by others.

Kahrl, William L. 1982. *Water and Power: The Conflict over Los Angeles' Water Supply in the Owens Valley*. Berkeley: University of California Press.

There are numerous accounts of how the city of Los Angeles obtained the water it wanted from California's Owens Valley, but this version is perhaps one of the most detailed. The author is specific in outlining who did what to whom, with backgrounds on all the people and companies involved.

Kaufmann, Obi. 2019. *The State of Water: Understanding California's Most Precious Resource*. Berkeley, CA: Heyday Books.

Illustrated with watercolors, this is a short (144-page) book that deals less with the history of water in the California and more on some practical solutions. There is a hopeful tone to the writing, and the author shows that responsible water conservation can be an important tool in helping animals and people to survive.

Krist, Gary. 2018. *The Mirage Factory: Illusion, Imagination, and the Invention of Los Angeles*. New York: Crown.

In a style that is more story-telling than scholarly work, the author describes how this "implausible city" grew up to be "an urban giant where no city should rightly be." Krist explains the people and process by which Los Angeles underwent an amazing transformation, and how three iconic innovators—William Mulholland, David Griffith, and Aimee Semple McPherson—facilitated an image of a blossoming city in the desert.

Kuhn, Eric, and John Fleck. 2021. *Science Be Dammed: How Ignoring Inconvenient Science Drained the Colorado River*. Tucson: University of Arizona Press.

You need not be a math major to figure out that the original division of the waters of the Colorado River overestimated the amount of water available to the seven states that divided it up. And yet the allocation formula that was developed has been in place for more than a century, and it has taken that long for officials to agree that it needs to be changed. The current crisis over the Colorado, the authors say, is due to decisions made long ago and never corrected or confronted until now.

Kurlansky, Mark. 2020. *Salmon: A Fish, the Earth, and the History of Their Common Fate*. Ventura, CA: Patagonia Books.

Part coffee table book, part cookbook, part historical narrative, this best-selling author's love affair with salmon is beautifully explained in both prose and photography. He takes what could have been a scholarly edition about the fish and turns it into a love story with endnotes.

Laflin, Rose. 2005. *Irrigation, Settlement, and Change on the Cache la Poudre River*. Fort Collins: Colorado State University.

This short (172-page) university publication outlines the changes that began in the early 1860s on the Cache la Poudre River, which drains 1,890 miles of land in the mountain ranges of Wyoming and Colorado. Settlers envisioned that the canals and reservoirs they built would turn the arid grasslands into fertile agricultural acreage, and that was partly true as the population boomed. But the Bureau of Reclamation's Colorado-Big Thompson Project also brought unintended consequences and clashes among the water users and environmentalists.

Marks, Paula Mitchell. 1998. *In A Barren Land: American Indian Dispossession and Survival*. New York: William Morrow.

Written by a historian who is not a Native American, the author nonetheless has provided a comprehensive and well-written chronology of the treatment of Indian people from their arrival in the New World in the early 1600s to 1996. She writes of the forced marches, the injustices, the attempts to assimilate tribes into Anglo culture, and the contemporary efforts to remain independent and not tied to federal assistance. Remarkably, there is coverage of so many tribes in different parts of the country that the reader gets a broad view of regional and tribal differences.

Martin, Russell. 1989. *A Story that Stands like a Dam: Glen Canyon and the Struggle for the Soul of the West*. New York: Henry Holt.

The rich telling of the story of the building of the Glen Canyon Dam is due in part to the author's ability to introduce the reader to the individuals involved, from the controversy over whether the dam should be built to its construction. This is an unbiased account, filled with detail at every phase of the dam's history.

McCool, Daniel. 1987. *Command of the Waters: Iron Triangles, Federal Water Development, and Indian Water*. Berkeley: University of California Press.

It is hard to find a volume that puts Native American water rights in context, but McCool does a good job of doing so with this book. Although it does not cover the more recent developments in the law, there is more than enough explanation of the role of federal agencies in these conflicts, especially the relationships among them and the Bureau of Indian Affairs.

McPhee, John. 1971. *Encounters with the Archdruid*. New York: Farrar, Straus, and Giroux.

Published when the word ecology was just beginning to find its way into our lexicon, McPhee's biographical narrative has become a classic account of the war that took place between David Brower of the Sierra Club and Floyd Dominy of the Bureau of Reclamation. McPhee explores the ideas at the core of the environmental movement versus those of the reclamation and development worldview.

Melosi, Martin. 2011. *Precious Commodity: Providing Water for America's Cities*. Pittsburgh: University of Pittsburgh Press.

Questioning whether access to water is an inalienable right, Melosi looks at the historical basis for water resource use, the role of government, legal jurisdictions, and privatization.

Midkiff, Kenneth. 2007. *Not A Drop to Drink: America's Water Crisis*. Novato, CA: New World Library.

What do you do when the water spigot runs dry? Blaming irrigated crop production and other water-intensive agricultural practices, the author calls for local involvement in water decision-making and increased efforts at conservation.

Moeller, Beverly Bowen. 1971. *Phil Swing and Boulder Dam*. Berkeley: University of California Press.

Called "The Father of Boulder Dam," the name Phil Swing is perhaps not as well known as it should be. A progressive Republican elected to the House who served in the House from 1921 to 1933, Swing spent seven years trying to persuade his colleagues to authorize legislation to build Boulder (Hoover) Dam, although he is rarely mentioned in the chronicle of the dam's origins.

Mumme, Steven P. 2023. *Border Water: The Politics of US–Mexico Transboundary Water Management, 1945–2015*. Tucson: University of Arizona Press.

Author Mumme looks at the 1,900-mile-long border between the United States and Mexico from the perspective of three distinct periods and the issues that frame the debate over water in each one. He sees water policy as part of a longer, larger binational relationship between the two countries that reflect changing events, including the terror attacks of 9/11.

Nies, Judith. 2014. *Unreal City: Las Vegas, Black Mesa, and the Fate of the West*. New York: Nation Books.

This journalistic account of the battle for resources focuses on the Black Mesa strip mining operation in northern Arizona, the Navajo and Hopi Land Settlement Act, the smog that found its way into the Grand Canyon, the role of Mormons, and the author's belief that in an arid climate, water assumes a mystical power.

Norris, Jane E. and Lee G. Norris. 1990. *Written in Water: The Life of Benjamin Harrison Eaton*. Athens: Ohio University Press.

This biography of Eaton explores how the founder of the Greeley (CO) Colony moved from serving as a railroad surveyor, prospecting for gold, being a prominent landowner/farmer who helped establish modern irrigation farming in the state, to building irrigation canals and reservoirs, to serving in political office as justice of the peace and county commissioner, moving on to the territorial legislature and serving as governor of Colorado.

Pearce, Fred. 2018. *When the Rivers Run Dry: Water—the Defining Crisis of the 21st Century*. Boston: Beacon Press.

Based on his travels to thirty countries, Pearce predicts that by 2025, water scarcity will be severe enough a problem to cut global food production by more than the current US grain harvest.

Pearkes, Eileen Delehanty. 2023. *A River Captured: The Columbia River Treaty and Catastrophic Change*, revised 2nd ed. Victoria, BC: Rocky Mountain Books.

The Columbia River Treaty examined in this book is also a story about First Nations. The author has previously written about the Arrow Lakes Indians, or Sinixt, and the loss of their Canadian rights. Now she covers how the treaty expires in 2024 and the debate over whether or not it will be renewed.

Pisani, Donald. 1992. *To Reclaim a Divided West: Water, Law, and Public Policy 1848–1902*. Albuquerque: University of New Mexico Press.

Environmental historian Pisani has an encyclopedic knowledge of the West and the development of its natural resources, which is illustrated by this collection of essays. The topic of water is featured throughout the book, which is one of several he has published on this topic.

Powell, John Wesley. 1879. *Report on the Lands of the Arid Region of the United States*. Washington, DC: Government Printing Office.

Although this report is somewhat difficult to obtain in its original format, it is the one that is often cited and an interesting first-person account.

Powell, James Lawrence. 2009. *Dead Pool: Lake Powell, Global Warming, and the Future of Water in the West*. Berkeley: University of California Press.

Sometimes, photographs add an element of understanding to a subject that cannot be explained well in words. In this book, the historical images paint a detailed history of the reservoir. This is not a scholarly work, but worth looking at nonetheless.

Qadir, Manzoor, Vladimir Smakhtin, Sasha Koo-Oshima, and Edeltraud Guenther, eds. 2022. *Unconventional Water Resources*. New York: Springer International.

Using global security as a frame, the authors have collected essays on six broad categories of unconventional water sources from scientists and practitioners, covering topics from cloud seeding, deep offshore groundwater, agricultural drainage water, and desalination as ways to increase freshwater resources during times of water scarcity.

Reisner, Marc. 1986. *Cadillac Desert: The West and Its Disappearing Water*. New York: Viking.

This award-winning classic chronicles the story of early settlers in California who thronged to what they thought was a new Eden—Los Angeles. He explains the competition between the US Bureau of Reclamation and the US Army Corps of Engineers, along with ruthless politicians and business interests, to transform the arid desert and to profit from the city's growth. If you read only one book about the West and its development, this would be the one.

Reisner, Marc and Bates, Sarah. 1990. *Overtapped Oasis: Reform or Revolution for Western Waters*. Washington, DC: Island Press.

There is plenty of water available, the authors believe, if only it were to be used efficiently. Published after Reisner's *Cadillac Desert*, some critics have called it a sequel to his award-winning book.

Richter, Brian. 2014. *Chasing Water: A Guide for Moving from Scarcity to Sustainability*. Washington, DC: Island Press.

Local community members, not state or federal leaders and bureaucrats, should make water policy in areas of scarcity, the author believes. Although the book uses case studies from around the world, his examples have, at their core, collaboration, dialogue, and a broader view of water use.

Righter, Robert W. 2005. *The Battle Over Hetch Hetchy: America's Most Controversial Dam and the Birth of Modern Environmentalism*. New York: Oxford University Press.

The building of the dam that flooded California's Hetch Hetchy Valley in 1934 marked a pivotal chapter between the country's conservationists and preservationists. The purpose of the dam was to provide drinking water for the people of San Francisco, but it polarized the West in an epic battle of ideas.

Robison, Jason Anthony, ed. 2022. *Cornerstone at the Confluence: Navigating the Colorado River Compact's Next Century*. Tucson: University of Arizona Press.

In the four sections of this edited volume, with a forward by climate scientist Brad Udall, the varied authors take on the 1922 agreement that governs the allocation of water from the Colorado River. Unlike the original document, they cover issues related to the apportionment among the basin states, the environment, Native American tribal participation in decision-making, and the potential alternatives for a different structure for a new agreement.

Rowley, William D. 1996. *Reclaiming the Arid West: The Career of Francis G. Newlands*. Bloomington: Indiana University Press.

Nevada historian Rowley has written a meticulously researched book that expands the more traditional biographical material about Newlands. He portrays him as a complex and sophisticated Progressive Democrat whose view on the role of government in regulating society would become an important element of administrations that followed.

Rowley, William D. 2006. *The Bureau of Reclamation: Origins and Growth to 1945*. Washington, DC: U.S. Department of Interior, Bureau of Reclamation.

For someone looking for a basic understanding of the agency, the author provides a clear synopsis of almost every major activity in the Bureau's history. The book is heavily illustrated, and explores both the engineering aspects of reclamation as well as the financial components.

Sabatier, Paul, et al., eds. 2005. *Swimming Upstream: Collaborative Approaches to Watershed Management*. Cambridge, MA: MIT Press.

Written at a time when collaboration was rarely mentioned as a strategy, the author shows how the traditional top-down model of management is outdated. He argues, instead, for the role of negotiation that encompasses many different stakeholders in decision-making.

Sauder, Robert A. 2009. *The Yuma Reclamation Project: Irrigation, Indian Allotment, and Settlement Along the Lower Colorado River*. Reno: University of Nevada Press.

Little attention has been paid to this 1904 reclamation project near Fort Yuma, one of the first in the region, and one that drew upon the irrigation experiences of Spanish colonists and the Indigenous Quechan people.

Schulte, Steven C. 2016. *As Precious as Blood: The Western Slope in Colorado's Water Wars, 1900–1970*. Denver: University Press of Colorado.

Unless you have lived in Colorado for a century or so, you may not be familiar with the political divide that brought water from the snowy range west of the Continental Divide to the more populated Front Range—the battle of urban developers, members of Congress, and state officials for this precious resource.

Standiford, Les. 2015. *Water to the Angels: William Mulholland, His Monumental Aqueduct, and the Rise of Los Angeles*. New York: Ecco.

Biographies of William Mulholland tend to be written from one of two perspectives, arguing that the man was a visionary who met the challenge of bringing water to Los Angeles, or an exploiter of rural residents who stole their water. Standiford tends to do the former in this book, giving credit to Mulholland for his decades of public service to the city and giving its residents what they wanted.

Stegner, Wallace. 1954. *Beyond the Hundredth Meridian: John Wesley Powell and the Second Opening of the West*. Boston: Houghton Mifflin.

Pulitzer Prize-winning author Stegner is a prolific author, and his love for the West is in evidence in this historical account of John Wesley Powell's explorations. For those unfamiliar with the subject of this book, Stegner reminds us of Powell's interest in geology and ethnography, and how he was much more than a river runner. Powell faced politics, bureaucracies, and the Grand Canyon with equal fervor.

Stevens, Joseph E. 1988. *Hoover Dam: An American Adventure*. Norman: University of Oklahoma Press.

Some might argue that the term "adventure" might not be an appropriate way to describe the building of the Hoover Dam, but the author does bring the task that involved thousands of workers to life.

Tyler, Daniel. 2003. *Silver Fox of the Rockies: Delphus E. Carpenter and the Western Water Compacts*. Norman: University of Oklahoma Press.

Despite his importance in the development of western water policy, there are few biographies of Delph Carpenter. This one ties the man and his impact on the Colorado River Basin together in weaving a story with a biography.

Wahl, Richard W. 1989. *Markets for Federal Water: Subsidies, Property Rights, and the Bureau of Reclamation*. Washington, DC: Resources for the Future Press.

Not for the timid, this is a book that provides a wealth of information about how the reclamation movement developed and how subsidies were used to help fund major irrigation efforts like the Central Valley Project. He analyzes potential solutions for dealing with water scarcity, including the development of water markets in the 1990s, the need for water conservation strategies, and efficient pricing. There is a strong emphasis on the economics approach to problem solving, and less attention paid to the politics of how this might be accomplished.

Walton, John. 1992. *Western Times and Water Wars: State, Culture, and Rebellion in California*. Berkeley: University of California Press.

Unlike purely historical accounts of how Los Angeles' officials decided to bring water from the Owens Valley, this is a study of social movements and activism. It explains how collective action, whether by a rural community or an urban one, or by a David and Goliath clash of economic classes, can be reflected in western history.

Ward, Diane Raines. 2003. *Water Wars: Drought, Flood, Folly, and the Politics of Thirst*. New York: Riverhead.

The author notes that most people do not understand the complexity of water issues, and that this is one reason the problems are so intractable. She argues that water scarcity problems are unique from one case to another, demanding different solutions rather than a one-size-fits-all approach.

Wehr, Kevin. 2004. *America's Fight over Water: The Environmental and Political Effects of Large-Scale Water Systems*. New York: Routledge.

Using the case studies of the Grand Coulee, Hoover, and Glen Canyon dams, the book outlines the fight over water in the West, examining the environmental, political, and social aspects of the contemporary debate. The material is not especially new or controversial.

Wescoat, James L., and Gilbert F. White. 2003. *Water for Life: Water Management and Environmental Policy*. New York: Cambridge University Press.

This book provides a useful background on groundwater, rivers, floods, and wetlands. It provides an overview of the governmental policies that have developed, and the role of non-governmental organizations in policymaking. The material is more for gaining an understanding of water policy rather than its depth.

Wiley, Peter Booth, and Robert Gottlieb. 1985. *Empires in the Sun: The Rise of the New American West*. Tucson: University of Arizona Press.

Written from both a historical perspective and a pessimistic one, the authors tell a different story of western development than most others, viewing the region's expansion and growth as capitalism and manipulation at its best.

Wilkinson, Charles F. 1992. *Crossing the Next Meridian: Land, Water, and the Future of the West*. Washington, DC: Island Press.

This classic in American and environmental history explores the role of law and those he terms "the lords of yesterday" who have shaped the nation's policies on land, its natural resources, and its Native people. He argues the need for a rethinking of those roles, coupled with the need for legal reform.

Williams, Richard N., ed. 2006. *Return to the River: Restoring Salmon to the Columbia River*. Burlington, MA: Elsevier Academic Press.

This edited volume consisting of thirteen chapters and over 650 pages reads like a scientific journal. The book covers the problems that have faced salmon populations in the Pacific Northwest, describes their habitat and salmon recovery efforts. The photographs are helpful in understanding the mechanical side of harvesting and restoring the salmon, along with seeing the problems of dealing with hydroelectric plants along the way.

Worster, Donald. 2001. *A River Running West: The Life of John Wesley Powell*. New York: Oxford University Press.

Historian Worster has written what is likely to be called the definitive biography of Powell, one that he admits avoids the perception of the explorer as the Man of the West. Instead, he looks at the way in which Powell's immigrant family roots, the rise in the importance of the natural sciences, and his relationship to the native peoples he met made him one of the most important influences on the rise of the conservation movement in America.

Young, Herbert C. 2003. *Understanding Water Rights and Conflicts*. Denver: BurgYoung.

If water is a complex natural resource, then water law is even more complex. This author explains the basics of water rights, legal rulings, and concepts that explain water scarcity for the novice.

Yudelson, Jerry. 2010. *Dry Run: Preventing the Next Urban Water Crisis*. Gabriola Island, BC: New Society Publishers.

From a global perspective, in what the author calls the Age of Scarcity, he interviews more than twenty-five water researchers and industry experts who propose solutions to reduce consumption and "net zero" water use.

Articles

"Nevada Ex-Sen. Alan H. Bible; Political Force for 40 Years." *Los Angeles Times*, September 14, 1988. https://www.latimes.com/archives/la/xpm-1988-09-14-mn-1677-story.html.

"New Permanent Water Conservation Rules are Coming to California—See How Your City Will Be Affected." *San Jose Mercury News*, August 31, 2023. https://www.mercurynews.com/2023/08/31/2023/new-permanent-water-conservation-rules-are-coming-to-california-see-how-your-city-will-be-affected.

"Pat Mulroy: Secrets to Success on the Colorado River." *Municipal Water Leader*, Vol. 8, No. 1, January 2021. https://municipalwaterleader.com/pat-mulroy-secrets-to-success-on-the-colorado-river/.

Alexander, Kurtis, Carlos Avila Gonzalez, and Guy Wathen. 2023. "The Big Melt Transformed California." *San Francisco Chronicle*, August 23, 2023. https://www.sfchronicle.com/projects/2023/california-big-melt-water.

Arrington, Debbie. 2023. "Finding Room for Cost-Effective Water Storage: Roseville and Neighboring Communities are Tapping into Groundwater as a Long-Term Solution." *Sacramento News & Review*, August 1, 2023. https://sacramento.newsreview.com/spotlight/finding-room-for-cost-effective-water-storage.

Baumhardt, Alex. 2023. "Oregon Has Failed to Address its Water Security Crisis, Government Report Finds." *Oregon Capital Chronicle*, January 26, 2023. https://oregoncapitalchronicle.com/2023/01/26/Oregon-has-failed-to-address-its-water-security-crisis-government-report-finds.

Beamish, Rita. 2023. "California's Mountain Parks: When All That Snow Melts," *National Parks Traveler*, April 28, 2023. https://www.nationalparkstraveler.org/2023/04/update-californias-mountain-parks-when-all-snow-melts.

Becker, Rachel. 2022. "Water-Hungry California Suffers Setback with Rejected Desalination Plans." *Governing*, May 16, 2022. https://www.governing.com/now/water-hungry-california-suffers-setback-with-rejected-desalination-plans.

Benanav, Michael. 2023. "In Drought-Plagued New Mexico, a City Loses Nears Half Its Water—To Leaky Pipes." *Searchlight New Mexico*, February 15, 2023. https://www.searchlightnm.org/in-drought-plagued-new-mexico-a-city-loses-nearly-half-its-water-to-leaky-pipes.

Berwyn, Bob. 2014. "Mono Lake Tribe Seeks to Assert Its Water Rights in Call for Emergency Halt of Water Diversions to Los Angeles." *Inside Climate News*, February 14, 2023. https://insideclimatenews.org/news/14022023/mono-lake-los-angeles-water-diversions/.

Bittle, Jake. 2023. "Arizona is Evicting a Saudi Alfalfa Farm, but the Thirsty Crop Isn't Going Anywhere." *Grist*, October 6, 2023. https://grist/org/agriculture/arizona/fondomonte-farm-saudi-alfalfa-groundwater-lease.

Brean, Henry. 2014. "Exit Interview: Mulroy Talks about Her Life as Las Vegas Water Chief." *Las Vegas Review-Journal*, February 1, 2014. https://www.reviewjournal.com.news/exit-interview-mulroy-talks-about-her-life-as-las-vegas-water-chief-2.

Caccese, Robert T., and Lara B. Fowler. 2021. "Come Hell or High-Water: Challenges for Adapting Pacific Northwest Water Law." *Pace Environmental Law Review*, 37. https://digitalcommons.pace.edu/cgi/viewcontent.cgi?article=1839&context=pelr.

Cahill, Nick. 2023. "New California Law Bolsters Groundwater Recharge as Strategic Defense against Climate Change." *Western Water*, September 7, 2023. https://www.watereducation.org/western-water/new-california-law-bolsters-groundwater-recharge-strategic-defense-against-climate.

Clyde, George D. 1959. "History of Irrigation in Utah." *Utah Historical Quarterly*, Vol. 27, No. 1. https://issuu.utah10/docs/uhq_volume27_1959_number1/s/97357.

Cook, Benjamin. 2022. "Megadroughts in the Common Era and the Anthropocene," November 15, 2022. www.drought.gov/news/megadroughts-common-era-and-anthropocene-2022-11-15.

Cox, John. 2023. "Where'd the Water Go? Underground Storage." July 8, 2023. https://www.bakersfield.com/news/whered-the-water-go-underground-storage/article_1f55c944-1ce4-11ee-bd06-a7e175f29700.html.

Davis, Martha. 2023. "Why Pausing Water Diversions to Los Angeles Honors Landmark Mono Lake Deal." *Cal Matters*, March 14, 2023. https://calmatters.org/commentary/2023/03/mono-lake-water-los-angeles.

Davis, Robert. 2023. "Colorado River Officials to Expand Troubled Water Conservation Program in 2024." *Colorado Newsline*, September 30, 2023. https://www.coloradonewsline.com/2023/09/30/colorado-river-water-conservation-program.

Davis, Tony. 2021. "Once Again, Arizona Hopes to Import Out-of-State Water in Face of Crisis." May 29, 2021. https://tucson.com/news/local/once-again-arizona-hopes-to-import-out-of-state-water-in-face-of-crisis/article_c47bf80a-be-39-11-eb-918b-13b88dd52f2f.html.

Davis, Tony. 2023. "Arizona Changes Course in Push to Import Water." *Arizona Daily Star*, October 29, 2023. https://tucson.newspapers.com/image/1014892228.

Desormeaux, Erik. 2023. "Is Seawater Desalination Right for California?" *WaterWorld*. https://www.waterworld.com/drinking-water/treatment/article/14294072/is-seawater-desalination-right-for-california.

Elliott, Gary E. 1989. "Senator Alan Bible and the Southern Nevada Water Project 1954–1971." *Nevada Historical Society Quarterly*. Vol, 32, No. 3: 181–196. Epubs.nsla.nv.gov/statepubs/epubs/210777-1989-3Fall.pdf.

Flavelle, Christopher. 2023. "Arizona, Low on Water, Weighs Taking It from the Sea." *The New York Times*, June 10, 2023. https://www.nytimes.com/2023/06/10/climate/arizona-desalination-water-climate.html.

Focht, Malya, and Sebastian Cahill. 2023. "The US Has Pumped So Much Groundwater That It's Literally Splitting the Ground Open across the American Southwest." *Business Insider*, September 11, 2023. https://www.businessinsider.com/american-southwest-mile-long-cracks-pumping-groundwater-2023-9.

Frederick, James. 2023. "Mexico Steps Up Rain-Making Project amid Intense Heatwave and Drought." *The Guardian*, July 23, 2023. https://www.theguardian.com/world/2023/jul/23/mexico-cloud-seeding-heatwave-drought.

Garrison, Jessica, Susanne Rust, and Ian James. 2023. "Fears Grow as Floodwaters Threaten to Drown this California City and Prison Complex." *Los Angeles Times*, April 24, 2023. https://www.latimes.com/california/story/2023-04-24/floodwaters-threaten-to-drown-a-california-city-and-prison.

Gerlak, Andrea K. 2006. "Federalism and U.S. Water Policy: Lessons for the Twenty-First Century." *Publius*, Vol. 36, No. 2: 231–257. https://doi.org/10.1093/publius/pji032.

Gilmer, Ellen M., and Jennifer Kay. 2020. "Water Wars at the Supreme Court: 'It's Only Going to Get Worse.'" *Bloomberg Law, Environment and Energy*. September 17, 2020. https://news.bloomberglaw.com/environment-and-energy/water-wars-at-the-supreme-court-its-only-going-to-get-worse.

Gomez-Van Cortright, Guanani. 2023. "Recharge Alone Won't End California's Groundwater Drought." *Bay Nature*, July 5, 2023. https://baynature.org/2023/07/05/recharge-alone-wont-end-californias-groundwater-drought.

Halaly, Alan. 2024. "'Phenomenal Progress'": Water Use in Southern Nevada Inches toward Goal." *Las Vegas Review-Journal*, January 18, 2024. https://www.reviewjournal.com/news/politics-and-government-nevada/phenomenal-progress-water-use-in-southern-nevada-inches-toward-goal-2984009.

Harris, Richard W. 2021. "Nevada's Public Lands: Who Owns and Controls Nevada?" *Nevada Lawyer*, October 2021. https://nvbar.org/wp-content/uploads/NevadaLawyer_Oct2021_who-owns-nevada.pdf.

Harrison, Casey. 2023. "Interior Department Official, at Water Summit, Lauds Nevada as a Leader in Conservation." *Las Vegas Sun*, August 30, 2023. https://lasvegassun.com/news/2023/aug/30/interior-department-official-at-water-summit-lauds.

Heinz, Mark. 2023. "Water Scientist: It Will Take 21 Years of Massive Runoffs & Wet Springs like This One to Fix Colorado River Crisis. *Cowboy State Daily*, June 8, 2023. https://www.cowboystatedaily.com/2023/06/08/it-would-take-21-more.

Heydinger, Timothy A. 1990. "The Mono Lake Controversy and the Evolution of California's Public Trust Doctrine." *Environs*: Environmental Law and Policy. https://environs.law.ucdavis.edu/volumes/13/2/articles/heydinger.pdf.

Hudson, Bill. 2019. "Editorial: The Murder and Resurrection of the Colorado River, Part One." *Pagosa Daily Post*, October 15, 2019. https://pagosadailypost.com/2019/10/15/editorial-the-murder-and-resurrection-of-the-colorado-river-part-one.

James, Ian. 2023. "The River's End: Amid Colorado River Cuts, Mexico Seeks to Restore Its Lost Oasis." *Los Angeles Times*, January 31, 2023. https://www.latimes.com/environment/story/2023-01-31/colorado-river-in-crisis-the-rivers-end.

James, Ian. 2023. "Battle Rages over 'Sweetheart Deal" between Trump Administration and Giant Water District." *Los Angeles Times*, August 10, 2023. https://www.latimes.com/environment/story/2023-08-10/environmentalists-praise-court-ruling-against-water-district.

James, Ian. "Saudi Firm that Grows Hay in California and Arizona to Lose Farm Leases over Water Issue." *Los Angeles Times*, October 5, 2023. https://www.latimes.com/environment/story/2023-10-05/arizona-ends-saudi-fondomonte-water-farmland-leases.

Johnson, George. 1996. "Social Strife May Have Exiled Ancient Indians." *The New York Times*, August 20, 1996. https://www.nytimes.com/1996/08/20/science/social-strife-may-have-exiled-ancient-indians.

Kaplan, Sarah, and Brady Dennis. 2023. "Great Salt Lake on Track to Disappear in Five Years, Scientists Warn." *The Washington Post*, January 6, 2023. https://news.yahoo.great-salt-lake-track-disappear-004427524.html.

Kaur, Anumita. 2023. "The Breakthrough Deal to Protect the Colorado River, Explained." *The Washington Post*, May 23, 2023. https://www.washingtonpost.com/climate-environment/2023/5/23/Colorado-river-deal-water-cuts-explained.

Kim, June. 2023. "As Companies Eye Massive Lithium Deposits in California's Salton Sea, Locals Anticipate a Mixed Bag." *Inside Climate News*, August 26, 2023. https://insideclimatenews.org/news/26082023/salton-sea-lithium-mining-california.

Knobeloch, Payton. 2018. "Meet the Hoosier Engineer 'Who Made the Desert Bloom.'" *The Inbox*. July 20, 2018. https://indianapublicmedia.org/theinbox/elwood-mead.php.

Landers, Jay. 2023. "Debate Centers on Diversions from California's Mono Lake Basin." *The Source*, August 3, 2023. https://www.asce.org/publications-and-news/civil-engineering-source/civil-engineering/magazine/article/2023/08/debate-centers-on-diversions-from-californias-mono-lake-basin.

LaRouche, Lyndon H. Jr. 1988. "The Outline of NAWAPA." January, 1988. https://archive.schillerinstitute.com/economy/phys_econ_nawapa_1983.html.

Lash, Nat, Mark Olalde, and Ash Ngu. 2023. "Las Vegas Needs to Save Water. It Won't Find It in Lawns." *ProPublica*, June 7, 2023. https://projects.propublica.org/turf-wars.

Leal, Bob. 2023. "Feds Ease Colorado River Water Cuts for Thirsty Western States." *Courthouse News Service*, August 15, 2023. https://www.courthousenews.com/feds-ease-colorado-river-water-cuts-for-thirsty-western-states/.

Leslie, Jacques. 2018. "Where Water is Scarce, Communities Turn to Reusing Wastewater." *Yale Environment 360*, May 1, 2018. https://e360.yale.edu/features/instead-of-more-dams-communities-turn-to-reusing-wastewater.

Lochhead, Colton. 2023. "Agency Now Has Power to Limit Residential Water Use in Las Vegas." *Las Vegas Review-Journal*, June 7, 2023. https://reviewjournal.com/news/politics-and-government/nevada/2023-legislature/agency-now-has-power-to-limit-water-use-in-las-vegas.

Lochhead, Colton. 2023a "Las Vegas Water Use Down 25% This Year, but a Hot Summer Looms." *Las Vegas Review-Journal*, July 11, 2023. https://www.reviewjournal.com/local/local-nevada/las-vegas-water-use-down-25-this-year-but-a-hot-summer-looms.

Lochhead, Colton. 2023b. "'It's Excessive': Homeowners Push Back on Water District's New Fee." *Las Vegas Review-Journal*, July 18, 2023. https://www.reviewjournal.com/news/politics-and-government/its-excessive-homeowners-push-back-on-water-districts-new-fee.

Lochhead, Colton. 2023c. "How Cloud Seeding is Giving a Boost to Nevada's Water Supply." *Las Vegas Review-Journal*, July 28, 2023. https://www.reviewjournal.com/local/local/las/vegas/how/cloud/seeding/is/giving/a/boost/to/nevadas/water/supply.

Lubofsky, Evan. 2021. "Can Icebergs Be Towed to Water-Starved Cities?" *Oceanus*, January 6, 2021. https://www.whoi.edu/oceanus/feature/can-icebergs-be-towed-to-water-starved-cities.

Lustgarten, Abrahm. 2015. "The 'Water Witch': Pat Mulroy Preached Conservation while Backing Growth in Las Vegas." *ProPublica*. June 2, 2015. https://www.propublica.org/article/killing-colorado-pat-mulroy-las-vegas-water-witch.

McKuin, Brandi, and Roger Bales. 2023. "Opinion: This Idea Could Save California Billions of Gallons of Water while Generating Clean Energy." *Los Angeles Times*, August 16, 2023. https://www.latimes.com/opinion/story/2023-08-16/water-canals-aqueducts-solar-energy-climate-conservation-merced-turlock-central-valley.

Melillo, Gianna. 2023. "How Arizona, California, and Other States Are Trying to Generate a Whole New Water Supply." *The Hill*, January 22, 2023. https://thehill.com/policy/equilibrium-sustainability/3824483-how-arizona-california-and-other-states-are-trying-to-generate-a-whole-new-water-supply.

Mertz, Keiko. 2023. "Sites Reservoir Project is not the Water Solution California Needs." *Cal Matters*, August 30, 2023. https://calmatters.org/commentary.2023/08/sites-reservoir-dam-project-water.

Miller, Jeremy. 2023. "In California's Monterey Bay Area, a Proposed Desalination Plant Divides Wealthy Communities and Poorer Ones." *Sierra*, June 13, 2023. https://www.sierraclub.org/sierra/california-s-proposed-desalination-plant-divides-wealthy-communities-and-poorer-ones.

Mullane, Shannon. 2023a. "Colorado River Officials Weigh How to Cut Water, Include Tribes ahead of Looming Negotiations." *The Colorado Sun*, June 12, 2023. https://coloradosun.com/2023/06/12/colorado-river-negotiations-tribes-top-priorities-2026.

Mullane, Shannon. 2023b. "Colorado River Basin States Stake Out Positions on the Future of Mead, Powell Reservoirs." *The Colorado Sun*, August 23, 2023.

https://coloradosu.com/2023/08/23/colorado-river-basin-states-future-ofmead-powell-reservoirs.

Naishadham, Suman, and Ken Ritter. 2023. "Breakthrough Proposal Would Aid Drought-Stricken Colorado River as 3 Western States Offer Cuts." *AP News*, May 23, 2023. https://apnews/com/article/colorado-river-arizona-california-nevada-drought-climate-change-85bfbc63bfc6590613bb142347e1a014.

Navarez, Alfonso A. 1988. "Former Senator Alan Bible, 78; Nevadan Was Advocate of Parks." *The New York Times*, September 14, 1988. https://www.nytimes.com/1988/09/14/obituaries/former-senator/alan-bible/78-nevadan-was-advocate-of-parks.html.

O'Donoghue, Amy Joi. 2023. "New Analysis Says Great Salt Lake Can Be Saved, but Not Without Great Effort, and Expense." *Deseret News*, February 8, 2023. https://www.deseret.com/utah/2023/2/8/23588664/great-salt-lake-water-drought-saline-ecosystem-policy-conservation.

Owen, David. 2022. "The Biggest Potential Water Disaster in the United States." *The New Yorker*, May 11, 2022. https://www.newyorker.com/news/dispatch/the-biggest-potential-water-disaster-in-the-united-states.

Pitzer, Gary. 2021. "As Climate Change Turns Up the Heat in Las Vegas, Water Managers Try to Wring New Savings to Stretch Supply." *Western Water*, June 25, 2021. https://www.watereducation.org/western-water/climate-change-turns-heat-las-vegas-water-managers-try-wring-new-savings-stretch.

Powel, James, and Trevor Hughes. 2023. "'This Buys a Year': Hurricane Hilary Edges Up Lake Mead Water Level." *USA Today*, August 22, 2023. https://www.usatoday.com/story/news/weather/2023/08/22/hurricane-hilary-rises-water-level-lake-mead-70654623007.

Prokop, Danielle. 2023. "Rio Grande Settlement Proposal Is in Federal Judge's Hand." *Source New Mexico*, February 7, 2023. https://sourcenm.com/2023/02/07/rio-grande-settlement-proposal-is-in-federal-judges-hand.

Ramsey, Kelly. 2023. "Dear Los Angeles: You're Drinking Indigenous Water." *Sierra*, October 9, 2023. https://www.sierraclub.org/sierra/dear-los-angeles-you-re-drinking-indigenous-water.

Reichmann, Kelsey. 2023. "Tribe Seeking Colorado River Water Rights Spurned by High Court." *Courthouse News Service*, June 22, 2023. https://www.courthousenews.com/tribe-seeking-colorado-river-water-rights-spurned-by-high-court.

Richter, Brian D. 2023. "Decoupling Urban Water Use from Population Growth in the Colorado River Basin." *Journal of Water Resources Planning and Management*, Vol. 149, Issue 2. https://doi.org.10.1061/JWRMD5.WRENG-5887.

Ring, Edward. "Saving California's Salton Sea." *National Review*, August 29, 2023. http://www.nationalreview.com.2023/08/saving-californias-salton-sea.

Rivard, Ry 2023. "Central Valley Farmers are Having a Climate Reckoning." *Politico*, August 17, 2023. https://www.politico.com/news/2023/08/17/central-valley-farmers-are-having-a-climate-reckoning-00111593.

Robbins, Jim. 2019. "As Water Scarcity Increases, Desalination Plants Are on the Rise." *Yale Environment 360*, June 11, 2019. https://e360.yale.edu/features/as-water-scarcity-increases-desalination-plants-are-on-the-rise.

Robbins, Jim. 2023. "Beyond the Yuck Factor: Cities Turn to 'Extreme' Water Recycling." *Yale Environment 360*, June 6, 2023. https://e360.yale.edu/features/on-site-distributed-premise-graywater-blackwater-recycling.

Rogers, Paul. 2023. "California Weather: How This Year Ranks among the All-Time Biggest Rainfall Years." *The Mercury News*, June 30, 2023. https://www.mercurynews.com/2023/06/30/California-weather-how-this-year-ranks-among-the-all-time-biggest-rainfall-years.

Rojanasakul, Mira, Christopher Flavelle, Blacki Migliozzi, and Eli Murray. 2023. "America Is Using Up Its Groundwater like There's no Tomorrow." *The New York Times*, August 28, 2023. https://nytimes.com/interactive/2023/08/28/climate/groundwater-drying-climate-change.

Rust, Susanne, Jessica Garrison, and Ian James. 2023. "Their Land Is Sinking. But Tulare Lake Farm Barons Defy Calls to Cut Groundwater Pumping." *Los Angeles Times*, December 27, 2023. https://www.latimes.com/environment/story/2023-12-27/tulare-land-barons-defy-calls-to-cut-groundwater-pumping.

Sackett, Heather. 2023. "Aspen Journalism: Tribes Promised a Voice in Colorado River Negotiations." *The Aspen Times*, July 9, 2023. https://www.aspentimes.com/news/aspen-journalism-tribes-promised-a-voice-in-colorado-river-negotiations/.

Singleton, Hannah. 2023. "This Year's Record-Breaking Snowpack is Pouring into the Dried-Out Salt Lake." *High Country News*, May 15, 2023. https://www.hcn.org/articles/flooding-this-years-record-breaking-snowpack-is-pouring-into-the-dried-out-salt-lake.

Smith, Anna V., Mark Olalde, and Umar Farooq. 2023. "How Arizona Squeezes Tribes for Water." *High Country News*, June 14, 2023. www.hcn.

org/issues/55.7/indigenous-arrairs-colorado-river-how-arizona-stands-between-tribes-and-their-water-squeezed.

Smith, Hayley. 2024. "Earth Reaches Grim Milestone: 2023 Was the Warmest Year on Record." *Los Angeles Times*. January 9, 2024. https://www.latimes.com/environment/story/2024-01-09/its-official-2023-was-the-warmest-year-on-record.

Smith, Hayley, and Sean Greene. 2023. "Californians Were Asked to Cut Water Use 15% during the Drought. How Close Did They Get?" *Los Angeles Times*, June 12, 2023. https://www.latimes.com/california/story/2023/06-12/did/Californians-cut-water-use-15-percent-during-the-drought.

Staggs, Brooke. 2023. "Study: Salton Sea Has Enough Lithium to Make More than 375 Million EV Batteries." *The Press Enterprise*, November 28, 2023. https://www.pressenterprise.com/2023/11/28/study-salton-sea-has-enough-lithium-to-make-more-than-375-million-ev-batteries/.

Stanley-Becker, Isaac, Joshua Partlow, and Yvonne Wingett Sanchez. 2023. "How a Saudi Firm Tapped a Gusher of Water in Drought-Stricken Arizona." *The Washington Post*. July 16. 2023. https://www.washingtonpost.com/politics/2023/07/16/fondomonte-arizona-drought-saudi-farm-water.

Tracey, Caroline. 2022. "The History behind the New Mexico–Texas Rio Grande Settlement." *High Country News*. November 10, 2022. https://www.hcn.org/articles/south-water-the-history-behind-the-new-mexico-texas-rio-grande-settlement.

Udasin, Sharon. 2023. "How US–Mexico Collaboration Could Help Stabilize the Drought-Stricken Colorado River Basin." *The Hill*, July 22, 2023. https://thehill.com/policy/equilibrium-sustainability/4112918-use-mexico-collaboration-could-help-stabilize-drought-stricken-colorado-river-basin.

Vad, Jesse. 2023. "'Immense' Flow of Public Funds to Groundwater Agencies is Tapering Off." *SJV Water*, September 11, 2023. https://sjvwater.org/immense-flow-of-public-funds-to-groundwater-agencies-is-tapering-off.

Viani, Lisa Owens. 2023. "Farm to Water Table." *Landscape Architecture Magazine*, August 24, 2023. https://landscapearchitecturemagazine.org/2023/08/24/farm-to-water-table.

Walters, Dan. 2023. "Water Rights Reformers Scored only a Minor Victory in the Legislature." *CalMatters*, September 17, 2023. https://www.calmatters.org/commentary/2023/09/California-water-rights-reformers.

Whitman, Elizabeth Wang. 2021. "Meet Arizona's One-Percenters." *The Guardian*, April 5, 2021. https://www.theguardian.com/us-news/2021/april/05/arizona-water-one-percenters.

Whitney, Charles Allen. 1969. "John Eastwood: Unsung Genius of the Drawing Board." *Montana: The Magazine of Western History*, Vol. 19, No. 3: 38–49. https://www.jstor.org/stable/4517382.

Willcox, Kathleen. 2023. "A Simple Vineyard Strategy Cuts Water Usage by One-Third." *The Drinks Business*, August 30, 2023. https://www.thedrinksbusiness.com/2023/08/a-simple-vineyard-strategy-cuts-water-usage-by-one-third.

Wilson, Janet. 2022. "Pipe Dream or Possible? Experts Weigh in on Idea of Sending Mississippi River Water to West." *Palm Springs Desert Sun*, August 14, 2022. https://www.desertsun.com/story/news/environment/2022/08/14/sending-mississippi-water-west-feasible-experts-weigh/10282030002.

Zorn, Justin Talbot, and Israel Mirsky. 2023. "America Should Harvest a Trillion Gallons of Rainwater." *Time*, September 6, 2023. https://time.com/6311363/harvest-trillion-gallons-of-rainwater.

Monographs and Government Publications

Abbott, Benjamin W. et al. 2023. "Emergency Measures Needed to Rescue Great Salt Lake from Ongoing Collapse." January 4, 2023. pws.byu.edu/GSL%20report%202023.

California. Department of Water Resources. 2023. "DWR Captures and Stores Water from Record-Breaking Snowpack." July 19, 2023. https://www.water.ca.gov/news/blog/2023/July-23/DWR-Captures-and-Stores-Water-From-Record-Breaking-Snowpack.

California. State Water Resources Control Board. 2023. "Next Phase of Recycled Water Begins for California." July 11, 2023. https://www.waterboards.ca.gov/press_room/press_releases/2023/pr20237711-recycled-water-next-phase.pdf.

Colorado Business Hall of Fame. *Benjamin Harrison Eaton*. https://www.businesshalloffame.org/benjamin-harrison-eaton.html.

Colorado. State Archives. *Benjamin Harrison Eaton*. https://archives.colorado.gov/collections/governors/benjamin-harrison-eaton.

Las Virgenes Municipal Water District. 2023. "OceanWell and LVMWD Announce Partnership to Pilot California's First Blue Water Farm." August 16, 2023. https://www.lvmwd.com/Home/Components/News/News/6028/22.

National Oceanic and Atmospheric Administration. n.d. U.S. Drought Task Force. *Drought Task Force Report on the 2020–2021 Southwestern U.S. Drought.* www.drought.gov/documents/noaa/drought-task-force-report-2020-2021-southwestern-us-drought.

Public and Environmental History Center. Colorado State University. n.d. "Delph E. Carpenter." https://pehc.colostate.edu/digital_projects/dp/poudre-river/moving-storing/biographies/delph-e-carpenter.

San Diego County Water Authority. 2022. "Carlsbad Desalination Plant Shields Region from Megadrought." March 16, 2022. https://www.waternewsnetwork.com/carlsbad-desalination-plant-shields-region-from-megadrought.

Southern Nevada Water Authority. n.d. "Water Smart Landscape Rebate." https://www.snwa.com/rebates/wsl/index.html.

Southern Nevada Water Authority. 2023. *Water Resource Plan.* https://www.snwa.com/universal/pdfjs/?file=/assets/pdf/water-resource-plan-2023.pdf#page=35.

U.S. Army Corps of Engineers. Civil Works Directorate. 2012. "Water in the U.S. American West: 150 Years of Adaptive Strategies." March 2012. Naturalresourcespolicy.org/docs/water-in-the-west.pdf.

U.S. Army Corps of Engineers. Institute for Water Resources. 2020. "Managed Aquifer Recharge and the U.S. Army Corps of Engineers: Water Security Through Resilience." April 2020. Aqua.doc.typepad.com/files/usace_march2020april.pdf?mc_cid=85ce7c0431&mc_eid=ffff8e049e.

U.S. Bureau of Reclamation. n.d. "Mark Wilmer: Arizona's Water Master." https://www.usbr.gov/lc/phoenix/AZ100/1950/mark_wilmer.html.

U.S. Bureau of Reclamation. 2022. "Request for Input on Development of Post-2026 Colorado River Reservoir Operational Strategies for Lake Powell and Lake Mead Under Historically Low Reservoir Conditions." June 24, 2022. https://www.federalregister.gov/documents/2022/6/24/2022-13502/request-for-input-on-development-of-post-2026-colorado-river-reservoir-operational-strategies-for-Lake-Powell-and-Lake-Mead-Under-Historically-Low-Reservoir-Conditions.

U.S. Bureau of Reclamation. April 20, 2023. "Above-Average Snowpack and Projected Runoff Will Send More Water from Lake Powell to Lake Mead." https://www.usbr.gov/newsroom/news-release/4492.

U.S. Bureau of Reclamation. April 20, 2023. "Reclamation Bolsters Central Valley Project 2023 Water Supply Allocations, https://www.usbr.gov/newsroom/news-release/4493.

U.S. Bureau of Reclamation. May 3, 2023. "Secretary Haaland Announces $12.6 Million from Bipartisan Infrastructure Law for Desalination Research Facility in Southern New Mexico." https://www.usbr.gov/newsroom/news-release/4507.

U.S. Bureau of Reclamation. August 15, 2023. "Reclamation Announces 2024 Operating Conditions for Lake Powell and Lake Mead." https://www.usbr.gov/newsroom/news-release/4603.

U.S. Bureau of Reclamation. 2023. "Scoping: Summary of the Federal Register Notice Input Received." https://www.usbr.gov/coloradoRiverBasin/post2026/scoping/summary-input.html.

U.S. Department of Energy. Federal Energy Management Program. n.d. "Best Management Practice #14: Alternative Water Sources." https://www.energy.gov/femp/best-management-practice-14-alternative-water-sources.

U.S. Department of the Interior. National Park Service. n.d. "Senator Francis G. Newlands." https://www.nps.gov/people/senator-francis-g-newlands.html.

U.S. Department of the Interior. Office of Saline Water. Research and Development. n.d. Progress Report No. 470. *An Economic and Engineering Analysis of the Electrodialysis Process.* https://www.crl.edu/news/office-saline-waters-research-and-development-progress-reports-digitized-trail.

U.S. Department of the Interior. 2014. "United States and Mexico Celebrate Partnership for Historic Release of Colorado River Water to Delta, Benefitting Both Nations." March 27, 2014. https://www.doi.gov/news/pressreleases/united-states-and-mexico-celebrate-partnership-for-historic-release-of-colorado-river-water-to-delta-benefitting-both-nations.

U.S. Environmental Protection Agency. 2017. "Outdoor Water Use in the United States." *WaterSense.* January 19, 2017. https://19january2017snapshot.epa.gov/www3/watersense/pubs/outdoor.html.

U.S. Environmental Protection Agency. 2022. "Aquifer Recharge and Aquifer Storage and Recovery." October 26, 2022. https://www.epa.gov/uic/aquifer-recharge-and-aquifer-storage-and-recovery.

U.S. Geological Survey. 1880. *First Annual Report.* Washington, DC.

Other Sources

n.a. 1965. *CQ Almanac 1965.* "Desalination Program." 21st. ed. 764-766. https://library.cqpress.com/cqalmanac/document.php?id=cqal65-1257810/.

n.a. 2023. "Achieving Groundwater Access for All." Press release. June 28, 2023. https://www.groundwaterresourcehub.org/content/dam/tnc/nature/en/documents/groundwater-resource-hub/AchievingGroudwaterAccessforAll.

Alvarez, Christopher, and Kristen DeSilva. 2022. "Former Southern Nevada Water Authority Chief 'Very Worried' about Lake Mead Level." *KNPR's State of Nevada*, May 26, 2022. https://knpr.org/show/knprs-state-of-nevada/2022/05/26/former-southern-nevada-water-authority-chief-very-worried-about-lake-mead-level.

Butler, Kirstin. 2022. "Soledad Luna and the St. Francis Dam Disaster." Public Broadcasting System, "An American Experience," April 5, 2022. https://pbs.org.wgbh/americanexperience/features/flood-desert-soledad-luna-st-francis-dam-disaster.

Butler, Kirstin. 2023. Press release. "New Report Addresses Findings that Most Groundwater Sustainability Plans Fail to Protect Vulnerable Communities and the Environment." June 27, 2023. https://cleanwater.org/releases/new-publication-finds-most-ca-groundwater-sustainability-plans-fail-protect-vulnerable.

Center for Biological Diversity. 2023. Press release. "Nevada Sen. Cortez Masto Pushes Bill for Colorado River Water to Feed Las Vegas Sprawl." June 15, 2023. www.biologicaldiversity.org.w.news.press-releases-nevada-sen-cortez-masto-pushes-bill-for-colorado-river-water-to-feed-las-vegas.

Clean Water Action. 2022. "SGMA and Underrepresented Farmers: Impact of Groundwater Sustainability Plans on Underrepresented Farmers." May 31, 2022. https://cleanwateraction.org/publications/sgma-and-underrepresented-farmers-impact-groundwater-sustainability-plans.

Colorado Public Radio. 2023. "How Might We Save the Colorado River?" July 5, 2023. https://www.cpr.org/2023/07/05/how-might-we-save-the-colorado-river.

Dungan, Ron. 2023. "Arizona's Groundwater-Supplies-Are-Essentially-Unregulated." KJZZ. July 24, 2023. https://kjzz.org/content/1852694/arizonas/groundwater/supplies-are-essentially-unregulated-means-rural-wells-are.

Felbab-Brown, Vanda. 2020. "Not Dried Up: US–Mexico Water Cooperation." The Brookings Institution. October 26, 2020. https://www.brookings.edu/articles/not-dried-up-us-mexico-water-cooperation.

Fuller, Craig. n.d. "Irrigation in Utah." *Utah History Encyclopedia*. https://www.uen.org/utah_history_encyclopedia/i/IRRIGATION.shtml.

Helfgott, Alexandra. 2021. "Bilateral Water Management: Water Sharing between the US and Mexico along the Border." Wilson Center. January 4, 2021. www.wilsoncenter.org/article/bilateral-water-management-water-sharing-between-us-and-mexico-along-border.

Hooton, LeRoy W., Jr. 1997. "What is Our Water Legacy?" Paper presented at the American Water Resources Association Conference, Salt Lake City, Utah. www.slcdocs.com/utilities/NewsEvents/news2013/news922013.html.

Hult, J. L., and N. C. Ostrander. 1973. "Antarctic Icebergs as a Global Fresh Water Resource." Prepared for the National Science Foundation. October 1973. www.rand.org/content/dam/rand/pubs/reports/2008/R1255.pdf.

Iowa State University. n.d. "Elwood Mead." *Biographical Dictionary*. https://isubios.pubpub.org/pub/pq0duz3v/release/1.

Kennedy, John F. 1961. "Remarks in Phoenix at the 50th Anniversary Dinner Honoring Senator Hayden." November 17, 1961. https://www.presidency.ucsb.edu/documents/remarks-phoenix-the-50th-anniversary-dinner-honoring-senator-hayden.

Klein, Kerry. 2023. "In Normally Dry Kings County, Tulare Lake has Carved a Long, Soggy Road Ahead for Farmers." KVPR, July 27, 2023. https://www.kvpr.org/local-news/2023/07/27/in-normally-dry-kings-county-tulare-lake-has-carveed-a-long-soggy-road-ahead-for-farmers.

McFarland, K. D. n.d. "North American Water and Power Alliance." Ucanr.edu/repository/fileaccess.cfm?article=164087&p=MCJMUC.

Mono Lake Committee. 2022. Letter to E. Joaquim Esquivel, December 16, 2022. https://www.waterboards.ca,gov/waterrights/water_issues/programs/mono_lake/docs/12162022-mlc-letter.pdf.

Northwest Power and Conservation Council. n.d. "Endangered Species Act, Columbia River Salmon and Steelhead, and the Biological Opinion." https://www.nwcouncil.org/reports/columbia-river-history/endangeredspeciesact.

Purdue University Archives. n.d. "Mead, Elwood, 1858-1936." https://archives.lib.purdue.edu/agents/people/604.

Rettig, Patricia J. 2023. "Delph E. Carpenter." *Colorado Encyclopedia*. https://coloradoencyclopedia.org/article/delph-e-carpenter.

South Coast Water District. n.d. "Doheny Ocean Desalination Project." https://www.scwd.org/about/district_projects/doheny_ocean_desalination_project/index.php.

Stanford University. Water in the West. n.d. "Recharge" Groundwater's Second Act." https://waterinthewest.stanford.edu/groundwater/recharge.

Stokley, Tom. 2023. “Flowing Downhill to Money.” California Water Impact Network, July 17, 2023. https://www.c-win.org/cwin-water-blog/2023/7/17/flowing-downhill-to-money.

Vad, Jesse. 2023. “State Pays Valley Farmers Millions to Keep Water in the Ground.” *SJV Water*, July 25, 2023. https://sjvwater.org/state-pays-valley-farmers-millions-to-keep-water-in-the-ground.

Walkem, Ardith. n.d. “Indigenous Peoples Water Rights: Challenges and Opportunities in an Era of Increased North American Integration.” https://www.uvic.ca/research/centres/globalstudies/assets/docs/publications/IndigenousPeoplesWaterRights.pdf.

Wilson, Janet, and Nat Lash. 2023. “The Historic Claims that Put a Few California Farming Families First in Line for Colorado River Water.” *ProPublica*, November 9, 2023. https://projects.propublica.org/california-farmers-colorado-river.

Electronic Media

Ambrose Video Publishing. 2009. *When the Water Tap Runs Dry*. New York: Ambrose Video Publishing. https://www.ambrosevideo.com.

CBS. 2023. *Not Enough Water to go Around: Colorado River Basin, Ravaged by Drought, Plans for a Drier Future*. 60 Minutes. https://www.youtube.com/watch?v=gmeWydWm2MU.

CNBC. 2021. *How the West Coast Drought Could Cause More Water Wars*. https://www.youtube.com/watch?v=aOQ0FHxeRTs.

Detrow, Scott and Taylar Dawn Stegner. Interview with Daryl Vigil. All Things Considered, National Public Radio. Podcast audio, July 2, 2023. https://www.npr.org/2023/07/02/1185721736/who-gets-a-say-in-the-colorado-rivers-water-supply.

Flint, Anthony. Interview with Jim Holway, Lincoln Institute of Land Policy. Land Matters Podcast: Water in the West. Podcast audio, October 31, 2023. https://www.lincolninst.edu/es/publications/articles/2023-10-land-matters-podcast-water-in-the-west.

Grist. 2023. *The Very Bad Math Drying Up the Colorado River*. https://www.youtube.com/watch?v=AzpYHXgfbbI.

Innovative Techs. 2022. How We Destroy the Colorado River. https://www.youtube.com/watch?v=Og_ruapbqXI.

Kilmer, Natlie. Interview with Clifford Lee. Apple Podcasts. *Protecting California's Water Before It Runs Out*. Podcast audio, 2023, https://podcasts.apple.com/us/podcast/protecting-californias-water-before-it-runs-out/id1587526639?i=1000582266375.

Los Angeles Times. 2022. "Desert Suburbia is Growing. But the Colorado River, and Arizona's Groundwater, Cannot Keep Up." https://www.youtube.com/watch?v=6sidQzMicXY.

National Public Radio. 2023. *Some Say the Century-Old Water Rights System in the West is Unfair and Racist*. https://www.npr.org/2023/07/10/1186827238/some-say-the-century-old-water-rights-system-in-the-west-is-unfair-and-racist.

Newsto. 2023. *Would You Drink Toilet Water? California Approves Wastewater for Human Consumption*. https://www.youtube.com/watch?v=4hFF0NusTrs.

Practical Engineering. 2023. *Why Is Desalination So Difficult?* https://www.youtube.com/watch?v=mxqOPdEUNTs.

Public Broadcasting System. 2016. *Beyond the Mirage: The Future of Water in the West*. https://www.pbs.org/show/beyond-mirage-future-water-west/.

Public Broadcasting System. 2022. *The Great Thirst: William Mulholland*. www.pbs.org/video/the-great-thirst-william-mulholland-fcbrjm.

Public Broadcasting System. 2022. *Water Wars: Whose Water is it Anyway? American Experience*. https://www.pbs.org/wgbh/americanexperience/features/conversations-water-wars/.

Stanford Wood Institute for the Environment. Stanford University. 2023. *Whiplash Weather: Lessons from California's Deadly 2023 Storms*. January 26, 2023. https://www.youtube.com/watch?v=qidpkV8FsbE.

Terra Mater. 2021. *How to Turn Sea Water into Fresh Water without Pollution*. https://www.youtube.com/watch?v=KdFIHecZDfc.

The Los Angeles History Project. 1989. *William Mulholland: The Dream Builder*. https://youtube.com/watchPV=Wu4Q7WrzQjE.

The New York Times. "7 States, 1 River, and An Agonizing Choice." https://www.nytimes.com/2023/01/31/podcasts/the-daily/colorado-river-water-cuts.html.

Toray Water. 2023. *Beyond the Current: San Diego's Water Reuse Revolution*. https://www.youtube.com/watch?v=gqiJON6XmcU.

VICE News. 2021. *The Town Trying to Pump Billions of Gallons of Water to Their Desert Community*. https://www.youtube.com/watch?v=rWpui1P9cAY.

Vox. 2022. *Who's Really Using the Water in the American West?* https://www.youtube.com/watch?v=f0gN1x6sVTc.

Wall Street Journal. 2021. "Why the Western Drought Will Have Major Ripple Effects." https://www.youtube.com/watch?v=kYsrGaHX7M4.

Watering the West. 2022. *Who Owns the Water in Colorado?* https://www.youtube.com/watch?v=blN0pKtxrRc.

Watering the West. 2023. Crisis on the Colorado. https://www.youtube.com/watch?v=3ZJ4seo6pZo.

Wertz, Louis. Interview with Wade Crowfoot. On Land. podcast audio, March 9, 2023. https://onland.westernlandowners.org/2023/podcast/water-in-california-with-ca-secretary-of-natural-resources-wade-crowfoot.

Western Resource Advocates. 2023. *Growing Water Smart in Utah*. https://westernresourceadvocates.org/podcasts/growing-water-smart-in-utah.

World History Summarized. 2023. *Why California Is Running Out of Water*. https://www.youtube.com/watch?v=TnDAlFQvPMo.

7

Chronology

Late 1500s Much of the Southwest experiences a drought over several decades, lasting twice as long as droughts in recent history.

1850 California enters the Union and the state legislature adopts the law of riparian rights. The legislature also incorporates the city of Los Angeles, eventually giving the city responsibility for water allocation.

1877 Drought kills off most of the sheep in the San Fernando Valley, California, ending livestock-rearing as the area's dominant land use. Landholders shift to raising wheat, becoming exporters of the commodity to Europe and Asia.

1891 The city of Phoenix, Arizona is inundated by floodwaters, signaling the need for flood control measures.

1902 President Theodore Roosevelt signs the Reclamation Act (also known as the Newlands Act) establishing the Reclamation Service within the Division of Hydrography in the US Geological Survey, providing federal funding

---

Aqueduct outside of Los Angeles, California. William Mulholland's ambitious project to bring water from the Sierra Nevada to the growing city of Los Angeles via the 233-mile California Aqueduct was completed in 1913. (Iofoto/Dreamstime.com)

	and expertise to develop dams and irrigation projects.
1905–1911	US Bureau of Reclamation builds Roosevelt Dam on the Salt River, north of Phoenix, Arizona, the largest (and last) masonry dam ever built by the agency. Cheap hydropower leads to tremendous agricultural and industrial growth in the area.
1906	President Theodore Roosevelt signs the Convention Between the United States and Mexico for the Equitable Distribution of the Waters of the Rio Grande. The United States agrees to pay the whole cost of the storage and delivery of water to Mexico.
1907	The Reclamation Service becomes an independent bureau within the US Department of the Interior.
1908	In the US Supreme Court case *Winters v. United States*, the court rules that when the federal government creates an Indian reservation, it also reserves adequate water necessary to achieve the purposes of the reservation.
1908	Construction begins on the Owens Valley Aqueduct from the Owens Valley to Los Angeles.
1909	Boundary Waters Treaty is signed, establishing the International Joint Commission and a framework for resolving shared riverine resources between the United States and Canada.
1919–23	Construction of the O'Shaughnessy Dam and a reservoir flood the Hetch Hetchy Valley in California after federal legislation allows the city of San Francisco to divert water from the Tuolumne River to serve its residents.

1922	The Colorado River Compact divides the Colorado River into the Upper Basin (Wyoming, Colorado, Utah, and New Mexico) and a Lower Basin (Nevada, Arizona, and California) to divide the river's annual flow equally between the two basins.
1923	The Reclamation Service is renamed the Bureau of Reclamation.
1928	By enacting the Boulder Canyon Project Act, Congress authorizes the building of the Boulder Canyon Dam after debates over the federal government's role in large power projects. The act also apportions the Lower Basin states' allotment of Colorado River water.
1930	Interior Secretary Ray Wilbur announces that the Boulder Canyon Dam will be called Hoover Dam, honoring the president of the United States, Herbert Hoover. The name change is ratified in April 1947.
1931	Construction begins on Hoover Dam on the Arizona/Nevada border of the Colorado River.
1931	California's Seven Party Agreement reaches consensus on the amount of water to be allocated between the state's municipal and agricultural interests.
1933	Construction begins on the Bonneville Dam on the Columbia River between Washington and Oregon.
1935	Black Sunday duster strikes Oklahoma on April 14 and becomes the most infamous of the dusters that rolled across America's "dust bowl" during the 1930s.
1937	First power is generated at Hoover Dam.

1938 The Rio Grande Compact apportions the waters of the Rio Grande from its headwaters in Colorado to above Fort Quitman, Texas between Colorado, New Mexico, and Texas.

1944 Arizona ratifies the Colorado River Compact for 2.8 million acre-feet (maf) of water from the Colorado River, the last state to do so.

1944 The Mexican Water Treaty and Protocol allots Mexico a guaranteed annual 1.5 maf of water from the Colorado River.

1946 The Bureau of Reclamation develops its primary laboratory in Denver to professionalize the study of technologies on subjects ranging from construction design and evaporation control to ecology and hydraulic structures.

1949 The Upper Colorado River Basin Compact is approved by Congress, creating the Upper Colorado River Basin Commission.

1948 The Pecos River Compact between Texas and New Mexico, administered by the interstate Pecos River Commission, is charged with allocating the waters of the Pecos River.

1950 The Canadian River Compact is approved by New Mexico, Texas, and Oklahoma to allocate water from the Canadian River, a tributary of the Arkansas River that flows through the three states.

1952 Arizona files suit against California asking the US Supreme Court to determine how much water each state has a legal right to use out of the waters of the Colorado River and its tributaries. Nevada, New Mexico, and Utah were later added as party to the suit. After two years of trial, testimony of over 340 witnesses and thousands of exhibits, the court issues its opinion on June 3, 1963 in favor of Arizona, becoming the longest case in Supreme Court history.

1952 Congress, under what is commonly known as the McCarran Amendment, agrees to judicial adjudication of federal reserved water rights in state courts, as long as the adjudication includes all water rights in a basin. This means the federal government waives its sovereign immunity for adjudicating western water rights.

1952 Congress authorizes $2 million in appropriations for a five-year program to convert sea water and brackish water into fresh water, administered by a new Office of Saline Water within the Department of the Interior.

April 1956 The Colorado River Storage Project Act is approved by Congress, authorizing Glen Canyon Dam with Lake Powell as one of four major storage reservoirs along the Colorado River and its tributaries. The dam is completed in 1966 at a cost of $135 million.

1961 The Columbia River Treaty is signed for development of the third powerhouse at Grand Coulee Dam and three upstream dams in Canada and one in the United States.

1964 The US Supreme Court issues a decree in the case *Arizona v. California*, granting Arizona 2.8 maf under the Colorado River Compact, but agrees the 1 maf from the Gila River is not considered part of the original allotment. The court also rules that 1 maf be reserved for Indian reservations in Arizona, California, and Nevada.

1965	First International Symposium on Water Desalination is held in Washington, DC, and President Lyndon Johnson announces the beginning of a "Water for Peace" program.
1966	Glen Canyon Dam is dedicated by the First Lady of the United States, Lady Bird Johnson.
1968	Congress enacts the Wild and Scenic Rivers Act to protect rivers in their natural states and excluding them from serving as hydroelectric power sites.
1968	The Colorado River Basin Project Act is enacted, authorizing several projects in four western states, including the Central Arizona Project.
1973	Construction begins on the Central Arizona Project (CAP), a 336-mile irrigation canal.
1973	Minute 242 of the US–Mexico International Boundary and Water Commission requires the United States to take actions to reduce the salinity of water being delivered from the Morelos Dam to Mexico.
1974	Under the Colorado River Basin Salinity Control Act, Congress authorizes desalting and salinity control projects to improve Colorado River quality, including a plant in Yuma, Arizona.
June 5, 1976	Teton Dam fails on the Snake River, resulting in 11 deaths, 350 businesses destroyed, and an estimated $2 billion in damage.
1974	The Office of Saline Water is incorporated into the Office of Water Resources Research.
1979	The New Melones Dam is built in California by the US Army Corps of Engineers, and turned

over to the Bureau of Reclamation as the last of the large power plants.

1979 Montana's legislature creates the Reserved Water Rights Compact Commission to negotiate the equitable division and apportionment of waters and Indian tribes claiming reserved water rights.

1979 The Bureau of Reclamation changes its name to the Water and Power Resources Service, but reverts back to the Bureau of Reclamation in 1981.

1980 The Northwest Power Act creates the Northwest Power and Conservation Council to implement the Columbia River Treaty among the four states.

1982 President Ronald Reagan signs the Reclamation Reform Act, changing the provisions (and costs) for which individuals could receive low-cost Reclamation project water.

1982 The Office of Water Resources Research is abolished as part of President Ronald Reagan's desire to eliminate most non-military, government-funded science programs.

1985 The first water deliveries from the CAP begin along the Granite Reef Aqueduct, later renamed the Hayden-Rhodes Aqueduct.

1986 Passage of the Water Resources Development Act begins to shift the responsibility for the management of federal water projects to the private sector and makes environmental considerations factors in federal water resources planning.

1988 In the US Supreme Court case of *Texas v. New Mexico*, the court appoints a River Master to compile data, calculate, and report any shortfalls or overages of water delivery under the Pecos River Compact.

1988 The Colorado Ute Indian Rights Settlement Act affirms the Utes' right to surface streams and tributary groundwater.

1989 In a closed-door meeting, members of the Las Vegas Valley Water District are told that in four years, they will have no more water to give to any new construction developments.

1991 The Southern Nevada Water Authority (SNWA) is formed to represent the water interests of Las Vegas and surrounding communities.

1992 The total investment for Bureau of Reclamation project facilities reaches $11 billion.

1993 The US Supreme Court rules that New Mexico has been in violation of the Canadian River Compact since 1987 and requires that the state release some of the water stored in its reservoirs.

1998 California's Department of Water Resources forecasts a gap between water supply and demand ranging from 2.4 maf in normal years up to 6.2 maf in drought years by 2020.

2003 Las Vegas bans lawns from being installed in front yards and grass is prohibited in commercial developments. The Southern Nevada Water Authority pays homeowners to get rid of their grass or pays for grass replaced with water-smart landscaping.

2004 President George Bush signs the Arizona Water Settlements Act that provides the Gila River Indian Community with 635,000 acre-feet of water annually, sourced from the CAP, the Gila River, the Salt River, and groundwater.

2005	Colorado's legislature establishes the Colorado Inter-Basin Compact Committee to engage locally based stakeholders in discussions about the state's water policies.
2007	The Colorado River Interim Guidelines outline what steps can be taken to provide Lower Basin water users more certainty about both the timing and volume of water delivery reductions due to massive drought conditions.
2010	PacifiCorp agrees to remove four dams on the lower Klamath River, marking a significant shift in the nation's policy of damming rivers.
2010	President Barack Obama signs the Claims Resolution Act of 2010 to settle claims with the White Mountain Apache Tribe to waters of the Salt River and the Little Colorado River watersheds, the headwaters of which are on or near the Fort Apache Reservation.
2011	The Western Governors' Association and the National Oceanic and Atmospheric Administration agree to improve the development of climate science and services to the western states to help inform their planning and management decisions.
2012	California Governor Edmund G. Brown, Jr. signs a law that makes California the first state in the nation legislatively recognizing the human right to water.
2014	In response to continuing droughts, California enacts the Sustainable Groundwater Management Act, requiring local groundwater agencies to take responsibility for protecting groundwater supplies for future generations.

2015	Poseidon Water's Claude "Bud" Lewis Carlsbad Desalination Plant to turn seawater into drinking water goes online in northern San Diego County.
2015	The Arizona State Land Department signs an agreement with the Saudi Arabian agribusiness company, Fondomonte, to lease desert farmland west of Phoenix for about one-sixth of its market value to grow water-intensive alfalfa. The lease also allows the firm to pump groundwater from Phoenix's water reserves to irrigate its crops.
2020	By the fiscal year, the Bureau of Reclamation operates seventy-eight hydropower plants, generating 15 percent of the hydropower generating capacity of the United States.
January 2020–August 2021	The Southwest has its lowest precipitation totals on record since 1895, as well as the third-highest daily average temperatures.
2020	Drought in the southwestern United States leads to $11.4–$23 billion in economic losses, including those from the 2020 wildfires, which burned over 10 million acres, about three times the acreage typical between 2001 and 2018.
2020	US Supreme Court hears original jurisdiction arguments in *Texas v. New Mexico* over the Pecos River Compact.
2021	Nevada Governor Steve Sisolak signs legislation requiring unused grass landscapes, and landscapes covered with turf grass for solely aesthetic purposes, to be replaced by the end of 2026 as a water conservation measure.
August 2021	The Secretary of the Interior begins implementing a Tier 1 water shortage declaration, reducing the amount of water

	available to water users—both cities and agricultural users—in 2022. The declaration requires emergency releases of water from reservoirs in Wyoming and Colorado to boost the water level at Lake Powell to protect water supplies and hydropower facilities' ability to turn the turbines in their dams.
December 2021	The three Lower Basin states (California, Arizona, and Nevada) agree to temporarily reduce the amount of water they take from the Colorado River to stabilize water levels in Lake Mead.
May 2022	The California Coastal Commission rejects a proposal, after twenty years of planning and debate, to construct a $1.4 billion desalination plant in Los Angeles.
May 2022	The federal government decreases mid-year water releases from Lake Powell for the first time, as well as reduced releases from Glen Canyon Dam.
May 2022	The Navajo Utah Water Rights Settlement Act is finalized, giving the Navajo Nation 81,500 acre-feet of water in Utah, and authorizing $220 million in funds for water infrastructure development.
June 2022	The Bureau of Reclamation asks the seven Colorado River Basin states to come up with a water use reduction plan by August 15, 2022. The states are called upon to save between 2 and 4 maf in 2023, about the same amount as the total allocation for Arizona and Colorado.
July 2022	More than 32 percent of land in the western states is classified as experiencing extreme or exceptional drought.

August 15, 2022	The seven Colorado River Basin states fail to reach an agreement on a Colorado River water use reduction plan.
August 16, 2022	The Secretary of the Interior declares a Tier 2a water shortage for calendar year 2023 to further reduce water available from the Colorado River, asking Arizona, Nevada, and Mexico to reduce their allotment by 4.2 maf of water annually through 2026 to make sure there is sufficient water to serve the region.
August 2022	The Colorado River Basin's two reservoirs, Lake Mead and Lake Powell, are at a combined 28 percent of their capacity.
December–March 2022	A storm pattern of moisture-laden atmospheric rivers bring well above normal precipitation and below normal temperatures to the West, although the Pacific Northwest is generally drier and warmer than normal. In Arizona, California, Nevada, and Utah the snowpack is well above normal, with some sites reporting more than 150 percent of normal.
2023	By the end of January, the US Drought Monitor reports that 61 percent of the West was in drought, with 6 percent in extreme or exceptional drought.
2023	Tulare Lake in California begins to reappear for the first time since 1997, fed by heavy rain and a melting snowpack.
January 2023	Colorado becomes the first state to develop rules for the use of treated recycled water as a source of potable water.
June 1, 2023	Arizona governor Katie Hobbs announces a moratorium on future housing development in

	some areas of the state due to insufficient water supplies.
March 2023	The US Supreme Court hears arguments in *Arizona v. Navajo Nation*, a lawsuit that seeks more water for Native people under the federal government's obligation to provide the reservation water, alleging a breach of trust under an 1868 treaty.
March 2023	The Bureau of Reclamation announces an increase in Central Valley (California) water allocations due to record-breaking snowpack in the Sierra Nevada.
April 2023	The Bureau of Reclamation releases a study projecting water levels at Lake Mead and Lake Powell resulting from above-average snowpack and projected runoff in the Colorado Basin from recent storms. The study indicates that there will be some opportunity to help replenish the lakes in the near-term, but notes that the drought conditions in the region have been more than two decades in the making.
April 2023	The Bureau of Reclamation releases a Supplemental Environmental Impact Statement (SEIS) to potentially revise the operations of Hoover Dam and Glen Canyon Dam in 2024 through 2026 in the event of potential shortages
April 2023	The Bureau of Reclamation and the US Army Corps of Engineers release the Annual Operating Plan for the Rio Grande, noting that above-average mountain snow and storms during March 2023 have improved the snowpack and steamflow predictions for the Pecos River, Conejos River, and the Rio Grande.

May 2023	Arizona, California, and Nevada propose to reduce water withdrawals from the Colorado River by 3 maf of water in exchange for federal money in order to break the stalemate over allotments due to droughts.
Late 2022–early 2023	Unexpected precipitation, along with Hurricane Hillary, bring rain and snow to the West, allowing for all or partial refilling of reservoirs.
October 2023	The federal government releases a draft SEIS to revise the 2007 guidelines for managing the Colorado River.
January 2024	The European Union's Copernicus Climate Change Service announces that 2023 had officially become Earth's hottest year on record.
January 1, 2024	The California Water Solutions Act of 2023 makes groundwater recharge the state's primary strategy for dealing with the impact of climate change.
February 2024	Record precipitation in many California cities causes flooding and property damage after back-to-back atmospheric rivers and warm Pacific Ocean temperatures from El Niño conditions reflect the changing climate. Much of the West remains in a snow drought as concerns are raised about snowmelt and spring flooding due to La Niña conditions forecast to arrive earlier than usual.
August 2024	The last of four dams on the Klamath River are removed allowing the river's salmon population to swim freely. This becomes the largest dam removal project in US history, and is considered a victory for native people and conservation groups.

Glossary

Like many topics related to science or the environment, the subject of water resources has a vocabulary all its own. The list below includes many of the terms commonly used in describing how water is managed.

acequia: simple water channels, often made of dirt, used to funnel water, usually to irrigate crops in the Southwest.

acre-foot: the amount of water needed to cover an acre of land (43,560 square feet) one foot deep, or 325,851 gallons.

active storage capacity: the amount of water that can be gravity flow released from a reservoir when it is not spilling over.

aqueduct: a method of transporting water using gravity from a source of water to a user, through channels, pipeline, channel, or another conduit.

aquifer: a permeable, water-bearing geological formation where water is stored or transferred underground, often used as a source of drinking water.

bathtub ring: a term used to describe the visible line of calcium carbonate that attaches to sandstone that marks previously higher levels of reservoir water.

beneficial use: the water that is diverted through a water right for a purpose, such as irrigation or drinking water.

channelization: the process of deepening or straightening a body of water such as a stream to allow it to run faster.

compact: an agreement between two or more parties.

conjunctive use: combining water from both surface and groundwater sources to reduce any negative effects of a single source.

conveyance loss: the amount of water that is lost through evaporation or leaks when it flows through a pipe, aqueduct, canal, or other channel.

cubic feet per second: a measurement of the rate of a stream or other body of water as it flows, equal to a volume one foot high and one foot wide flowing a distance of one foot in one second, or 448.8 gallons per minute.

dead pool: term applied when the level of water in a storage reservoir drops too low to spin the hydroelectric turbines inside its dam.

desiccation cracks: a type of fracture in the ground's surface that results when the soil is dried out, such as by high temperatures.

desalination: the process by which salts are removed from water to produce fresh water, often used by coastal communities to increase the availability of water.

diversion: the artificial removal of water from its natural or original source.

drawdown: the condition where water is pumped out of a body of water, causing the groundwater surface to be lowered.

full pool: the total capacity of a reservoir.

gage height: a measurement taken at a site on a river or stream where observations of a stream or river are taken to determine the height of the water surface.

gravity flow: the movement of water downhill generated by the force of gravity.

groundwater: water that seeps down into rocks and soil and is then stored in naturally occurring geologic formations.

headwaters: the original source of a stream that becomes a river, including tributaries.

hydrological cycle: the process by which water evaporates from bodies of water such as lakes or oceans, then is returned to the earth through precipitation, flowing back into the earth, and is repeated.

leaching: the process where soluble salts, nutrients, and contaminants such as fertilizer are washed into the soil, or carried away by flowing water.

levee: a barrier, often built, alongside a river, lake or other water feature designed to protect the land from flooding.

megadrought: a persistent, multiyear drought event considered exceptionally extreme, factoring in severity, duration, or spatial extent compared to droughts over the last 2,000 years.

non-potable: water that is not suitable for use as drinking water because of contamination.

outfall: the location where a stream, river, or other conveyance discharges, such as a river into a basin.

overdraft: the withdrawal of water from a source that takes place faster than the water can be replaced by recharge methods.

peak flow: the amount of discharge from a stream or a river, usually occurring when the water source is at its maximum stage.

percolation: the replenishing of groundwater through openings in the rocks, soil, or other ground surfaces.

perfected water right: a fully developed water right authenticated or certificated by a court, official, or through legislation.

point of diversion: the place or location specified in a water right where water is moved from its source.

potable water: water of sufficient quality according to federal standards to be used for drinking.

prescriptive rights: rights that are authorized or agreed upon by long-standing historical use.

recharge: the process of adding water to an aquifer, either naturally through rain or snowmelt, or by human means, such as spray irrigation.

recycled water: water that is used more than once before it reenters the natural hydrological cycle.

runoff: water that does not evaporate or soak into the ground after a storm.

safe yield: the amount of water that can be pumped or withdrawn from a basin over time without affecting its quality or ability to be recharged.

snow water equivalent: the amount of water that would be produced if snow were to be melted.

subsidence: the sinking of the ground in an area where the underlying level of material has been pressed down, or compacted.

surface water: any body of water that remains on top of the ground as a lake, stream, reservoir, or ocean.

tribal consultation: the formal, government-to-government process between tribal and federal negotiators to discuss projects before a final decision is made.

unappropriated water: areas of groundwater found in streams, rivers, lakes or other sources that are not already being used to satisfy water rights.

watershed: the land area between the two highest elevations on a map where precipitation such as rain or snow, runs off to form streams, lakes, and other bodies of water.

water year: a measurement of hydrological phenomena during an annual calendar period, such as the US Geological Survey's data from October 1 to September 30.

Index

About the Author

Dr. Jacqueline Vaughn is Professor Emerita at Northern Arizona University, where she taught in the Department of Politics and International Affairs and in the university's School of Earth and Sustainability. She holds a PhD in Political Science from the University of California, Berkeley, an MA in Political Science from San Jose State University, and a BS in Education from Boston University. She previously taught at the University of Redlands and at Southern Oregon State University. In addition to her academic career, she worked for the California legislature, the district attorneys offices in both San Bernardino and Riverside County, the South Coast Air Quality Management District, and in the Environmental Affairs division of Southern California Edison. She is the author of more than fifteen books dealing with environmental issues and public policy, including three ABC-CLIO volumes: *Environmental Activism*; *Waste Management*; and *Conflicts Over Natural Resources*. Her most recent book, coauthored with Dr. Hanna Cortner, is *Philanthropy and the National Park Service*. Dr. Vaughn has written extensively in academic journals and presented at professional conferences on a wide range of topics such as managerial discretion, American government and elections, disability rights, child abuse, forest management, wildfires, and wildlife policies.